Beyond the Pale

The best of Ireland's local news stories

DONAL HICKEY

**MENTOR
BOOKS**

First Published in 2007 by

MENTOR BOOKS
43 Furze Road
Sandyford Industrial Estate
Dublin 18
Republic of Ireland

Tel: + 353 1 295 2112 / 3   Fax: + 353 1 295 2114
e-mail: admin@mentorbooks.ie
www.mentorbooks.ie

ISBN: 978-1-84210-391-3

A catalogue record for this book
is available from the British Library

Editor: Adam Brophy
Design and layout: Kathryn O'Sullivan
Cover: Anú Design
Cover Image: Fintan Taite www.fintantaite.com

Printed in Ireland by ColourBooks Ltd.
1 3 5 7 9 10 8 6 4 2

CONTENTS

FOREWORD

The typical front page of an Irish regional newspaper today could have a photograph of smiling Polish triplets at school in a country town; a story about a drunken riot in another town late on the previous Saturday night; a tale of a cat trapped under a car bonnet; or of a bottle of coke being hurled across a courtroom and barely missing its target – a bewigged judge sitting on the bench.

Such stories offer unique insights into a rapidly-changing Ireland and all human life as lived 'beyond the Pale' (i.e. outside usual social conventions and/or the geographical area of Ireland excluding Dublin and parts of the surrounding counties). In spite of the growth of modern communications, the internet and local radio, Irish people remain loyal to their local newspapers, with some counties supporting three or four newspapers. Far more people, almost 60 per cent, read their regional press than they do national broadsheets.

Week in week out, the regional press provides a solid service to its readers by faithfully covering the news of interest. Many of the stories may seem humdrum but the issues they cover are important to people living in the circulation area of a particular newspaper. Council meetings and court cases provide bread-and-butter fare and often throw up quirky and humorous stories.

During a working lifetime in journalism, I have always been intrigued, entertained and sometimes bamboozled by what appears in many of these venerable newspapers which, despite their great longevity, have in most cases moved with the times. I've drawn from roughly 200 of the best stories – some hilarious, some unbelievable, others sad and many more downright bizarre – in an attempt to reflect what's happening outside the Pale in the early 21st century.

This book would never have seen daylight but for Danny McCarthy, publisher of Mentor Books, whose idea it was and who persuaded me, eventually, to write it. Thanks also to Adam Brophy, an ever-patient editor and, of course, to the newspapers for allowing me to quote from their columns.

In contrast to times past when many papers were shy about reporting on hush-hush and sensitive matters that might offend the Church and other bastions of the local establishment, most nowadays adopt a 'publish and be damned' policy within the constraints of the defamation laws.

A far cry, surely, from the notable week in 1946 when *The Kerryman* broke new ground. The Tralee organ forever dampened the ardour of many rural bulls by being the first Irish newspaper to publish an illustrated feature article highlighting the value of artificial insemination in cattle. Conservatism in society at the time, reservations about interfering with nature's way and unspoken fears that the practice could progress to a human level made newspapers hesitant to propagate such a radical idea.

But now nobody would be shocked if they read about cloning, test tube babies or other new-fangled means of procreation in their local newspaper – all grist to the ever-turning mill that is the regional press. Now read on . . .

Donal Hickey

ACKNOWLEDGEMENTS

The author and publishers wish to thank the following managers and editors of the regional newspapers for permission to reproduce copyright material.

Unison Group [Independent Newspapers] Ger Walsh – *Wexford People, The Anglo-Celt, Bray People, Carlow People, The Corkman, Drogheda Independent, Enniscorthy Guardian, Fingal Independent, Gorey Guardian, The Kerryman, The Meath Chronicle, Nenagh Guardian, New Ross Standard, Offaly Independent, The Sligo Champion, The Southern Star, The Argus, The Tuam Herald, Westmeath Examiner, Westmeath Independent, Wicklow People.*

Irish Examiner [TCH Group]: Colin Walsh – *Carlow Nationalist, Kildare Nationalist, Laois Nationalist, Sligo Weekender, Roscommon Herald, Western People, The Kingdom, Waterford News & Star, The Enniscorthy Echo, Gorey Echo, New Ross Echo, Wexford Echo, Down Democrat, Newry Democrat, Irish Post [UK].*

Johnston Press Group: Joe Flaherty – *Longford Leader, Leitrim Observer, Dundalk Democrat, Tallaght Echo, Limerick Leader, Clonmel Nationalist, The Nationalist and Tipperary Star.*

Derry Quinn – *Leinster Express, Leinster Leader, Kilkenny People and Offaly Express.*

Independents: Kieran Walsh, *The Munster Express;* Dave O'Connell, *The Connacht Tribune;* Austin Hobbs, *The Clare Champion;* Michael Daly, *Donegal Democrat;* Pádraig Kennelly, *Kerry's Eye;* Columba Gill, *Donegal News;* Gerry Collison, *The Clare People.*

The Sporting Irish

Flaunting and Snorting at the Galway Races

If you have it flash it – money, cars, houses, boobs, jewellery, helicopters or an SUV. Time was, and not that long ago, when Irish people were shy and even embarrassed about their wealth, but now we love to flaunt our status symbols. And what better place to show off the new brashness than the Galway Races!

On a week when there were signs of an economic downturn, the well-heeled at the races were certainly not easing up. All were in party mood even though shares were in freefall, house prices dropping, construction firms letting workers go and multi-nationals moving out to foreign, more cost-effective labour destinations. It looked as if all of Ireland's 33,000 millionaires were having a right auld time of it at Ballybrit.

Old-fashioned male chauvinists were also keeping an eye on the other 'filly stakes' and eyeing the two-legged form. A few of the codgers couldn't hide a chuckle as stylish women in trademark Chanel sunglasses who were 'trying' in the fashion competition faced a dilemma in the rain.

To have any chance, the ladies had to be seen first and foremost. That involved strutting around and posing in the area between the champagne bar and the hospitality tents. It also meant getting wet, which left the feathers in hats limp and some amber legs dripping with fake tan. But that was the price they were prepared to pay for the opportunity of taking gold and getting their photos in the papers.

Some of the hats looked as if trees were growing out of them and cost a fortune. Other headgear was from another era with women telling of how they raided dusty boxes under the bed or on top of the wardrobe at home.

Anything goes in Galway during race week – the mother and father of all parties. High society takes over with the Dublin middle classes getting lost in the west and giving it a lash for a few days.

The Armani and Gucci set hung around the champagne-soaked VIP tents at the track but the real craic was in the fancy hotels at night. According to reports, the city was full of cocaine with well-dressed, middle-aged men and women snorting away blissfully. Some wealthy Dubs reportedly brought their own 'Devil's Dandruff' down with them as they didn't want to take any chances with unfamiliar dealers in Galway.

Even the term Galway hooker, the name of a traditional sailing boat with an honourable reputation, had a new resonance. Five-star prostitutes flown into the city were reckoned to have netted €500,000 during the festival. Numerous brothels operated in the city centre and Salthill areas with clients reportedly preferring darker, exotic girls. The visiting hookers, including a few male escorts, also operated from apartments and advertised their services on websites with mobile phone numbers provided.

Investigative work by Galway media found that prices ranged from €250 per hour to €4,000 for the most expensive call girls. Five girls were flown over from London to Galway for the week, with one source commenting:

These girls aren't your average prostitutes. They regularly entertain high-flyers in Dublin and London and would even travel on weekend European breaks with multi-millionaires. It's the Galway Races and there's nothing that money cannot buy, although it may cost you around €4,000 or €5,000 per night.

The Connacht Tribune

The number of helicopters in the air had the place resembling a Vietnam war zone. And people hadn't the slightest reluctance about shelling out €360 for a return trip by chopper from locations on the edge of the city to the race course, a journey of less than five minutes each way. Crowds were slightly down on 2006 which, according to the organisers, was due to the rain and not the downturn in the building trade. But the bookies' satchels were still bulging.

On the same week, a retired Dublin property developer treated himself to a €1.5 million Bugatti sports car with a top speed of 280 kilometres per hour, whatever use that is to him given that the top speed limit is 120 kilometres. But wasn't he putting it up to the crowd in the Mercs and Beamers in Galway who thought they were the front runners?!

Culchies Closet Snobs in Croker

Whether you bump into them on 'The Hill' or at matches in Thurles or Castlebar, the Dubs are always the same. Home or away makes no difference. They're cocky, act as if they know it all and feel compelled to give opinions on every subject under the sun usually trailing off with the phrase, 'Yez know whar I mean', even though you mightn't have a clue what they're at.

Now the true-blue 'Dubalin' man or woman is the best type of individual you can meet and is capable of extraordinary kindness. But what's in them that makes people from beyond the Pale feel inferior in their company? Is it because Dublin is bigger than any other place in Ireland, or that nobody celebrates quite like them on the odd occasion they win All-Ireland finals, or that, very simply, they are just convinced they are better than the Culchies in every way?

Undoubtedly the average Dub regards himself as being smarter than any redneck – smarter maybe but definitely not cuter. Let's try to define the difference between smart and cute. We'll start by assuming that both Dub and Culchie have roughly the same level of intelligence. The voluble Dub, with that peculiar nasal twang, can't help showing off his ocean-deep knowledge and insights. He's at his best when planked on a high stool with a pint of plain sitting in front of him and comes across as being smart. The Culchie is the opposite: he's just as clever but doesn't want to show it and tends to understate himself in a self-effacing way – more of a behind-the-door type. That's your cute Culchie who confidently believes he'd buy and sell any Dub.

Traditionally, people from the country going to Dublin have looked upon the metropolitans with jaundiced eyes and aren't long in the capital before they realise that, yes, there are differences between Dub and Culchie. The different worlds were observed by sportswriter Owen McCrohan from Valentia when he first started going to Kerry v Dublin matches in Croker in the heady days of the Fifties.

> The urban/rural divide always remained paramount and took precedence over most other things in life . . . A true story of a Dublin man who was carried semi-conscious into the casualty ward of the Mater Hospital on a drunken Saturday night illustrates the point. On being undressed by the nursing staff, the reluctant patient kept shouting, 'Let me go yez bleedin' Culchies.'
>
> The moral of the story should not be lost on sociologists who might be conducting a future survey for the enlightenment of the masses. And it is this. Every normal, patriotic Dubliner looks upon certain professions with a high incidence of rural

recruitment as bastions of anti-city antagonism and as such are deserving of public odium. These include members of the Gardaí, civil servants, traffic wardens, construction workers and elderly parish priests.

Let's be honest about it. City people have little in common with their country cousins who invariably look upon the denizens of Hill 16 with a mixture of tolerance and amusement. Tolerance because the rustic in Croker is a closet snob who considers himself to be of superior bloodlines. Amusement because he firmly believes that Dublin people are deprived in their origins.

And why wouldn't they be deprived seeing as they never saw the dog jump the half-door, never heard a blackbird sing, never ate a salty mackerel, never warmed their shins at a turf fire and were seldom further west than Inchicore.

The Kerryman

Now, yez know whar I mean!

Jerry's Heart Beats for Cork

Life began again for Jerry O'Leary the day he left the Mater Hospital with a new heart beating inside his Cork hurling jersey. It was 14 March 2007. Jerry had no plans for a world tour, a seat on a space mission or any other epic adventures. His big hope was, simply, that Cork would win the All-Ireland later in the year.

He had spent 311 days tethered to an artificial heart machine beside his bed before a suitable donor was found in December 2006.

It was a trip to Croke Park in 1995 to see his beloved Cork play which changed his life, when he got his first heart attack.

The Corkman

Three years later a second heart attack put an end to his working life as a welder. When his heart started to fail in 2006, he was connected to an artificial heart machine and so began a patient wait for a suitable donor. The cumbersome machine, which pumped blood in and out through his body, was his only hope of staying alive until he got a new heart.

At times he got depressed, but never gave up hope, encouraged along by the Mater staff. Then a suitable donor heart became available in December and an eight-hour transplant operation was carried out successfully. Freddie Wood, the cardiac surgeon who led the operating team, gave Jerry a prognosis of 15 to 18 years of very active life.

Uppermost on the mind of the 50-year-old Kanturk man for the rest of his days will be the donor and the donor's family who gave him a second chance at life. Nor will the self-confessed hurling fanatic ever let go of his favourite item of clothing – that red jersey bearing the autographs of the Cork team.

Ghost of Harris in Thomond Park

The spirit of the late actor and rugby player Richard Harris was surely in Thomond Park when the famed Limerick ground hosted its last major game on 20 January 2007 before redevelopment.

It was a chilly Saturday and Limerick was festooned in the familiar red. Nostalgia filled the Shannonside air. Old ghosts returned for a final time to the spiritual home of Munster rugby for the Heineken Cup fixture between Munster and Leicester Tigers. On a day when emotions took over and heroic feats of times long since past were recalled, victory went to the English side.

The words of curmudgeonly Harris, a true Limerick man, echoed from beyond the grave. He was a devoted Munster rugby fan all his life, something which radiates from the following extract from an article he penned in 2002:

> I adore Thomond Park, which I could see and hear from my bedroom in our house on the Ennis Road. It is a citadel of Munster rugby; we have never lost a European Cup game there. If Ireland played there we would never lose. Did I ever tell you I scored 19 tries and one dropped goal on the hallowed turf in various schools and junior games?
>
> I can recall every score in intimate detail . . . I was a second row at school, but seriously miscast. I should have been a flanker. I loved roving, snaffling tries, putting in big hits – though we called them tackles in those days.
>
> I attended Crescent College, played in two Munster Schools' finals and represented Munster schools and Munster under-20. I still wear that very red shirt and intend to be buried in it. I have left instructions . . . before TB struck and I discovered books, women and a hitherto unsuspected, or submerged, desire to act and show off.
>
> God, they were great days. To play rugby and glory in your fitness. To feel invincible. If you could just bottle that moment. Rugby was life in Limerick. It was a love of sport and also a parish thing. The junior teams were based around parishes and local pride was always at stake. We were tribes and you needed visas to move safely between parishes. Inter-marriage was almost unthinkable. Garryowen man/Shannon girl? Scandalous.
>
> *Limerick Leader*

No More Chicken Wings for Top GAA Players

As millions poured into GAA coffers, Mick O'Dwyer once berated the association for being miserly with leading players and feeding them chicken wings after matches in Croke Park.

According to O'Dwyer, players need more sustenance than chicken wings if they're to win All-Irelands. Thoroughbreds such as the Kerry footballers have to be well fed. In 2006, for instance, €72,023 was spent on meals and accommodation for the All-Ireland winning Kerry team. And that doesn't include an end-of-season holiday abroad for the team and officials.

But Kerry sports reporter Kieran McCarthy has been playing against a veritable gale in his attempts to get a detailed breakdown of the Kerry County Board's annual accounts.

> What hotels did our senior players stay in? What was the room rate? How many nights did the players stay in hotels? Are they fed fillet steak, or bangers and mash? Where exactly did the €72,023 go?
>
> This is not a question about being nosy or trying to dig the dirt but if the Kerry public is paying for it, those that contribute have a right to know where the money is going. The man that chips in a euro at the church gate has as much a right to information as the captains of industry that splash out over €1,000 to be wined and dined at a corporate dinner . . .
>
> 'What expenses do players get? How much per mile do they receive for travelling to training? If they miss work to train or play, are they compensated?
>
> Is the manager paid expenses? At what rate? What about his selectors and backroom staff? Are the county board officials claiming travelling expenses to attend training sessions or games?
>
> *The Kingdom*

Après match conversations inevitably turn to what managers and coaches are earning, even at club level. Being an 'amateur' organisation, the GAA won't confirm anything, but it's well-known that some managers are commanding huge sums, nearly always paid in the form of expenses.

Payments can, reportedly, be up to several hundred euro per training session, with annual sums well into five figures being commonly paid over, not to mention bonuses, cars and other incentives.

Little wonder then that county players, who don't get paid despite providing all the entertainment and swelling the GAA's ever-growing coffers, are getting increasingly resentful at being excluded from the gravy train.

Despite the official protestations of the GAA, big money is being paid to people to look after teams by both rich and poor clubs that are prepared to go to any expense to achieve success. According to reports, €13,000 is the 'wage-bill' that one Limerick GAA club has agreed to 'pay' their senior hurling management for the 2007 season.

> Individual coaches can now make up to €120 in expenses per session. Of the 16 senior hurling clubs in the county, ten have changed their management teams for 2007 with most opting for 'big names'. Five of the clubs have gone outside of the county in the search of someone to lead them to the promised land.
>
> *Limerick Leader*

A Knock-Out Letter from Muhammad Ali

When Jack and Grace McCrae read in the newspaper that the iconic boxer, Muhammad Ali, was not feeling too well on his 65th birthday, they decided to send him a letter to cheer him up.

Like Ali, Jack has Parkinson's disease and has taken a special interest in the former world champion's personal struggle with Parkinson's, as well as being a long-time fan of the man who styled himself 'The Greatest'.

On learning of Ali's birthday in January 2007, Grace sent him a birthday card with a short note enclosed and addressed it to a PO box in Berrier Springs, USA. The McCraes wanted him to know they were thinking about him.

Grace didn't think any more about it until three months later when their postman delivered a personal letter and signed photograph from the fighter to their home near Killarney. They were almost knocked out by the surprise.

And Grace could tell by the uneven writing on the photograph that the signatory had Parkinson's.

> In thanking the surprised McCraes for their kind words, Ali wrote that it was especially warming to know that he had touched their life in some way.
>
> *Kerry's Eye*

He concluded with the following nugget of wisdom: 'Here is one of my favourite sayings which I think both of you might enjoy. "What is man's wealth? His wealth is in his knowledge. If his wealth was in the bank and not his knowledge, then he doesn't possess it because it's in the bank. Keep smiling." '

Doing an 'Ali Shuffle' around the Club Bore – The Qualities of an Ideal Golf Club Captain

Important-looking men that strut around golf clubs wearing snazzy blazers emblazoned with gold-braided badges are entitled to look proud. For they earn the right to have their names up there on their club's mahogany roll of honour the hard way.

They have to act with skill and diplomacy, on and off the course. And they must also be able to appease female golfers, who still have an inferior status to men in some of the high-brow clubs and are not allowed to be 'full' members.

Countless men that work hard and thanklessly in their clubs over a virtual lifetime would give their right hand to wear a coveted captain's blazer for a year. But many indeed are the special qualities required by the perfect captain of a golf club, according to columnist Nicky Barry:

> Blazzerati are all very personable fellows. As a rule they are not short of bobs and have shiny foreheads. An outgoing personality would seem to be the first prerequisite, ie the ability to smile when under attack from the club gripe or, worse again, when cornered by the club bore.
>
> With the latter, it helps to be adept at the 'Ali Shuffle', while with the club comedian it is mandatory to laugh heartily, even if you heard it before!
>
> The ideal captain is a charming diplomat, a golden tenor, silver orator, raconteur – a man's man.
>
> Seriously, he must have a sense of humour, the constitution of an elephant, the heart of a lion, play mixed foursomes and be able to see around corners. Bi-location also helps.
>
> He must be a psychiatrist to handle the thorny wires, a hit-man to neutralise the fools and a many-faced rogue to placate the mother of his children . . . his liver must be sound and his neck as hard as a jockey's strap . . . verily, folks, this paragon must not only be a gentleman and a rogue, he must be Superman himself.
>
> Enjoy every minute for it will be all over before you know it. Oops – I nearly forgot. May Fido and the kids recognise you when the year is up!
>
> *The Kingdom*

Micko Mania in the Wicklow Hills

TV cameras, flash bulbs and bumper attendances are almost as rare at Aughrim GAA grounds as All-Ireland medals won by Wicklow people. But the media and the crowds turned out in force on a memorable Saturday in early January to see the Wicklow footballers play their first match under the renowned manager, Mick O'Dwyer.

A carnival atmosphere prevailed and around 4,000 paying customers went through creaking turnstiles that generally squeeze in hundreds. Even replica Wicklow jerseys that nobody previously wanted were selling briskly and school teachers had their pupils writing essays about the new phenomenon that was Wicklow football.

The presence of the charismatic 70-year-old, who had previously managed Kerry, Kildare and Laois, was the reason for all the hullabaloo. So-called 'Micko-mania' had swept through the Garden County since his appointment as team boss had been announced in late 2006. Wicklow, the perennial losers, had won only a single match, against Waterford, in the 2006 National League.

With even one victory O'Dwyer would have equalled the previous year's performance by Wicklow. The hype that accompanied his arrival raised expectations sky high, though he himself typically tried to calm things. After being cheered onto the Aughrim turf, he posed for photographs with a clinched fist and started on a winning note, Wicklow defeating neighbours Carlow in the O'Byrne Cup.

> Without getting carried away, O'Dwyer was happy to get off to a winning start and was particularly heartened at the way his players fought back in the closing stages to snatch victory from the jaws of defeat.
>
> *Wicklow People*

Some people had wondered why O'Dwyer, a man so accustomed to victory in Croke Park and other stadia, would bother with lowly Wicklow. But he knew things could only get better in the Garden County where he was already being compared with another Michael O'Dwyer, a home-grown rebel and folk hero.

By mid-February, Wicklow had won three of their first four games and Wicklow fans, so long denied success, had a team to follow at last. In June, Wicklow were beaten in the Leinster championship by Louth but O'Dwyer promised to fulfil his two-year commitment to the county.

But the boy who sold tomatoes and oranges to buy his first football in Waterville long ago gave a lift to people who welcomed even the hope of modest success.

Bertie's Speed Record for Getting Team off the Pitch

Bertie Coleman was a GAA legend known for sending hundreds of teams out onto playing fields all over Ireland. But part of his legend was the speed with which he got a team off the pitch way back in 1962.

His club, Dunmore MacHales, was playing in a Galway county football final against Tuam Stars when a storm disrupted play and the teams were forced to retire, temporarily, to the dressing rooms. Dunmore were being hammered so Bertie eagerly welcomed the break.

After the tempest had passed, the referee came knocking on the Dunmore dressing room asking the players to resume hostilities on the field only to discover that Bertie had already sent half the team home.

> It was a measure of the cuteness of Coleman, and also his love for the club, that he used the opportunity to wrangle his team out of a losing situation.
>
> *The Connacht Tribune*

The match was rescheduled and Dunmore lost but that did not diminish Bertie's commitment one whit and he continued to serve the club until his death in early June 2007 at the age of 84. His insurance office in Dunmore was a friendly port of call for GAA people and the scene of many sporting debates.

Bertie was a Galway selector for 30 years and was secretary of his club for 28 years running. He was president of three GAA organisations in Galway at the time of his death and GAA luminaries from all around the country attended his funeral.

Rugby to Cause Grave Ructions in Clare

Croke Park may now be opened up to rugby but that doesn't mean all GAA people, especially dead ones, approve of the game. The thought of rugby gaining a foothold in the GAA heartland of west Clare would make long-departed Gaels turn in their graves, according to the RTÉ sports commentator on mainly GAA affairs, Marty Morrissey, who is himself an avid Clareman.

His profound warning came when he claimed to be first with the hush-hush, sensational revelation in his local newspaper column. Marty's shocking news was that young boys and girls in the pure Gaelic parishes of Miltown Malbay (Kilfarboy) and Kilmurry Ibrickane were coming together to form a rugby club.

Gaels, who for years tried to keep the despised oval ball game and its sheepskin-clad followers out of the GAA enclave of Clare, would roll in their places of repose. Such would be the deadly impact of this ground-breaking event.

> Yes indeed, thanks to a few creative, imaginative individuals,
> rugby will be coached in the nine national schools in the two

parishes and will give young children in the area the opportunity to be coached in the skills of a game that is growing in popularity every season.

The Clare People

Let's hope that in the best traditions of Clare hospitality, the 'true Gaels' provide comfortable seats at local rugby matches for the flask-swilling auld lads with the rugs around their knees.

Harry Potter Casts Spell on Munster Hurling Final

All was set for a memorable day out for the Lynch family at the glamorous première of the latest *Harry Potter* blockbuster at the Savoy cinema in Dublin. Ivanna Lynch was in the movie.

Donal Lynch had been prepared to go to any lengths to get his daughter Ivanna the part. She beat off 15,000 other girls to win the role of Luna Lovegood in *Harry Potter and the Order of the Phoenix*, set to become one of the box office hits of the year.

There was an unfortunate clash of events, however, on the day of the première, 8 July. Donal is a passionate Limerick hurling fan and his native county happened to be playing Waterford in the Munster Final in Thurles on the same day. Seeing that the Shannonsiders don't get to that many Munster finals it was an event he was reluctant to pass up.

'It's a lovely dilemma to be in but there was never a chance that I'd be anywhere but Thurles on Sunday. I've been following Limerick since 1958 and I've only missed a handful of games and that was only because I was out of the country,' said Donal who moved from Murroe to Drogheda in 1972.

Limerick Leader

However, despite his best intentions Donal had to choose the Savoy over Semple Stadium and went along to the première with Ivanna and his wife, Marguerite. But there was never any hesitation from the two other Lynch children, Máiread and Patrick, about which event they wanted to go to. They share their father's love of Limerick hurling and duly went to the match.

All of the children were born in County Louth but a green and white Limerick flag flew over their home at the height of the summer hurling frenzy. For some reason Ivanna has escaped the hurling bug. Donal took her to an All-Ireland quarter-final against Wexford in Croke Park in 2001, but she read a *Harry Potter* book through the whole game.

Her dream always was to get a part in a *Harry Potter* film and Donal flew her specially to London for an audition. When she was younger she even sent a letter to JK Rowling telling her how much she wanted to play Luna, but feared it would never happen because she was from Termonfeckin, a 'humble village where not much happened'.

But to Ivanna's surprise, JK Rowling wrote back: 'Don't be too hard on Termonfeckin; it does have a brilliant name! And I come from a very sleepy place.'

Ivanna's star will continue to shine for she will also be in the next *Harry Potter* film.

Raging Bull Lands Loughnane in Trouble

Though never far away from conflict, the last thing on hurling guru Ger Loughnane's mind must have been a confrontation of any sort as he motored along a quiet country road.

The Galway hurling manager was being driven home to Clare in his brand new Lexus by selector Louis Mulqueen when they came face to face with a bull on the road between Craughwell and Ardrahan. The men got out of the car and grabbed a couple of hurleys from the boot before trying to 'lure' the beast off the road. The bull was in no mood for appeasement, however.

> Instead, the animal attacked the Lexus causing enough damage to the front and side for it to be returned to Tom Hogan Motors for extensive repairs.
>
> *The Connacht Tribune*

That particular match was clearly won by the bull and the duo were glad to beat a hasty and battered retreat. Afterwards, Ger, himself a former Clare hurler and Clare hurling manager, learned that the bull had strong Clare hurling connections. Could it be that the animal was unhappy with Ger's decision to defect to neighbouring Galway?

The bull was owned by Seamie Ryan, a brother of the Chairman of the Galway Hurling Board, and had been bought from the mother of Clare hurler Niall McInerney.

The incident came at a tempestuous time for Ger Loughnane. In the week coming up to the All-Ireland qualifier second round between Clare and Galway, which Clare won, he started stirring the pot by calling for the resignation of Clare County GAA Board Chairman Michael McDonagh. Loughnane said he did not think Michael was capable of holding the office.

He also expressed surprise that Michael hadn't resigned last year following a County Board Awards controversy – something that still stung Ger.

For some amazing reason, the board snubbed Ger from the awards despite the fact that he had played for Clare for 15 years, was an All-Star and trained Clare to two All-Ireland victories ending a long spell in the wilderness. Michael said he was 'very hurt' by the comments but had no intention of stepping down.

If the Cap Fits (Or Not) . . . Wear It!

Wearing exactly the right cap is all important when you're the manager of a top GAA team. In an era of €1 million 'gates' at Croker, the GAA is immersed in cash from the ordinary punter. But businesses that put their money into sponsorship also have to get their credits.

Sporting the sponsor's boots, shirts, tops and caps and having the sponsor's revitalising drink in your hand when in the media glare (making sure it's right in the eye of the camera at that) is all part of the deal for players.

Managers must also show the sponsor's wares at every opportunity, as Clare hurling boss Tony Considine was reminded after he gave the obligatory television interview following a match with Cork. Tony must have struck a discordant note when he wore a baseball cap bearing a name that wasn't that of the sponsor, Pat O'Donnell & Co, but rather of a fashion store.

> It set tongues wagging and triggered off mischievous minds, begging the question: if Considine, who also enjoys the benefits of a courtesy car as previous incumbents of the Clare job also did, had done his own private deal with the menswear shop?
>
> *The Clare Champion*

Pat O'Donnell, whose company is one of the country's leading suppliers of heavy machinery, noted what had happened and took precautions to ensure it would not be repeated. As he set out on the long trek to Belfast for the next game, he was armed with a selection of baseball caps with the O'Donnell business logo clearly emblazoned on them.

Tony and other members of the management team were each handed a cap so that when Tony went before the TV cameras, it was the team sponsor – and only the correct sponsor – that was being promoted. Which is as it should be, Pat and the powers-that-be in Clare GAA would undoubtedly argue.

The Crusheen businessman, who stepped in as Clare's sponsor last year after Vodafone pulled out, had also been a sponsor years ago. He cemented his new deal with Clare GAA for a six-figure sum and they were only too glad to have Pat, and his caps, back.

Waterford Mayor 'Sidelined' at Munster Hurling Final

It had all the makings of a memorable occasion for the newly-elected Mayor of Waterford City, Mary O'Halloran. There she was in the VIP section of the Thurles stadium in one of the best seats and with a great view of the Munster hurling final between Waterford and Limerick.

It was one of her first important official engagements and she turned out in her best style, proudly wearing her shining chain of office.

There at the invitation of the GAA, she was seated with many other luminaries, including President Mary McAleese and Taoiseach Bertie Ahern. What looked like being a perfect day was crowned by a Waterford victory. But an unexpected snub awaited Mary.

As GAA bosses tripped over themselves pandering to all the dignitaries present, the first citizen of Waterford was brushed aside in the spell of unbridled elation that followed the final whistle. Mayor O'Halloran was, incredibly, denied an opportunity to congratulate the Waterford players by the Taoiseach's and the President's security personnel.

They prevented her from approaching and shaking the hand of Waterford captain Michael 'The Brick' Walsh. Stiff protocol had got in the way and Mary was dismayed.

'I was dying to get to shake the hand of the captain but I couldn't get in because the Taoiseach and President were there,' she said. Neither was the Mayor introduced to either the Taoiseach or the President throughout proceedings. The Mayor said she had been officially invited to attend by the County Secretary but was unsure who was responsible for protocol on the day.

Munster Express

Somebody clearly made a *faux pas* on the occasion and Mary was none too pleased, though she made the best of things afterwards saying that she had not been personally offended. But it was a slight to the mayoral office.

A long-time hurling fan and regular supporter at Waterford matches, she said she would nonetheless have loved a handshake with the captain and team and, as the first citizen, to tell them well done.

'Even though I was just a stone's throw away from them, the security teams prevented me from doing so,' she continued. 'I have no gripe with the security teams of either the Taoiseach or President, they were simply doing their jobs. But I hope at future matches, say if Waterford gets to the All Ireland final, this situation will be rectified. I'd want to be there shaking the team's hands that day,' she said.

Love and Relationships

Western Men Awake on Valentine's Day

The men of the west were wide awake, lusty and snapping up underwear for their lovers on St Valentine's Day.

Lorraine Kirrane, who has a lingerie shop in Claremorris, Co Mayo, reported brisk business as Romeos forked out generously for gifts for their partners. Many shuffled shyly in at the last minute, but always knew what they wanted, Lorraine noted.

Neither were the men of the west asleep when it came to ensuring tables for two were available on the night. Some tables had been booked well before Christmas. On the day itself, there wasn't a hope of getting a table in a hotel or restaurant; the five-star Ashford Castle in Mayo had taken its first Valentine's booking in November. In early February, a hotel spokesman described it as a very romantic year, with the men taking the initiative and booking up the non-residents' restaurant. Only three free rooms were left at €232 each.

Florists were hard pressed to ensure enough red roses were available to go around, with bunches of 24 roses walking out the door for around €200 each.

In sharp contrast, there was no great love for the V-Day 'racket' in Kerry where romance was in short supply. Some cute Kerrymen believed the event was over-commercialised, a rip-off and a waste of money. No flowers and expensive meals for them.

> What we found simply showed the steady and practical nature of the people who live in these parts. Teddy bears and love hearts? Not on your life boyo, there are far more subtle and tasteful ways of getting your affections across.
>
> *The Kerryman*

Mayo County Council was also being practical, sending out 1,000 cards to young men around the county. Instead of the usual love poem, the message inside the card was an appeal to keep their girlfriends safe by driving carefully.

> With flowers on the outside, the card looks like every other one for the feast of love but once opened young men will see a picture of a crashed car with the message reading, 'I'm sorry, I didn't mean to kill you. I miss you.'
>   The 'For My Girlfriend' campaign will also feature posters in the men's toilets of pubs and nightclubs, featuring a graphic picture of a crashed car.
>
> *Western People*

Such grim images were certainly not on the mind of a Carlow man whose honest profession of love captivated radio listeners. His text message about his girlfriend of four years won them an evening away in a romantic castle. Tom McDonald, from Bagenalstown, landed the Valentine's prize on Beat FM when he decided, on a whim, to pull his car over and voice his affections for Rachel O'Connor, from Tramore, County Waterford.

The loved-up couple were given Gucci watches, beautiful roses and a romantic night in the presidential suite at Waterford Castle on Valentine's Day. The evening was completed with champagne and their own taxi service ready to whisk them to whatever location they desired.

Carlow Nationalist

Spies under the Bed in the West

Spies are on the trail of cheating spouses in the west. They are doing whatever it takes to catch out those being unfaithful. The aptly-named 'Gotcha' company has been operating in England for eight years and is now spreading its tentacles here.

Cheating spouses could be in for a nasty shock with private investigators due to open an office in Castlebar in the coming months.

Western People

The investigators' undercover work could start with a simple stakeout. They might just remain in one place for a week. If the person under observation is staying in a hotel, they simply book the room next to them. The fee to 'getcha' could be a few thousand euro depending on the amount of work involved. The probe starts with some basic information about a partner – place of work, times he or she goes out and a photograph. The agency then starts tracking. A team of spies builds up a file of photographic and video evidence for their clients who are often high-powered women. Women, of course, are also investigated.

News of a cheating partner is always hard to break to someone, but Gotcha works on the basis that people are better off knowing. It investigates up to 30 people in Britain every week. While the service is still new here, problems remain the same and the company promises to find out everything clients want to know.

ACCORD, the voluntary Catholic organisation which helps people in troubled marriages, believes it can offer a more helpful service – free *gratis*. Working on the basis that honesty and trust are paramount in marriage, ACCORD says that hiring investigators to spy on a partner goes against those ideals.

Infidelity is usually the result of an emotional detachment in the marriage. For no cost, people can come along to an ACCORD meeting if they are worried about their marriage and – according to the organisation – be guarded onto a path much better for their marriage than any private investigator.

A True Love Story from 'Bundy' Beach

A wave of romance rolled over Bundoran's famous surf beach on Christmas morning as David, from Lucan in Dublin, went down, literally, on bended knee to propose to his lovely girl from Donegal, Sabina.

Other hardy souls were shivering as they ran down to the water for their annual Christmas Day swim, but David's heart was warm and beating faster than usual. So, what inspired this dramatic gesture in a most unlikely setting before nearly 100 onlookers?

> David Buckley explained: 'Well, last weekend, Beenie and I were in Dublin and, as we were passing a jeweller's shop, I just casually asked her if there was anything she would like. She replied, "A gold ring wouldn't be a bad idea." The excuses I had to make to be able to slip off and buy that ring were unbelieveable. At least I know now that I'll be able to get away

with the odd white lie in the future.'

As for Sabina (Beenie) Byrne? 'As far as I was concerned we were just going for a nice walk on Christmas morning. I nearly dropped dead when he got down on bended knee and asked me,' she said.

And did she say yes? 'Now what do you think? It was so cold out there it was the quickest way of getting off that beach!'

Donegal Democrat

Taking Love to New Heights

There they were, lovers Gerard and Claire, battling rain, wind and the worst of the elements on top of the highest mountain in South East Asia. An unlikely romantic setting.

Before taking on Mount Kinbalu, however, Gerard had decided that proposing to Claire at the summit, with the sunrise in the distance, would be a 'unique' experience for them both. They had first met in December 2004, when Gerard O'Loughlin, who was planning the climb, felt he needed a personal trainer and asked for Claire Byrne's help. She consented. Before long, Cupid struck and they fell madly in love.

They set off on their trek up the mountain with their guide on Claire's birthday and found the climb wasn't easy. But Gerard, an IT consultant from Sligo, was determined that this rocky adventure was not a sign of things to come.

After resting at 3,000 metres on the first night, the pair began the second leg of their journey before bad weather intervened. Though they were advised it was too dangerous to climb, Gerard was determined to keep going. So they struggled on up the mountain, wearing ponchos that looked like plastic bags, socks on their hands and six layers of clothes as the temperature had dropped to minus one.

They could barely stay on their feet and the lack of oxygen made every step suck the last ounces of energy from them. Twenty metres from the top, Claire, from Dublin, decided she couldn't go on, describing it as 'the most awful experience' of her life.

Wet and freezing, she couldn't breathe. She burst into tears and just sat down on a rock. Gerard came over, calmly sat beside her and said, 'We don't have to go the rest of the way up, we nearly made it.'

Then, saying to her he wanted to take a photograph of what they had just achieved, he reached into his pocket and pulled out an engagement ring. Her tears gave way to beaming smiles.

> 'At the highest point of South East Asia, 4,000 metres above sea level, he asked me to marry him and I, of course, said yes,' Claire revealed.
>
> *The Sligo Champion*

On their return to Dublin, Claire told her story to 98FM as part of its Ireland's Wedding of the Year promotion. The couple won the top prize of a €50,000 wedding, including a honeymoon in Australia worth €10,000, €16,500 for a room organiser and wedding planner and a wedding dress costing €3,000.

A date of 4 February 2008 has already been set for Finnstown Country House Hotel, Lucan.

Friendship Goes Sour in Row over Girl

Tom believed his good friend Des was seeing his ex-girlfriend behind his back. So he decided to start sending Des text messages – up to 80 in all over a three-month period – threatening him.

One text sent in September 2006 read: 'The law can't do anything about this Des. If I kicked the head off you and the time is right you p***k.' Another read: 'If you don't tell me the truth I will beat you up and I will do time. I am not afraid of the law.'

Des Barrett complained to the gardaí that he was receiving a number of threatening text messages from Tom McLellan's phone number. When questioned by the gardaí, Tom admitted sending the messages.

> Kenmare Court was told the two men had been 'very good friends' but Tom became suspicious that Des was seeing his ex-girlfriend and the friendship then 'went sour'.
>
> *The Kerryman*

Tom, from Ballyduff, County Kerry, was ordered to pay €200 to Des and €800 into the poor box. Judge James O'Connor gave a lengthy adjournment of the summons for sending threatening text messages. The judge also warned Tom that he would be jailed for a month if he misbehaved in the meantime.

Model Viv's Comeback Has Set Male Hearts Aflutter – Again

When former top model Vivienne Connolly came back on the fashion scene after taking a break for family reasons, male hearts in her native Carlow began to beat a little faster.

Lovely Viv returned from domestic bliss to the cut-throat world of style and glamour to launch 'Fly with 3' – the holiday giveaway from 3, Ireland's mobile media network. And Carlow was all agog, according to the Barrowside media.

The press gang reached for superlatives in their anxiety to burst forth with the exciting news that 'one of Ireland's original beauties', who had made a name for herself on the catwalks since the early 1990s, was again basking in the limelight.

She was described as Carlow's most famous and beautiful export. They had her ahead of other local worthies such as TV travel programme presenter Kathryn Thomas – no slouch herself in the glamour stakes – and the less glamorous singer Richie Kavanagh of JCB and combine harvester fame. Now read on:

> Guess who's back boys?! Yes, take a deep breath and sit yourselves down because the very luscious Vivienne Connolly has dusted off her stilettos.
>
> The Carlow-born supermodel, who is responsible for sending many a man's heart into flutter overdrive with her dazzling physical attributes, is back on the modelling scene.
>
> After taking two years out to raise a family, the down-to-earth stunner made her comeback during a sunny beach-scene photocall for the phone network and, dare we say it, she is looking as hot as ever.
>
> Despite by now being considered an old-timer in the business, the Carlow woman's classic looks still make her stand out against the rest of the Irish models.
>
> So, it's no surprise that her every move was documented in this here paper, from her early days as a discovery of local photographer Thomas Sunderland, to the rise and rise of her career, her society wedding to Mark Dunne (of the clothing dynasty) and the birth of her children.
>
> But jealousy isn't a word we use when it comes to our Viv because she has remained as down-to-earth as ever and is well known for making regular trips home to Carlow.
>
> Her comeback is sure to set tongues wagging in the fashion industry where it is notoriously difficult to maintain a career with the amount of new faces on the scene. But sure, what's a two-year break when you look like Vivienne Connolly!
>
> *Carlow Nationalist*

Women Looking for Drumlish-ious Men

Funny the way some people with inventive brains can interpret the driest and coldest of statistics. Who, for instance, would ever realise that a modest town in north Longford had more single and virile men per head of population than any other town in Ireland, if Michael Nugent hadn't looked at the statistics in a particular way?

Since the revelation, Drumlish has become known to women in the know as 'Drumlish-ous'. It has one single man in eight, a ratio that trumps all other parts of the country. The next nearest place is Castlerea, County Roscommon, which has a ratio of one in ten. Other towns of interest with large single male ratios include Belturbet, County Cavan, Ballaghaderreen, County Mayo and Ballyjamesduff, County Cavan.

Also high in the ratings is Templemore, County Tipperary, reputedly a great place to cop a man because of large numbers of young men attending the Garda Training College there.

> The Drumlish community braced itself for an influx of women on the prowl, with unreliable reports suggesting an increase in sales of breath fresheners and Lynx locally. Interestingly, if the influx materialises these women will more than likely come from the well-known urban areas around the country, including Galway and Dublin.
>
> *Longford Leader*

And what about the towns with the most available women? The south and west of Galway City take first and sixth respectively, with the former having one single woman in every seven. Dublin has most of the top ten places to find unattached women – Stillorgan, Blackrock, Dún Laoghaire, Crumlin/Kimmage, Clontarf and Rathmines.

The figures were compiled by Michael Nugent, co-writer of hit musical, *I, Keano*, who used recent census statistics as his source. He also compiled a list of the best places to find a party, based on non-family household figures, which was published on his blog http://thatsireland.com.

Unfortunately, Drumlish, the undisputed male singleton capital of Ireland, or any other Longford town did not feature among the leading party towns. So it looks as if the best option for men from those parts is to head in droves to suburban south Dublin to take on the Ross O'Carroll Kelly types.

According to Michael Nugent, anyone seeking out a party in Ireland should start in Maynooth or Galway City, where one house in every six is a non-family household containing no related persons.

Again based on census figures, the following are his top ten places to party: Maynooth, Galway, Annacotty in Limerick (one house in eight), Carrick-on-Shannon in Leitrim (one in ten), Sligo town (one in ten), Limerick City (one in eleven), Ballyhaunis in Mayo (one in twelve), Westport in Mayo (one in twelve), Athlone in Westmeath (one in twelve) and Cork City (one in thirteen).

Man Tormented by Former Lover

The real trouble between Michael and Kathleen, both in their sixties, started after she had met him with another woman. They had been in a relationship for about ten years and were friends after they broke up – until the other woman came into the picture.

Torture began for Tralee man Michael O'Regan on 18 December 2004, the day Kathleen saw him with that other lady. He was hardly able to go outside his door without fear of being accosted. He claimed she assaulted him, sometimes made up to 80 phone calls a day, hung her underwear on his van, took his mobile phone and, on the day of his daughter's funeral, his phone rang during the service.

At Tralee District Court, Kathleen O'Rahilly admitted assaulting him at his workplace in Rock Street, Tralee. He told the court he was afraid to walk around the town and never knew where she was going to spring out of.

'When I was walking after my daughter's hearse, the phone was ringing and she was abusing me. The gardaí have a thick file on the activity of this lady. It was not just a one off,' he said.

> The court heard that after the prosecution was served Ms O'Rahilly came to Mr O'Regan's workshop and threw an envelope with € 1,000 inside and told him not to press charges. 'She did apologise numerous times but came back again afterwards,' he said.
>
> *Kerry's Eye*

Even during an interval on the day of the court, he claimed she marched up and down in front of him, 'coming close and pulling faces'. She was a law unto herself and told him the gardaí would do 'f°°° all'. On one occasion, she parked her car across his drive and refused to move for the gardaí.

Michael said that he walked away from confrontations as he only wanted peace, but eventually went ahead with the prosecution when she verbally abused him outside his art gallery and punched him in the groin with her fist.

In court, Kathleen defended herself and denied being in a relationship with Michael for ten years. She suggested he was telling lies. 'I wasn't really with him. I hired him to do work and we became great friends,' she stated.

Telling Kathleen she was old enough to have more sense, Judge James O'Connor warned her she was in danger of going to jail if she did not stop tormenting Michael. She was also ordered to stay away from his home, business address and where he socialised. Judge O'Connor put the case back for review at the end of the year.

Lovers Kiss and Make Up on Courthouse Steps

Love conquers all even when you are in trouble with the law. Take the case of Brendan, who was caught driving his girlfriend Geeta's car without having insurance or a licence.

Geeta O'Neill wasn't a bit happy with him when he related his sorry tale to her and they split up. He had told her he had garage insurance and a licence but he was sorry afterwards for doing that. He took full responsibility for breaking the law and claimed Geeta knew nothing about it.

'We broke up on the night about all this, but we got back together just before the court here this morning,' he told Tullow District Court with a happy smile.

> Judge Donnchadh Ó Buachalla clarified that the reunion had happened as they waited for the court sitting to begin, much to the amusement of the court.
>
> *Carlow Nationalist*

The judge then fined Brendan Payne of Burrin Manor, Carlow, €800 for driving without insurance and put him off the road for six months.

Tom and Jerry's – The Best Place for a Wedding Bash

It was a meeting with Garryowen man Paddy Gleeson in France five years before that led a Welsh couple to tie the knot in Limerick. The message from Paddy was simple – if you're ever in Ireland, go to Tom and Jerry's pub because they'll look after you. Paddy was bang on, as ever after that any excuse at all brought 36-year-old Anthony Greszea to Shannonside.

The craic was only ninety and Anthony got an added bonus when he married the woman of his dreams in Limerick – a weekend celebrating in Tom and Jerry's homely pub in Lower Glentworth Street.

And just to show that Las Vegas-style opulence, glitz, helicopters, celebrities and multi-million euro receptions in country mansions are not typical of all Limerick weddings, Anthony and his bride, Louise Morgan, chose the simplest possible bash.

The couple got hitched in Limerick's registry office and spent the rest of their weekend in the pub where staff had been working around the clock preparing for the big day.

'There really was nowhere else we would have liked to hold it. It wasn't an option. At least 30 people here have never been to Ireland before and they all want to come back again,' Anthony said.

He and Louise, a 26-year-old nurse, are both from Ireharris in south Wales and 50 people attended the nuptials. Friendship is the biggest single attraction of the pub according to Anthony. 'We walked in here and were immediately accepted as family. We keep in contact with Jerry and Tommy all the time.'

Mr Greszea, a mechanic, has made such good friends here that local man Patrick Kelly from Garryowen was his usher on the big day. By Saturday, the group were out of their gladrags and back in their Welsh rugby jerseys in the pub.

'We've become very good friends with the barman, who has practically organised everything for us. We love Limerick. The people are so friendly and make you feel so welcome, that's why we keep coming back,' Louise said.

But Friday was also a day of double jubilations as their best friend John Jones was celebrating his 51st birthday. 'I've been told to celebrate my birthday tomorrow as the wedding is today, but that gives us another chance to celebrate,' he said.

Limerick Leader

Sex on the Net Countrywide

It's a planet removed from the days when the plight of lovelorn bachelors desperately seeking female company was highlighted by the late John B Keane. A click of a mouse can now bring internet users to a number of websites offering sexy escort services in many towns around Ireland.

The escort industry, which sees women advertising a range of services from girlfriend experiences to 'domination and submission', got some of the media in the north-east rather excited. Escort agencies promoting their services in towns such as Dundalk and Drogheda reportedly had no shortage of clients, a trend also reported in several other towns.

A male reporter decided to do a bit of pricing and contacted one of the County Louth agencies. He was greeted by a friendly girl with an English accent who informed him that it would cost him €160 for half an hour or €240 for an hour of her company.

The Candy Shop website described itself as a small, friendly cooperative of Irish and foreign female escorts working together in Dundalk. Clients were promised: 'If you like sexy ladies and you would like some erotic companionship in Dundalk . . . look no further.'

The advertising blurb claimed they provided very discreet top quality escort services at competitive rates to discerning gentlemen and couples in Dundalk and the surrounding area. The website included a photo gallery where potential clients could view the personal details of some of the girls available.

It boasted a good choice of ladies available to cater for all tastes, early until late, seven days a week. Contact could be made through a mobile phone number.

> Among the ladies stated to be available are a tall, slim, busty and very good looking black lady, friendly and adventurous.

Another is listed as a tall, slim, sophisticated and busty English blonde who is good company in public and great company in private.

Services offered include domination and submission, duos and trios, fantasies and fetishes, girlfriend experiences, private lap dances, role playing and massage.

The Argus

Websites also boasted a private member's club offering access to 'our super elite' escorts, adding: 'Superb quality, absolute honesty and integrity, impeccable personal attention, and the appropriate respect, are things our clientele have come to know and expect from Escorts Dundalk every time they make a booking with us.'

Animals and Pet Stories

A Big 'Merci' to Father of All Cows

He had fathered 100,000 daughters by the time he hit the age of 15 and was, unsurprisingly, dubbed a true hero of Irish agriculture. The prolific sire came from Holland leaving the tulips behind to ensure Irish cows were kept mooing with pleasure.

Galtee Merci arrived unheralded as a young buck to the fertile plains of Munster and has left his mark for ever more. He was the first Irish-registered artificial insemination (AI) bull to be let loose in County Cork and, given his short time on this earth, his achievements were quite remarkable.

He proved to be a full-blooded hot male with an eye for the ladies. The only time he left the comfort of celibacy was to make his donations to the bovine gene pool.

The 100,000 figure is based on a count of 33,400 of his daughters which were milk-recorded. According to one report, only 30 per cent of Irish cows are milk-recorded and it was taken as fact that he was the father of the girls. So far, no cow has come forward demanding a DNA test be undertaken.

Last week, with great sadness, a true beast left this world for pastures new and probably left whole herds grieving their brief, yet fulfilling, encounter with Galtee Merci, a Holstein bull. However, at 15 years he was showing his age, and had to be put down with great regret.

The Corkman

But the sense of sadness in farmyards all over Cork was tinged with joy as he had also fathered a lot of sons who are set to follow their old man into the trade. And grandsons will also carry on his legacy.

Which ensures a lot of cows will be mooing contentedly for years to come in the Golden Vale and along the foothills of the Galtee Mountains.

A Traffic-Stopping Waddle

Mammy Duck and her 11 ducklings brought traffic to a halt in Carlow and taught everybody a lesson in the safe cross code at the same time. She made sure her offspring used a pedestrian crossing at Kennedy Avenue.

A large crowd gathered to watch the procession all the way to the river bank. Even the regular hang-out area at the town centre fountain was deserted by youngsters who were distracted by the event.

The photographer, John Courtney, was on hand to snap the proceedings. Soon, up to 50 people had gathered to witness the traffic-stopping episode which went on for nearly half an hour.

'They were stuck to their Mam like glue and various people stepped out onto the road to stop the traffic but, in truth, no drivers were in a hurry to miss the show,' said John Courtney.

Carlow Nationalist

After Mammy Duck and her brood made it safely across the road in 12 pieces they meandered down to Penney's car park and were ushered through a fence to the river. The family, undoubtedly tired after their waddle, jumped into the river to the sounds of applause from the onlookers.

But Daddy Duck missed out on the drama. The drake turned up a few minutes later as the crowd was dispersing.

Cat-Astrophe as Feline Sparks Electricity Chaos

A cat which ran out of lives left thousands of homes in the Drogheda area without power for several hours. The cat had come in contact with a 110 kv line, one of the major lines supplying power in the north east.

The unfortunate moggy managed to make its way through two wire barriers and into the Drybridge substation before being blown to bits by the huge electrical current. The bang was heard by local residents and the explosion could be seen as far away as Ardee.

Local ESB staff had the job of collecting feline body parts in the machinery on the following day. The ESB head office, however, was more circumspect, saying officiously but not very informatively that 'initial indications are that an external object came into contact with the components within the substation.' Although they would not confirm it was a cat, they agreed that it was likely.

> The rambling cat left approximately 20,000 homes and businesses without power, mainly in Drogheda but also those in Louth and Meath served by the 110kv line in Drybridge. Users include businesses, shopping centres and factories in Dundalk who were also left without power.
>
> *Drogheda Independent*

The ESB afterwards reviewed the situation in the hope of preventing a similar cat-astrophe in the future.

Dead Cow Found Standing Up

In February 2006, gardaí were called to a farm at Meelin, in north Cork, after receiving reports that dead animals were not being properly buried there. Dorina Humphries was in charge of the holding but was not there when the gardaí arrived.

A dead cow was plainly to be seen in the mud. 'The cow was found standing up and was deep in mud. It was there for a considerable period of time and there was a bad odour,' Inspector Senan Ryan told Mallow Court.

An official from the Department of Agriculture also told of finding the cow and another 'deceased bovine animal'. In his opinion, the cow was an old one as it had an ear tag predating 1996.

> The court was told Ms Humphries wasn't at the holding when the animal died as she was taking care of her seriously-ill daughter who had cancer at the time. Her son, James, was in charge and he told her about what had happened. He phoned the knackers to take the carcases away but they refused to come out.
>
> *The Corkman*

Her partner, Robert, said they had the vet out to the premises a few times and had phoned the knackers' yard twice to collect the animals. 'We were told to bury the animals and we did it by hand,' he said.

He told the court that they had got a track machine to move the animals and he said he did not tell his partner at the time as she had 'enough on her mind'.

A picture of tough circumstances was painted before the court which heard there were 'plenty of rushes and bad land' in Meelin. Judge Leo Malone fined Ms Humphries €500.

Kelly the Seal Takes a Stroll in Limerick

It was a sight that made building workers almost fall off their scaffolding. A young seal climbed out of a river bank and slithered up the road in front of them in the Corbally area of Limerick. The three-month-old seal, nicknamed Kelly, was most likely separated from her mother during a storm and was blown in along the River Shannon.

The builders immediately downed tools and, before the young seal could make her way into the path of oncoming traffic, encircled the mammal. They then made an urgent call to Niamh Allen of Limerick Animal Welfare. Niamh, who is more accustomed to getting calls about dogs in trouble, couldn't believe what she was hearing.

> 'The seal was really dehydrated and her eyes were rolling back in her head. She should have been about 40kgs and we reckoned she was 20kgs. Seals can die very fast when they lose all their fat.'
>
> *Limerick Leader*

The seal received some initial veterinary treatment in Limerick and Chelsea Collins of the Seal Sanctuary in Cork was then called. Once she heard the unusual details of the story, Chelsea dropped everything and headed straight to Limerick. Chelsea gave the seal some sugar glucose. The patient started flapping her flippers, fell asleep shortly afterwards and snored like a baby.

After the week-long separation from her shoal, the seal was treated to mackerel and herring smoothies at the Irish Seal Sanctuary in

Garristown, Dublin, on her way to a full recovery and ultimate return to the sea.

Watching Fish Replaces TV as Tank Craze Takes Off

Is this a plasma TV or a 21st century fish tank? A question that some people might ask on entering modern homes in the north-east of Ireland.

Like many another 'fishy' idea, it came from America – the notion that home aquariums might even take over from televisions, or at the very least share living-room space with the telly. Some homeowners in Louth, Meath and north Dublin are part of a growing trend towards purchasing the latest in wall-mounted fish tanks, which look like plasma TVs.

Brisk demand is being reported in Drogheda for this new-fangled equipment, which is similar in size and design to a plasma TV. It's a big hit with design conscious people, according to Adrian O'Donoghue, owner of the local pet centre.

The tanks look well, are relatively maintenance-free and are said to be the first of their kind in this country.

> Adrian enthused: 'They are making a big impact and there is a bit of a craze in Ireland for them at the moment, the visual impact is incomparable to any other aquarium. The biggest selling point is the visual impact, it has that wow factor as soon as you see it.'
>
> *Drogheda Independent*

The funky design and low maintenance means the aquarium appeals to those who may not previously have been interested in keeping fish. Most purchasers have never kept fish before.

Big Deal Fish Was Completely out of its Depth

Saint Patrick made a name for himself driving snakes out of Ireland but, clearly, his writ did not include the sea. He missed out on some serpent-like fish that live off our coast.

Years ago, in the early days of sailing ships, sailors spoke of sea serpents which sceptics believed were just other mythical creatures of the deep. But 'deal' fish, which occasionally turn up in trawler nets these days, fit the description of sea serpents in the view of Dingle marine life expert, Kevin Flannery.

One such fish was caught by a Dingle trawler skippered by Labhrás Courtney last March. It was the first recorded 'deal' landing in Dingle Bay in 35 years. These fish normally live at great depths, but sometimes come up at night to feed in shallow waters. The head looks like that of a horse or a dog.

> 'It is believed nowadays that what they [early sailors] saw were those deal fish swimming on the surface. Because they swim like a serpent, the body is totally flat as it has to survive under great pressure in the deep,' Kevin Flannery explained.
>
> *The Kerryman*

Undersea oddities regularly arrive in Kevin Flannery's post. As someone who has built up a national reputation as a specialist on rare fish, he is never fazed. One day, he received an envelope from Michael Fenton, a fisherman in Castlecove, County Kerry, containing a crab claw which had four pincers instead of the usual two.

It seems that crabs and lobsters have an amazing ability to do something humans have not yet achieved – re-grow body parts that are removed or damaged. It is believed that is what happened in the case of the Castlecove crab. According to Kevin, the damage in the claw caused a genetic malfunction which resulted in four pincers instead of two.

The strangest marine item he ever got was the skin of an Atlantic football fish. It was found by a woman walking on a beach near Waterville, County Kerry. It took ages to identify the skin because he had had never come across anything like it before. The skin is in the Natural History Museum, Dublin.

Chaos as Stag is Chased through Village and Schoolyard

All was peaceful in the Meath village of Kildalkey – until the Ward Union Hunt Club arrived on horseback. More than 80 huntsmen went through the village chasing a deer and causing pandemonium.

There were chaotic scenes on the quiet street and a stag was pursued through the grounds of Kildalkey national school. The pupils, who were about to leave school for the day, were upset and frightened by the incident according to the principal teacher, Kathleen Lynch. When she saw what was happening, she rushed around the classrooms to tell the other teachers to keep the children inside.

The upshot of it all was that a number of local landowners decided to ban all hunting on their property. And, with most townlands around the village being affected by the landowners' decision, this effectively ruled out all hunting in the area.

A local farmer, Tony Brady, said all hunting was being banned for the foreseeable future due to the 'arrogance of the huntsmen and total disregard for public and private property', of the Ward Union. The hunt secretary of the Meath Hunt and Tara Harriers was also notified in writing of the areas affected by the ban.

The Meath Chronicle

Oliver Russell, chairman of Ward Union Hunt, apologised for the incident which, he admitted, had caused 'anxiety and stress to staff and potential risk to the children'.

Hunting was suspended by the Ward Union to allow for a review of the incident and Oliver Russell said a number of measures were to be implemented.

Meanwhile, in Limerick, people were shocked following the alleged killing of a pet cat by hounds belonging to Limerick Harriers on St Stephen's Day.

The 13-year-old cat was in a private garden in Ballyclough and could not escape the hounds as its legs were disabled. Neighbours saw the cat being killed by a hound, Mary Cooke, a local resident, claimed. Parents were also concerned for the safety of young children who may be playing in gardens and faced with a pack of hounds.

The cat was owned by Mary's neighbours and she called on the Limerick Harriers to let homeowners know when they were holding a hunt in an area so that people could protect their domestic pets. They were not aware a hunt was being held on St Stephen's Day, she pointed out.

According to John McNamara, joint master of the Limerick Harriers, a hound would never follow a cat and he could not say for certain if the cat was killed by one of the hunt's hounds.

> He went on: 'I genuinely believe the cat was dying or dead and one of the hounds picked him up. We meet cats all the time and the hounds would never follow a cat, but they would pick something up if they saw it on the ground. This has never happened before. I can't explain it. The cat had no visible injuries,' he said.
>
> *Limerick Leader*

The Limerick Harriers apologised to the cat's owners after the incident.

John McNamara also gave an assurance that the hounds posed no danger to young children. He also said that all farmers were sent out cards informing them that a hunt was taking place in their area, but it would be impossible to inform every householder in a particular area.

Obstacles Put in the Way of Petrina and her Guide Dog

Petrina Finn is almost blind and loves her guide dog, Fionn. Guide dogs for the blind are allowed in public places, under law, but not everybody accepts Petrina's faithful friend who is helping her to lead a 'near normal' life.

In the course of just one day, the Drogheda woman found herself barred from shopping in Aldi with Fionn while, later, a security guard tried to stop her entering the local Lourdes Hospital with her dog.

Petrina, who has a degenerative eye disease and is rapidly approaching total blindness, was very annoyed about the Aldi incident. She was shopping with husband, Kieran, and children, Aoife, aged five, and Pádraig, four.

> 'It is very embarrassing for the children and for myself to be stopped from going into a store. People could think you were shoplifting or something,' said Petrina.
>
> *Drogheda Independent*

It was the second time such an incident happened to her at the store. It should not have happened and turned shopping from an ordinary chore into an ordeal, she protested. After the first time she was stopped at Aldi, the store put up a sign saying guide dogs were accepted.

When she was stopped on the second occasion, she told a security guard that Fionn was a guide dog but he still wouldn't let her in. So she went to higher authorities and was eventually met by a deputy manager who apologised. He showed the sign to the original staff member and, by way of explanation, said the staff member was a foreign national who was not aware that guide dogs were permitted in shops.

That evening, Petrina experienced the same problem at the Lourdes Hospital. When she was outside the front door, a security guard 'bellowed' at her that she couldn't go in with the dog. However, a woman from a nearby shop shouted back that guide dogs were allowed and he then waved her in.

In the two years since her beloved dog Fionn arrived, Petrina has been stopped from entering public places five times, four of them in Drogheda.

Mee-ow from Mobile Phone Saves Day for Lucky Cat

The cries of a kitten alerted Limerick woman Sue Haskett as she made her way to work just before eight o'clock one morning. She could hear the plaintive sounds coming from a parked car and quickly discovered that a little feline was under the bonnet.

Soon up to a dozen people had gathered at the scene in Catherine Street, all trying to lure the kitten out of the car. A unit of the Limerick Fire Brigade was called but failed to have as much luck as the two locals who remained at the Toyota for over an hour and a half.

The owner of the nearby Coffee for Two café also placed a saucer of milk and some food on the ground in an effort to coax the kitten out. One passer-by commented: 'You wouldn't see as much fuss over a human being.'

George McElligott of Limerick Animal Welfare had a mobile phone with a cat's mee-ow ringtone and he lay on the side of the road holding the phone under the bonnet, assisted by Bernadette Keogh who eventually coaxed the cat out.

'Persistence always wins the day. I tried to explain that to the fire brigade as I've loads of cats myself,' said Bernadette, holding the shivering kitten in her arms.

> Eventually, the owner of the car arrived at the scene, unaware of all the commotion taking place over the previous two hours. 'She didn't know what was going on. She was just really embarrassed over all the hullabaloo,' said George McElligott.
>
> *Limerick Leader*

The kitten was afterwards named Little Diesel.

Cat in Tricky Position in Limerick

It looked like being another routine sort of day for Limerick animal lover Noel Shinnors. That was until a call for help came from a house in the Ennis Road area about a cat being in trouble.

A big, ginger feline had somehow got stuck about 15 feet in between the walls of two neighbouring houses which only had a six-inch gap separating them.

Noel, an inspector with the Limerick branch of the ISPCA, responded and Limerick Fire Brigade was also called to the scene. Firemen had to partially demolish the wall of one of the houses to free the cat from the narrow gap.

The owner of the house, Kathleen Ryan, allowed firemen drill a hole about six feet wide in the wall of an extension to her property and the cat was rescued after two hours of patient work.

Noel, who expressed gratitude to Kathleen and other neighbours for allowing them break the wall, said the cat would certainly have died only for their quick thinking. The cat was described as being very friendly and all concerned waited for the owner to come forward.

> 'It was a really unusual case and the officers got a huge round of applause once they managed to prise the cat out. I've called the vets since and she's going perfect; she's only lost two nails,' he said.
>
> *Limerick Leader*

Kathleen Ryan hadn't a clue how the cat had wedged itself into such a trap. 'Maybe she fell off the roof, as she had landed on her back when she became stuck,' she suggested.

Kathleen had been using the extension to her property as a garage and didn't mind forking out to have the wall fixed, as long as she didn't have to hear the cat crying any longer!

Is Comfy Cat Sleeping on Missing Wig?

A cat in Carlow is snuggled up in a missing barrister's wig, if anonymous ransom notes are to be believed. The story begins as Dublin-based barrister Agnes McKenzie is leaving Carlow courthouse after a busy day. On the way to her car, she loses the cherished symbol of her calling which had been tailored by one of the best makers of legal wigs in London.

Through the Carlow media, she offered a €100 cash reward as well as a 'complete amnesty' to whoever was unlawfully holding on to it. 'I don't care who took it, just so long as I get it back,' said the frustrated barrister.

Agnes may be accustomed to listening to strange stories in courtrooms, but she was unprepared for the bizarre responses to pleas she made for the return of the missing wig. A response came quickly to the *Carlow Nationalist* in the form of a ransom note reading as follows:

'Hello everyone in the *Nationalist* office, Carlow. I read your article about the barrister's wig. Well I am the anymous [sic] person that has got it. If she wants it back, she will have to put her price up to €1,000. The money she is offering is chicken feed. At the moment, my cat is enjoying it, using it as her bed. She loves it. So it's a case of cat versus wig. I will look out for next week's paper, and read all about this famous wig. Hopefully €1,000 will be up for offer. I will then contact the barrister in question. Until then, keep smiling.'

The paper responded by telling the ransom demanders to jump off a large cliff with two boulders tied to their ankles. But another letter was posted to its office the following week reading:

'Give her this message, Miss Wilmot: Money Up Front €1,000 or The Wig Gets It! Get a move on barrister. Cat v Wig! Miaow! PS Paitence [sic] isn't my strong point.'

> Her stolen wig holds particular value because it was a hard-fought battle to get it between money woes and sitting her exams because she came to law late in life . . . The wig is silver in colour and has stayed with Agnes since she first became a barrister. It has survived years of travel and made it safely from London to Dublin only to be lost in the car park of Carlow courthouse.
>
> *Carlow Nationalist*

Horsehair wigs cost from around €600 upwards and Agnes was not prepared to pay the ransom. Investigative reporters in the *Nationalist* never got to the bottom of the story and the location of the wig remains a mystery. But is a cat with a secret purring happily somewhere in Carlow?

Snakes Alive . . . Exotic Reptile Arrives Unexpectedly

Tom Smith was having breakfast at his home in Newbridge when an uninvited guest arrived from nowhere and slithered across his kitchen floor. He almost fell off his chair with shock when he saw the unfamiliar creature was a snake about two feet in length. Tom didn't know what to do but immediately decided to ring the gardaí. 'It gave me an awful fright,' he declared.

On hearing of the strange appearance, neighbours soon gathered in Tom's home in Anfield Terrace. And while everybody was curious for a peep, nobody wanted to take away the visitor. The gardaí guessed the snake was probably an escaped pet and began to look locally for the owner.

Looking tame and happy, despite all the drama that was going on around it, the snake was eventually coaxed into a cardboard box by the gardaí. Fiona O'Dwyer from nearby Jean's Jewellers was the bravest of the lot and agreed to take the snake until the owner could be identified.

> Fiona took the snake to the Exotic Pet shop in the industrial estate where it was identified as a Californian King Snake. 'They are not dangerous. They can grow to be about a metre long and as thick as a woman's wrist. In the wild they hunt and kill rattlesnakes. But they are not a danger to humans,' she assured concerned folk.
>
> *Leinster Leader*

'It was my first encounter with a snake but by the end of the day he was like my best friend!' Fiona remarked later.

Californian King Snakes can be found in the areas of Baja, California, Oregon, Arizona and Utah. They are one of the most popular and easy to keep species of snake to own. Adults can live on two frozen mice every 10 days.

The gardaí in Newbridge also put local minds at ease by telling people they were satisfied that the snake was not a danger to the public and that it was being cared for properly.

Old Irish Pucks in Danger – No Kidding!

Some Irish conservationists start jumping up and down about the plight of endangered faraway species such as the Polar bear or the Yangtze River dolphin, but few enough give a puck about the native Old Irish Goat. Interbreeding with less pure goats and rampant culling are threatening this noble denizen of the Burren. However, the threat of extinction has prompted an eleventh hour conservation effort.

The goat population of the Burren includes a large number of feral goats – animals that were once tame but are now living in the wild – and the Old Irish Goat is in a minority among these herds. The Burren Life Project and local farmer Patrick McCormack are now working to collect and breed an animal that can truly be described as one of our own.

Patrick has no time at all for people who say, 'Ah sure, they're only goats.' And he is also dismissive of those who are concerned only for the likes of the White Rhino and other threatened species in distant places.

Identification of the Old Irish Goat is a difficulty and the Old English Goat Society is helping to distinguish the breed. Just as 'there's no such thing as a purebred Irish man', it's the same with goats, according to Patrick.

'There are genes from other influences there. From a recent survey we know that unless something is done in the next three to five years this old type goat will be swamped by modern hybrids, the Sannan and the British Alpine and so forth. Unless something is done now the breed will be gone and lost for ever,' he said.

The Clare Champion

The plan is to get 20 obliging females who will be attracted to the dwindling number of male goats (pucks). But the temptresses could have some seducing to do as time is not on the side of the pucks who may be losing their libido. 'The old type goats, the few of them that are left in the hills, are old themselves and to knock another year or two breeding out of them is so important,' Patrick explained.

Bats Can't See Their Luxury New Home

The location of a new bat house in Clare is supposed to be a secret from the public for security reasons. Unfortunately, however, it also appears to be a secret to bats giving the term 'blind as a bat' a new resonance. Built at a cost of €175,000 to the taxpayer as part of the Ennis bypass project, it is intended as a home for the endangered Lesser Horseshoe Bat community which is protected under EU laws and listed as a vulnerable species.

All very well and fair dues to the powers-that-be in Clare for doing their bit for nature conservation, but the problem is that two years after the construction of the bat house it still had no bats. Electronic equipment and heaters were not operating in the bat house but this was an unlikely reason for the absence of bats according to Howard Williams of Inis Environmental Services.

'It is more likely that bats in the area have yet to discover and investigate the purpose-built house,' he opined. Another reason, he felt, might the presence of swallows just inside the entrance to the house.

> There are less than a dozen of these bat houses in Europe presently and the new bat house has been kitted out with infrared beams to monitor bat movements and a telephone line

has been installed into the home to enable the downloading of information.

The Clare People

But Howard Williams discovered that a refurbished old schoolhouse – a much less sophisticated roost – had attracted the Lesser Horseshoe Bat, with seven recorded bats at the house in June. He has not given up hope that the bats will eventually find their expensive new home.

Courtroom Dramas

Cash Scam on Friend 'Too Fanciful' for a Movie Script

In February 2006, Helen started to receive unsigned letters asking her for money. She thought the letters were from a man known to her and her close friend, Anne. She believed the man was in financial trouble. Six letters arrived over a six-month period asking Helen to leave cash at various hotels in Tralee. She left a total of €8,325 at the hotel reception desk and it was later collected.

However, Helen became suspicious after the final cash delivery. She made enquiries of the person she thought was receiving the money and discovered it was not him. The gardaí set up a surveillance operation and traced the scam back to her friend, Anne Buckley.

> The court was told that Helen Nash was very distressed when she found out what had happened and it had put her under terrible financial strain. Mrs Buckley was fully aware of the impact on her friend because it was mentioned to her in confidence and she was telling her at all stages what happened, said Judge James O'Connor.
>
> *Kerry's Eye*

Anne Buckley's solicitor, Pat Mann, said if anyone read the story as a script it would be too fanciful for a movie. The women, both from Tralee, were no longer friends, he added.

Helen did not give evidence but the prosecuting garda said Helen did not want to see Anne going to jail.

Anne pleaded guilty at Tralee District Court to six charges of deceiving her friend and paid back the €8,325 she had scammed. Judge O'Connor, who described the case as a 'right con job', also ordered her to pay €15,000 compensation to Helen. A scam that began on St Valentine's Day 2006 ended on St Valentine's Day 2007. It was a 'one-off blunder' that caused a lot of damage.

The Man from Tipp wanted his Wife killed.

In 1995 the marriage of Patrick and Mary began to break down. He became involved with another woman, Sinead, and had a baby with her. Soon after, his wife withdrew €70,000 of the €100,000 lying in the joint bank account she held with her husband. She also gave certain information to the Revenue Commissioners which resulted in tax judgements of €27,000 being made against her husband. Oddly enough, the €30,000 she left behind in the joint account just about covered this tax bill.

The wife, Mary Rafferty, mother of two children aged six and four, described in her victim impact statement how she lived in fear since June 2004.

Her life, she said, had been turned upside down and she had lived in fear since she was made aware that her life was in danger. She was forced to move out of her house until September of that year when she returned as one of her children was starting school.

In February 2005, she again had to move out of her home due to another threat being made on her life. She said she would now like to see justice done, move on with her life and raise her children in a safe, secure environment.

> The court heard that Mr Rafferty had not seen his two children from the marriage since the incident and that his wife had taken possession of the family home. Brendan Nix, the defending counsel, said his client was now in a stable relationship with another woman and that they had a child together. That relationship, the court heard, began during Mr Rafferty's marriage.
>
> *Limerick Leader*

In the autumn of 2004, Patrick made the first attempt to have his wife killed. He approached a well-known criminal figure who priced the job at €8,000. The streetwise conman, seeing Patrick as 'a soft touch', took 'the fee' and did a runner, knowing well Patrick could hardly make a complaint to the gardaí.

But Patrick didn't seem to be deterred by this setback. He approached another man and upped the offer to €15,000 and suggested that he 'could probably come up with another €5,000'. The only problem was this man (unknown to Patrick) was an undercover garda.

They met in the Five Alley pub just outside Nenagh, Co Tipperary. Taking the 'new hitman' on a 13-mile drive in his expensive four-wheel drive, Patrick discussed the plan. He suggested to the undercover garda that he stage a road traffic accident in which he would 'run her car off the road'. If this was not successful he was to 'do her neck in' – making a choking gesture with his hands on his throat.

Patrick, who is originally from Galway, left school at 14 to work in a steelworks. He soon became foreman and by age 27 he ran his own steel fabrication business. He also worked nights as a taxi driver. In court evidence, he was described as a 'hard-working man whose motivation in life was making massive amounts of money'. By the time he was arrested in February 2005, he was a haulier living in Ballina, County Tipperary.

Brendan Nix said it was of some comfort to Patrick that his two young children did not understand the 'terrible thing' he had done and he hoped as they grew older they would learn to forgive him.

On 30 January 2007, Patrick Rafferty [39] was sentenced to seven years in prison at Limerick Central Criminal Court for 'soliciting somebody to kill his wife.'

> In passing sentence, Mr Justice Carney said the offence of which Rafferty had been convicted was, fortunately, still a rare one in this jurisdiction. Only three other people have been convicted of soliciting for murder in the history of the state.
>
> *Limerick Leader*

The 'Genius' of Bare Hand Window Breakers

It's late on Paddy's Night and the unmistakeable sound of breaking glass echoes around a County Cork town. Gardaí come upon two men fighting in Kanturk; one admits smashing a window with his bare hand.

In a separate incident, a man was seen smashing windows in a house and was bleeding heavily from both hands.

The two cases and several others arising from mayhem in Kanturk on different nights came before Judge Seán Ó Donnabháin at the Circuit Court in the town. 'Is this a form of genius? Is this a particular form of stupidity in Kanturk? In fairness, I have not come across it before,' he declared.

One of the window smashers was given a suspended jail sentence and barred from every pub in Kanturk for a year. The other was put under curfew and ordered to stay at home from 10pm until 6am.

In yet another case at the same court, a man alleged to have a hatchet in a fight was barred from every pub in Kanturk for a year and bound to the peace.

> The defence solicitor had argued the man was extremely intoxicated and very annoyed and there was no evidence of a real attempt to do harm. Judge Ó Donnabháin commented that the punishment will 'test his sobriety'.
>
> *The Corkman*

Harmless Busker 'Sorry' for Enjoying Paddy's Day

Busker Ralph Perkins can entertain people both on the street and in the courthouse. He had been playing his bodhrán outside Dunnes Stores in Ennis on St Patrick's Day and was arrested for not obeying a garda's direction to get moving.

Ralph later came before Ennis Court where he represented himself. 'I'm sorry for enjoying Paddy's Day. I was just playing the bodhrán and got told to move on. I'm guilty of certain things. I used threatening words which is out of character for me . . . He [the garda] pushed me against a glass . . . I ended up missing a session because I was locked up,' he told Judge Joseph Mangan.

The Judge replied: 'Weren't you lucky.'

Ralph, from Cadamstown, Birr, County Offaly, said he would not move because his bodhrán had been taken from him earlier. 'I think he [the garda] was out of order. I was enjoying Paddy's Day. People were enjoying my music. They had smiles on their faces. He told me to go – "move now, move now." I was busking. I wasn't causing any harm.'

The case was struck out.

Judge Mangan said that he was worried about where and how
Mr Perkins would be celebrating St George's Day. Mr Perkins
bowed and thanked the court for hearing his story.

The Clare Champion

The Chicken Nugget Assault Case

Mark Francis entered his local chipper in Killorglin after quaffing a few
drinks too many. It was just after 1am and he ordered food.

After an exchange of words with a staff member at Micko's Takeaway,
Mark spat into his bag of chips and started throwing chicken nuggets at
the man. He then punched one of the tills and used his boot to break a
pane of glass on a teddy bear crane amusement machine.

At Killorglin Court, he was fined €400 for abusive and threatening
behaviour and made pay €1,500 for damage to the machine.

But the charge of assaulting a fast food worker with chicken nuggets
was dropped after he pleaded guilty. The court was also told the 19-year-
old had apologised to the worker, was staying away from drink since the
incident and was no longer using chicken nuggets as missiles.

Judge James O'Connor adjourned the matter until the end of the
year, saying Francis was on his absolute last chance and would
be jailed for ten months if there was any further misbehaviour.

The Kingdom

Called Judge a 'Pr − − k'

You don't call a judge a 'pr − − k' and get away with it, as a 20-year-old
Clare man learned to his cost at Scariff District Court. James Casey was
given a three-day sentence in St Patrick's Institution for referring to

Judge Joseph Mangan in such terms.

Casey, from Ardnacrusha, had public order charges against him adjourned, but caused a disturbance as he was leaving the court and was immediately called back. Having faced the judge and been sternly ticked off by him, Casey turned towards his seat and was heard to mutter, 'You're some pr – – k'.

Judge Mangan found him in contempt of court and offered him an opportunity to purge his contempt by apologising. Casey accepted the opportunity. He said he was sorry, adding that the reason he drank was that he had problems.

> Judge Mangan, who had a seven-day sentence in mind but reduced it to three days because of the apology, remarked: 'All you have to do is have manners like anyone else. Do you think you're the only one here with problems? Do you think that no one else has gone through that experience?'
>
> *The Clare Champion*

Nally Visits Grafton Street during 'Mighty Stressful' Fortnight

Being a typical countryman more used to spending his days walking the land, Pádraig Nally felt out of place on Dublin's busy streets. But the best-known farmer in the West, who was making one of his rare trips to the capital for his trial in the Four Courts, also took time to look around the city, including his first visit to Grafton Street.

The shy man became a celebrity of sorts during his two-week trial which cleared him of the manslaughter of John Ward, a Traveller, on Nally's farm in Mayo, in October 2004.

After the second day of the trial, Nally's solicitor and confidante, Sean

Foy, took him on a walk through the city, an adventure in itself. Because of nightly television coverage of the trial, he was easily recognised in his open-necked white shirt and dark suit.

> It was to be a memorable first visit (to Grafton Street). Every second person who met him on the street was eager to shake his hand, pat him on the back and wish him the very best in his trial. Complete strangers of all ages and from every walk of life gathered around the quiet-spoken Mayo man and, in messages from the heart, extended their very best wishes to him at such a difficult time.
>
> *Western People*

On the street outside the Four Courts, cars and vans honked their horns and waved their support. The 62-year-old accused and his supporters could hardly believe they had so many backers.

At O'Shea's Hotel on Merchant's Quay, where Nally and his supporters were staying, the diners at lunch and dinnertime would stop briefly at his table with further messages of encouragement. One evening, a lady was so supportive that she insisted in picking up the tab for an evening meal for the entire Mayo group.

People told him they prayed for him and he also got thousands of letters, cards and mass cards while in prison. Looking back later, the farmer said the trial had been 'mighty stressful' and that he was all the time worrying and on edge. He also spent a night in St James' Hospital after getting severe chest pains.

After the verdict was announced, he felt sorry for the Ward family who had lost a father and were left with 11 children. In O'Shea's, Nally, who normally doesn't drink, settled his nerves with a brandy but there was no hint of triumphalism.

'I didn't think it [the trial] would go my way but, thank God, it has. I was surprised at the outcome. I thought I'd be found guilty more than not guilty and I was prepared for prison, at least I'd been told I was anyway,' he admitted.

Travellers were furious, with Rose Mary Maughan, spokeswoman for the Mayo Traveller Support Group, declaring: 'Travellers fear this will send out the message to society that it is perfectly all right to kill a Traveller. We don't feel protected by the law of the land. Personally I feel my life is viewed as worthless by society.'

For Pádraig Nally, it was back to his 30 cattle, two dogs and a tranquil life on his 65 acres in south Mayo.

Man Who Takes on Burglar Hailed as a Hero

At about half past five on the morning of 15 August 2005, Michael Courtney was sleeping soundly at his home in Killarney. He suddenly awoke and saw the shadowy outline of a hooded man standing at the bottom of his bed rummaging through his wallet.

Michael shouted at the burglar who dropped the wallet and ran downstairs. Wearing only a vest and underwear, he jumped from his bed and gave chase. He caught the burglar outside the backdoor and a struggle ensued. The intruder then bit Michael in the arm. The attacker also pulled a screwdriver, but Michael eventually got the better of him and pinned him to the ground.

The gardaí soon arrived, but Michael Courtney had been bitten so hard and the bite mark had penetrated so far under his skin that he feared for his health. He received four hepatitis injections afterwards.

> His teenage attacker, Harry Clifden, formerly of Woodlawn Park in Killarney, was in court to face justice and his victim. Clifden told gardaí that he must have been sleepwalking or trying to find a bathroom. And he blamed Michael as the one who brandished the screwdriver.
>
> *The Kerryman*

Clifden's barrister pleaded with Judge Carroll Moran not to send him to jail. He was a young man who was experiencing some family difficulties at the time. It would not be in society's interest to jail him.

Judge Moran praised Michael Courtney for his courage. Not alone did he take on the burglar, but he restrained him until the gardaí arrived.

The judge also spoke about what an horrific ordeal it must be for somebody to wake up to a complete stranger at the end of the bed. 'It is an appalling intrusion of the innermost sanctum of a person's home. This is why burglary is so serious an offence. And when the person is there in the house, it's even worse.'

Clifden was made pay €2,000 as a token of apology or else go to jail for three years.

Corkman Man Conned in Deal 'Far Too Good To Be True'

The day conman James O'Gorman walked into the motor factors premises of James Crowley in Ballincollig, outside Cork City, is a day Crowley has ever since rued.

It was the day the businessman was made a money-making offer he just couldn't resist, but which was far too good to be true as he soon learned to his cost – €54,000 to be exact.

O'Gorman and another man came into Crowley's stores in 2000 looking to buy an exhaust and there followed a discussion between them concerning Sterling exchange. They told Crowley he could sell Stg£40,000 at IR£43,000 which would save him IR£10,000 on normal bank charges. Crowley discussed the tempting transaction with his wife Shauna and Ian Chadwick, his partner in Autopoint Rally Sports. They agreed to buy into the deal.

A meeting was then set up in an apartment and Crowley went there carrying IR£43,000 cash in a suitcase. He was told three men sitting round a coffee table wished to count the money which was in bags of IR£1,000. One of the three men, who James Crowley described as 'looking like film star Brendan Gleeson', picked up several bags and threw them back into the suitcase.

The three men then left the room with the suitcase and after 15 minutes he went downstairs as he heard Shauna calling him. She had started to shout for him after she saw three burly men, whom she described as looking like nightclub bouncers, leave the apartment complex with the suitcase he had taken in. She feared he had been shot.

> Crowley also left the apartment and returned later only to be confronted by an irate O'Gorman who said there was only IRL£41,500 in the suitcase and the men believed he was trying to 'scam' them.
>
> *The Corkman*

Crowley said he wished to call off the deal and demanded his money back. But the money was gone. Over the next few days, he received reassurances from O'Gorman that he would get his money back 'pound for pound'.

There was no sign of the money, however. He said he was fed a constant stream of false promises and lies for a number of months before he eventually went to the gardaí on 23 August 2000 after pleas from Shauna.

James O'Gorman, aged 34, of Maplewood Park, Tallaght, was convicted by a jury in March 2007 of defrauding James Crowley out of the money. O'Gorman had €10,000 in court and he asked for more time to gather the balance. Judge Desmond Hogan gave him until May 2008 to put together €60,000 in compensation, warning that sentencing would not be adjourned again.

The court was told Mr O'Gorman had 19 previous convictions, including one in 1998 for theft and deception in Melbourne, Australia. There, he received a 30-month sentence but left Australia by mutual agreement instead of serving the time. He also had three previous assault charges and the other convictions were for road traffic offences.

Jail for 'Fraudster' Galway Councillor over Fence

It was almost teatime at Kilcolgan Private Nursing Home when the gardaí arrived to escort a colourful, portly resident to jail. Even the prayers of his 96-year-old mother were not enough to keep Michael 'Stroke' Fahy, a Galway councillor of 27 years standing, out of the clink.

Fahy's woes began with a fence he had erected for almost two kilometres around his land – at the expense of Galway County Council, of which he is the longest-serving member.

At Galway Circuit Court, he was found guilty by a jury of causing €7,055 to be paid by the council to a fencing company for work done on his property in 2001 and 2002. He was also convicted of submitting further false invoices from Byrne Fencing, totalling more than €14,500.

Judge Raymond Groarke labelled the farmer and former insurance salesman as 'arrogant, greedy and a determined fraudster'. He imposed a one-year sentence and fined the former Fianna Fáil councillor, now an Independent, €75,000.

> In a country where corruption among politicians rarely makes it to court, let alone attracts a prison sentence, it was widely predicted by court watchers that Fahy might get a suspended sentence at worst, and a hefty fine at best. But Judge Groarke laid it on the line when he imposed sentence on Michael 'Stroke' Fahy.

The Connacht Tribune

The story took a surprise turn the night before he was originally due to go to Castlerea Prison. The 56-year-old, who has heart problems, became ill and was anointed prior to being rushed to University College Hospital in Galway. Neighbours said he was 'very poorly, very weak altogether' before being taken away in an ambulance from his home near Ardrahan.

His devout mother, Mae, with a rosary beads entwined around her fingers, was taken to Merlin Park Hospital for respite care ahead of his jail term. Mr Fahy spent 22 hours on a trolley, had a device inserted to keep an artery open, and was also treated for high blood pressure.

After coming out of hospital, Michael Fahy went to Kilcolgan Nursing Home for convalescence. On Tuesday, 24 April, he was due to be discharged from the nursing home and was expected to make his own way to Loughrea garda station to surrender himself for his sentence.

However, the gardaí, who two weeks previously had been left in the embarrassing position of not knowing where he was following his discharge from hospital, took no chances and went to collect him on Monday, 23 April. In the nursing home during the weekend, Fahy, an only child, had been re-united with his mother, for whom he is carer.

He had expected to be returning to the hospital for further surgery on his heart and maintained he was not in a fit state to go to prison for at least six weeks. But the gardaí did not share this opinion.

Fahy was confined to the open area of the prison, sharing facilities with the killers of Detective Garda Jerry McCabe and other men convicted of murder, sex offences, manslaughter, robbery, assault and drug offences. He also had work duties to perform and had choices of catering, woodwork or housekeeping.

In lambasting the errant councillor, Judge Groarke said he had knowingly implicated a 'totally innocent' man – the fencing contractor Thomas Byrne – leaving him open to vilification and ruin if the truth had not come out.

The judge also said Fahy had invented a non-existent agreement; alleging the fencing was in exchange for stone from his land. But the jury had no doubts that the agreement was a fiction. Judge Groarke said Fahy had used his long experience in the council to steal from the council, but he had gambled with the reputations of honest men in an effort to escape the consequences of his delinquency.

Fahy is believed to be the first serving councillor in Ireland to go to jail. He was determined not to resign his seat and indicated he would remain a councillor until his appeal was heard in the Criminal Court of Appeal.

Become Friendly with the Dogs – a Recipe for Neighbourly Harmony

Bad enough to have dogs barking non-stop next door, but things get really serious when neighbours start barking at each other as a result.

Brian and Attracta Walsh got fed up listening to two of their neighbour's dogs barking loudly and constantly all day long for 18 months. However, when they approached Rory Tyson, the owner of the dogs – a boxer and Labrador cross – all they got was verbal abuse and foul language.

Rory, from Ballinduff, Corrandulla, in County Galway, claimed the Walshs had never made an effort to get to know his dogs, saying the three times he had communication with them were when they complained about the noise.

Both Rory and his wife work during the day and the dogs are left alone, Tuam District Court was told.

Having listened patiently to lengthy and detailed evidence, Judge Mary Fahy concluded that Rory had done very little to sort out the problem.

'People are not obliged to become familiar with neighbouring dogs. The problem has been going for 18 months and nothing has been done. In fairness, they have not complained about dogs barking at night, but it is happening during the day when there is nobody around them (dogs),' the Judge observed.

The Connacht Tribune

Judge Fahy pointed out that Rory's wife had been aggressive and had promised to rectify matters but nothing had been done. Judge Fahy said dogs needed companionship and were probably barking for attention.

Even though she did not like separating pets from their owners, the judge felt this was the best course of action because no apparent action had been taken by Rory. She ordered that the dogs be handed over to the dog warden and that every effort should be made to find new homes for them.

No Sympathy for Getting Caught Short

Don't get 'caught short' if you've had a few pints in Carlow. That's the message from Judge Mary Martin who presides over courts in the area.

Alan Fenlon was summonsed after being found relieving himself against the wall of a shop in Tullow Street, Carlow. He was duly brought to court on a summons for disorderly conduct in a public place.

When asked by Judge Martin why he urinated up against a business premises, he replied: 'I got caught short.' She then asked: 'Why didn't you leave it where you got it?'

The Judge asked Alan, of Church Street, Graiguecullen, to give €1,000 to the Irish Kidney Association and to attend an alcohol awareness programme.

Carlow Nationalist

Hit Speed of 168 KPH as He Rushed for Girlfriend's Christmas Present

It was Christmas Eve and all the shops would be closed in a few hours. But John still hadn't bought a present for his girlfriend. He jumped into his car and reached a speed of 168 kilometres per hour on the Tralee-Killarney road in his rush to get to the shops on time. He overtook another car on a white line, with a junction to the right, and was duly caught by the gardaí.

Judge James O'Connor, who heard the case in Castleisland Court, commented that any speed over the maximum limit of 100 kilometres per hour was 'lethal' and there could have been terrible consequences had anything run across the road in front of his car.

> John Dunne, an apprentice electrician from Mountain Close, Tralee, admitted driving without consideration on the occasion, 24 December 2006. He was ordered to fit a controlling device that would limit the speed of his car to 100 kph and was also ordered to pay €750 into the court poor box.
>
> Asked by Judge O'Connor if he ever had exceeded the speed limit before, he replied that he did.
>
> *Kerry's Eye*

The speedster, who was told by the judge that he is not allowed drive any car without a speed limiting device, will be disqualified for a number of years if he doesn't obey the court orders.

Letting your Christmas shopping wait until the last minute can be a dangerous business, as John discovered.

Threat to Blow Bank Teller's Brains Out

It was another ordinary day at the AIB branch in Charleville on the Cork/Limerick border – until John Loughman arrived to do some business.

He wanted to cash a €481 cheque, but John's patience ran out as bank staff tried to contact the account holder so that the money could be transferred to his account. He vaulted the bank counter and threatened a teller, shouting at her and putting his fingers to her head in the shape of a gun.

> 'If I had a real gun, I would blow your f***ing brains out,' he screamed into bank teller Emer O'Shea's face after hopping over the counter, a court was told later. He also roared: 'I'm not f***ing leaving until I get the money. I've robbed banks before.'
>
> *The Corkman*

He was also 'ranting and raving' about being in Portlaoise for seven years for the 'likes of ye', the arresting garda told the court. However, John, aged 53 and of no fixed abode, had never robbed any banks. But the staff had no way of knowing that.

'They didn't know if he was armed or not, and they were quite shaken and scared by the experience,' the garda said.

John's solicitor, Pat Enright, said his patience had run out. He had been at a centre in Bruree, County Limerick, due to a drinking problem and was on his way to a hostel in Cork for which he needed money.

The case came before Listowel Court where John pleaded guilty to a number of charges including assault and putting a person in fear. Judge Mary O'Halloran imposed a €160 fine and a five-month suspended prison sentence.

Gift Horse Had No Mouth, Head, Hoofs, Tail . . . or Anything

In August 2006, Jeremiah O'Brien and another man called to Denis Murphy's farm near Cork city.

According to Denis, who had known Jeremiah for many years, they made a number of visits over several hours on the same day. Jeremiah's story was that he had been caught with illegal diesel and needed a loan to pay the fine.

At first, the two men offered to sell Denis a horse for €4,000 which he refused. They lowered the offer each time they came back and eventually a deal was struck for €2,500. Though he had not seen the horse, Denis paid in cash. The three men then went to Mallow to collect the mare but it was nowhere to be seen.

Denis waited for a while at the roundabout in Mallow but had to go home to milk his cows. Jeremiah told him he would wait on and bring the horse to his farm in Castlewhite, Waterfall, outside Cork. However, there was just no sign of the horse, Denis related.

He told Mallow Court he later made contact with Jeremiah who told him he would give him the horse the following Tuesday, but Jeremiah never turned up. Denis phoned Jeremiah again afterwards, but Jeremiah hung up.

When all hope of getting the horse failed, Denis went to the gardaí, following which he received a letter from Jeremiah's mother, on 8 December 2006, with a postal order and bank draft enclosed for €2,500.

The investigating garda, Michael Corbett, said he had no doubt in his mind that if Denis had not reported the matter he would not have got his money back. 'There have been other circumstances that, if a complaint is made, then a postal order is sent on,' Garda Corbett stated.

Jeremiah, from Deel Court in Rathkeale, County Limerick, told the court he had horses. He asked Denis for €2,500 so that he could get married in November. Should he have been unable to repay the 'loan' he would have given Denis a horse instead.

> When Judge James Hamill asked where exactly the money for the postal order and bank draft came from, Inspector Senan Ryan interjected saying: 'Your honour, I'm not sure if you're familiar with Rathkeale, but down in Rathkeale it's a cash business!'
>
> *The Corkman*

The judge gave Jeremiah, aged 28, a five-month jail sentence for selling the horse that never was – the charge was for making gain, or causing loss, by deception. The court was also told he had 11 previous convictions including a nine-month sentence for the theft of a colt worth €4,500. He had also appeared in Killarney Court for having 'dud' €50 notes and a forgery charge.

A Case of 'Bureaucracy Gone Wrong' for Pregnant Woman

In May 2006, Daire Byrne was caught driving at 25 kilometres per hour over the speed limit near Taghmon, County Wexford. On 20 June, a notice demanding payment of an on-the-spot fine of €80 arrived at her home. But Daire had other more important things on her mind the same day; she was within hours of going into labour and had a baby a day later.

Unsurprisingly, the fine was not exactly her top priority but she did pay it. However, the Central Processing Unit in Capel Street, Dublin, returned her cheque because she had not paid it within the 28 days allowed.

And that was not all, the fine had now jumped to €120 due to late payment.

More hassle was to follow. Because she sent off the €40 cheque and the original €80 cheque together to the fines office in Dublin, they were both returned.

'They said they couldn't accept two cheques and that I had to send them one cheque,' Daire told Judge Donnchadh Ó Buachalla at Wexford Court.

> And that was still not the end of the saga. When Daire sent the fines office a single cheque for €120 that, too, was returned because the payment was now outside the 56 days allowed. She was duly summoned to appear in court.
>
> *Wexford People*

'It seems to be bureaucracy gone wrong,' her solicitor remarked after Daire, from Curragh, Inch, came to court to explain the circumstances surrounding the case.

Judge Ó Buachalla agreed with her sentiments. 'I have no hesitation in striking out the summons,' he declared.

Next Puff Could Cost Publican a Small Fortune, Judge Warns

A 'thick haze' of tobacco smoke filled the air in a Galway pub when the anti-smoking inspectors swooped in the early hours of 5 November 2006.

It was 1.40am and reminiscent of the good auld nights for smokers as they puffed away contentedly in Divilly's Welcome Inn in Glenamaddy.

One drinker was sitting at a high table, pint in one hand, fag in the other. The floor was littered with 30 to 40 cigarette butts. There were also butts in ash trays and two packets of cigarettes were lying on the counter.

On looking around further, Marian Caulfield, one of two environmental health officers on inspection duties, found the hallway leading to the toilets to be very heavily littered with cigarette ends which also blocked the urinal. Official, no-smoking signs were on display but were being blissfully ignored.

'It was quite evident that a lot of smoking had gone on in the bar area and that the official smoking area had not been used for some time,' she told the local court.

The bar manager could only put his hands up when approached by the environmental health officer and he agreed with her observations of the scene.

> The owner of the premises, Joseph Divilly, told the court he was always telling staff about smoking and had never come across an instance where smoking was allowed. He was not there himself on the night and, according to the barman, he [the barman] was unable to stop people smoking while they waited for taxis.
>
> *The Connacht Tribune*

Judge Geoffrey Browne remarked that the customers were in the premises after hours and that it was 'crazy' to allow smoking in a pub as the anti-smoking laws had been in place for about two years.

Fining Joseph Divilly €750 with €500 costs, Judge Browne warned: 'It is not on. You cannot do this any more. It will cost you a small fortune. I know your customers don't take any notice.'

Flying Bag of Waste Hits Unmarked Patrol Car

Garda Noel Sexton was driving an unmarked patrol car along a quiet Cork road when, suddenly, an object bounced off the windscreen.

Brendan Lafferty, who was coming in the opposite direction, 'flung' a bag of rubbish, containing mainly food waste, out his car window and straight into the patrol car, near Derrinagree.

The garda told Millstreet Court that he then stopped Brendan who admitted throwing out the bag and said he was unaware that it was a patrol car that was coming towards him.

> Judge James McNulty imposed a €1,000 fine and remarked: 'Indiscriminate dumping is just a scandal in this day and age. It's shocking and it's disgusting and people who do this have no regard for the environment.'
>
> *The Corkman*

Brendan, from Gortlarry, Carndonagh, Co Donegal, was not in court. The Judge was told he had a previous conviction for assault and assault causing harm, as well as public order offences.

Man Wearing Stolen Earrings when the Gardaí Came to His Door

It was 13 days after the theft of valuable earrings from a jewellery shop in Killarney when the gardaí arrived with a search warrant at Karl Horvath's home in Cois Abhainn, Tralee.

But they didn't have any searching to do for when he answered the door to the officers, the Czech national was wearing the 'very distinctive' stolen earrings. He told the gardaí he had bought the earrings from an Irish gypsy two or three months previously in Tralee for €400. He also claimed he wasn't in Killarney on the day the earrings, which were priced at €945, disappeared.

Breda O'Leary was attending a customer in the Kerry Gold Jewellery, Killarney Outlet Centre, when three men, one with sallow skin, came in looking for expensive earrings. She showed them a selection, then locked the cabinet and told them she would attend to them shortly. But the earrings were missing when she returned.

Later, a member of the staff at another jewellery shop in Killarney noticed the earrings that had been reported stolen on a man who came into her shop inquiring about 18 carat gold earrings. She contacted Breda immediately.

Karl Horvath, a father-of-two who lived on €285 social welfare per week, plus rent allowance and children's allowances, was tried at the Circuit Court in Tralee.

Asked how he could afford to pay €400 for earrings, he replied through an interpreter:

> 'Who couldn't afford some luxury? My jeans cost €130. My mom gets €240 and I get €250 children's allowance a month. Sometimes I have money left over. Every week, I try to buy something expensive. Is it not allowed to wear diamond earrings in Ireland?'
>
> *Kerry's Eye*

After being found guilty by a jury of possessing diamond earrings that had been stolen, he was jailed for 18 months.

Judge Becomes Peacemaker in Ongoing Family Row

It was a phone call from a woman after an incident in a Connemara pub, that dragged a new generation into a bitter family row that had been going on for more than 20 years.

Agnes Folan was in Lee's pub where she claimed her brother-in-law, Tomás Folan, pushed her and made insulting comments towards her. She phoned her son, Bertie, aged 19, who later went to Tomás's house and attacked him as he lay asleep in bed, kicking and punching him and fracturing his cheekbone.

Bertie's father, Michael, had not spoken to his brother, Tomás, for 20 years. Bertie had never spoken to his Uncle Tomás in his life and the dispute between his father and uncle had happened before he was born.

At Galway Circuit Court, Bertie pleaded guilty to assaulting his uncle at Leitir Mór on 27 December 2005 and handed in €4,000 as a gesture of remorse.

> Judge Raymond Groarke called Bertie's father to the witness stand. Michael Folan said things had gone from bad to worse since his brother, who was the manager on a fish farm, fired him for no reason.
>
> 'Can the two of you sort it out?' Judge Groarke asked him.
>
> 'That is what I would like,' Michael Folan replied.
>
> 'Will you shake his hand publicly?' Judge Groarke ventured. Witness nodded.
>
> Judge Groarke invited Tomás Folan up to the witness box where the brothers shook hands briefly.
>
> *The Connacht Tribune*

Moments later, the judge – who observed one would have seen warmer handshakes in the Arctic – asked the brothers' wives, Eileen and Agnes, to shake hands in public before the court. But they flatly refused.

Referring to Agnes Folan, the judge said she had used her son to exact revenge for a push she claimed she got in a pub.

He went on: 'You are a disgrace. And I mean the whole lot of you. I see the smirks and sneering smiles on your faces but I'm telling you here and now that I will wipe them off your faces.

'The worst of it is you can't keep it to yourselves: you have to involve your children. If parents want to behave like young thugs – well and good – but you leave your children out of it.

'If you do not stop this here and now, I will jail you for as long as I possibly can. You owe it to your children. That handshake should mean something. I say to you men – take control of your lives.'

He urged the men to make their peace, regardless of their wives. Turning to Bertie Folen, Judge Groarke said he was not a fool and he [the judge] accepted he had acted on the spur of the moment in attacking his uncle. However, Bertie should have had more sense than to allow himself to be 'led to the slaughter' by his mother.

The judge told Bertie, who had no previous convictions, to stand on his own two feet and not to be encouraged by anyone to break the law.

Sentencing was adjourned for 12 months and Judge Groarke warned both couples to behave themselves and stay away from each other in the meantime, or else he would 'make it very hard' on them.

The court was told the families were small farmers and the ongoing acrimony between them had taken up a lot of the gardaí's time over the years.

Drugs Dealer Begs Judge to Send Him to Jail for a Long Time

Damien Quinn believed prison was the only place he could 'sort himself out'. Throwing himself at the mercy of the court, he pleaded with a judge to hand him a lengthy sentence for a drug dealing offence committed in June 2006.

He had been caught red-handed in Tuam by Detective Pat Shannon with four bars of cannabis worth €7,000 for supplying a person he would not name. When interviewed by the gardaí that evening, he confessed: 'I'm as guilty as sin.'

Damien, aged 23, has an address at Parkmore Estate, Tuam, but Galway Circuit Court heard he had no address other than Castlerea Prison at the time and he was happy to stay there. He expressed 'gratitude' to the detective for catching him.

He happened to be behind bars for a different offence when he came before Judge Raymond Groarke for dealing drugs and said he feared he would get involved in more crime if set free.

'I have peace of mind in there [Castlerea Prison] at the moment and I know I can't get into trouble. I want to be able to plan for the future and I don't ever want to see a judge, jury or guard again. I've missed two days of study because I've been waiting in the holding cells downstairs for this case to be called. I'm bored with it all,' he added.

If he was left to remain in prison, he could get 'stuck into' courses in Maths, English and Computing, he added.

The judge said the quantity of cannabis resin involved in the case, and the fact that it was in nine-ounce bars, suggested that Damien, who had previous convictions, had 'moved up the ladder' and was not simply selling the drug on the street.

He imposed a three-year sentence, but suspended the final year on condition that Damien attend a treatment centre following his release.

> Quinn beamed with delight as he was being led away by prison
> officers and nodded when Judge Groarke told him he hoped he
> would put his talents to good use.
>
> *The Connacht Tribune*

Damien's barrister, John Hogan, said it was the first case he had come across where an accused person had given clear instructions of his wish to go to prison.

Believes Pets Were 'Dognapped' and Sold on

The McKeown-O'Neill family were heartbroken when their three dogs disappeared mysteriously from their home in Tallow, County Waterford, in February.

Several weeks after the pets had gone 'missing' they received a phone call from a man who was convinced he had spotted them in Waterford city. He had seen photos of the dogs in the newspapers and there was a remarkable resemblance, he thought.

It seemed the much-loved canine members of the McKeown-O'Neill family were being offered for sale from the back of a van in Waterford – all of which led them to believe their pets had been 'dog-napped' for profit.

As a lot of time had passed and a pretty thorough search around the south-east had proved fruitless, they hadn't really expected any developments in response to their public appeals for help according to Tara McKeown-O'Neill.

> She said: 'He [the caller] said there was a white Hiace van
> parked in the Applemarket in the city on Good Friday. He said

there were about eight dogs in the van and men who looked like Eastern Europeans were offering them for sale. Three of them, he said, looked exactly like ours.'

Waterford News and Star

During their searches, the McKeown-O'Neills learned that a lot of dogs had gone missing in the west Waterford area in the previous months and their concern was that the animals were being mistreated. 'I found out a lot about the trade in stolen dogs and it's made me even more fearful,' Tara remarked.

She went on: 'We've been devastated since the dogs went missing on Valentine's Day and our two boys, Oisín and Tiarnan, who are aged just 7 and 11, are taking it particularly badly. These dogs have grown up with our children and we'd really love to get them back. Two of our dogs, Paddy and Ceilí, are terrier crosses and the third, Peter, is a Jack Russell – breeds which are popular for hunting or dog baiting.'

The absence of closed-circuit television coverage in the area meant that the gardaí were able to do very little to help them.

Threw Coke Bottle at Judge

Another day's sitting of Waterford District Court was slowly grinding to a conclusion and most of the litigants had left the building having taken their punishment. All of a sudden, a plastic bottle of Coca Cola was thrown across the courtroom in the direction of Judge William Harnett.

The bottle struck the wall above his bench spilling its contents and fell to the floor near the press bench, startling the reporters who were noting proceedings. The gardaí on court duty arrested a young man at the door of the courtroom and he was taken into custody.

When asked if the court wanted a brief adjournment, Judge Harnett replied, 'Not at all. He missed badly.'

Munster Express

On the following morning, the man who threw the bottle, Brian Veale, with an address at Boherduff Heights, Clonmel, pleaded guilty to assault in the court and was sentenced to four months imprisonment by Judge Gerard Haughton.

Woman Worker Bullied and Called a 'Floozie'

When Joy Porter started work at Atlantic Homecare in 2001, the atmosphere was good but things changed quickly for the worse after a new manager took over. Joy claimed the manager began to pick on people and started calling her names in 2002.

Insulting terms such as 'flirt' and 'floozie' were used and she was also referred to as a 'blonde bimbo'. The manager also called her 'Mrs Bouquet' over the tannoy, which signified a fussy old woman. Joy brought her case to an Employment Appeals Tribunal and told the tribunal she never knew what to expect. The manager was referred to as 'M'.

One day, she would be 'M's best friend and another day not. 'M' just picked on somebody every day, the Tribunal heard.

Donegal News

Joy, aged 35 and from Drumenan in Donegal, said she was shouted at so loudly at times that she could not understand what the manager was saying. Another employee told the Tribunal the manager had also called her names. She claimed she was branded as a 'smart cookie' or 'Ms Diana'.

Eventually, Joy began to get headaches and anxiety attacks. By May 2005 she could no longer take the name calling and verbal abuse. So she visited the doctor, went on sick leave for workplace stress and later resigned.

However, 'M' told the Tribunal it was totally untrue that she picked on people. When it was put to her about someone overhearing her calling Joy a 'blonde bimbo', the manager replied that it definitely didn't happen. 'I never name called as a manager for twenty years, it's schoolyard stuff,' she stated.

She also said no one complained to her that she shouted or was aggressive in manner or speech. The allegations, she said, were totally untrue.

But Joy Porter was awarded €12,480 in her claim against Atlantic Homecare after the allegation that she was bullied by her manager was upheld. The Tribunal found that her resignation was a case of constructive dismissal and not a voluntary decision.

Difference between a Whistle and a Cough

An experienced judge wasn't going to be fooled by a man who pretended that a whistle was a cough.

Kevin McMahon, who had 14 previous convictions, whistled when leaving Ennis District Court after receiving a five-month prison sentence from Judge Joseph Mangan. The judge called him back pronto and gave him a chance to purge his contempt.

'It was more of a cough than a whistle,' Kevin claimed.

'You think I don't know the difference between a cough and a whistle?' Judge Mangan retorted.

The judge then advised McMahon's solicitor, William Cahir, to have a chat with him adding that 'it better be good'.

The 21-year-old from Plunkett Drive, Kilkishen, later apologised profusely in open court, saying, 'I'm sorry for whistling. I wasn't trying to disrespect the court. I was nervous. It will never happen again.'

Kevin McMahon, who had appeared in court on public order charges arising from an incident in which he was said to have been extremely intoxicated and abusive, indicated he would appeal against the sentence.

> 'He indicated his behaviour was more that of a maggot than malicious. He took the fun further than anyone else and admits his conduct was out of order,' Mr Cahir said.
>
> *The Clare Champion*

Judge Tells Man to Be a Good Boy

The man who 'never got a break' was in court for the umpteenth time and ran the risk of getting extra time in the clink after telling off Judge Joseph Mangan.

Gary Byrne had amassed almost 100 convictions when he came before the judge at Ennis District Court on charges of being drunk and failing to give his correct address to the gardaí. He was given a three-month sentence and this sparked an outburst from Gary, described as a Trinity College student from Kilbarron Road, Coolock, Dublin.

> 'Forget about it. I've had enough. Let me back in the cells before I hit him. Every time I come here you send me back to prison. You never once gave me a break. 24 years I've spent in prison,' commented Byrne.
>
> *The Clare Champion*

Judge Mangan responded by telling 40-year-old Gary to conduct himself, saying: 'I'll find you in contempt and you'll serve concurrent sentences. Now be a good boy and leave here quietly.'

The court was told he was studying for a sociology degree in Trinity and was progressing through the education system. He studied while in prison and earned a place in Trinity.

Publican Hurt in Pocket on Pollution Charge

Reality dawned for a Clare publican when he had to fork out more than €5,000 for discharging polluting matter in a river.

Patrick Sexton's premises in the traditional music hotspot of Doolin was visited by an environment technician from Clare County Council who carried out a routine inspection to monitor discharges.

While Patrick had a licence to let a limited amount of waste into the river he was found to be up to six times over the limit. His counsel told the Circuit Court that he accepted responsibility and had tried to comply with the limits but had not been successful. He further claimed the council was happy Patrick was doing his best.

> However, the court heard that is the fourth time the defendant had been prosecuted on similar matters and to date had paid almost €4,000 in fines.
>
> *The Clare Champion*

Before imposing a further fine of €2,500, as well as ordering Mr Sexton to pay costs of €2,580, Judge Sean Ó Donnabháin remarked, 'It's funny how the reality only dawns when it begins to get costly.'

Solution to the Nuisance of Barking Dogs?

It's the ultimate neighbourly nightmare – the dog that never stops barking. A fortune surely awaits the person who can find a solution to this problem and Judge Aeneas McCarthy, sitting at Loughrea Court, was prepared to give one woman's proposal a chance.

People living beside Helen O'Neill brought her to court complaining about the nuisance her two Alsatians were causing them. Her neighbours queued up to give evidence. At one stage during the hearing, Judge McCarthy viewed a camcorder video of the dogs taken by one of the neighbours and listened to the barking which they said was continuous when the animals were left outside.

> Another neighbour, Liam Cunniffe, said the dogs barked all the time from when they were left out in the morning until dark and any movement seemed to trigger off the barking.
>
> *The Connacht Tribune*

Patrick Dolan had to take his children inside one day when the dogs came into his garden. His four-year-old son was always looking over his shoulder and didn't really want to be in the garden. Patrick's concern was about a two-and-a-half-foot wall in front of Helen's house which the dogs had no trouble in jumping over.

The court was told Helen, of Blackgarden, Craughwell, Co Galway, had spent €10,000 on erecting a secure fence around her house but Patrick said, 'I don't want the dogs there full stop. I am afraid of my life that my kids will be bitten by them.'

A solution offered by Helen was that she would get special collars which would stop her dogs from barking by giving them a small shock.

Judge McCarthy said he was happy Helen had secured the dogs in her property and they did not pose a threat of physical attack. But the barking was clearly a nuisance that had to be abated. He was happy to give the anti-barking collars a try and adjourned the case to allow time for that.

Loses Cool with Judge for Lack of Fags

The constant thud of feet kicking the door of a holding cell began to disturb Judge Michael Pattwell's District Court in Mallow. The judge asked a garda to go and tell the prisoner to stop making a racket or else he would face contempt of court.

The garda duly did as he was bid and there was silence for a few short minutes before the banging started again. This time Judge Pattwell was in no mood for sending out further messages to behave. Garda White left the courtroom to investigate and the prisoner, Shane Frayne, was hauled in before the bench.

Shane, from Castleview Estate, Newcastle West, County Limerick, had become irate when he wasn't allowed smoke in the cell. He immediately said to the judge, 'Look, all I got all day long was thirty fags and I want to smoke some fags.'

Judge Pattwell then addressed Garda White and asked him what did the defendant say when he was requested to stop banging the cell door. 'He said he wanted cigarettes and I told him he could not smoke in the cell. I told him if you don't stop the banging, Judge Pattwell will hold you in contempt of court and he said to me, "F*** Judge Pattwell",' said Garda White.

Mr Frayne interjected once again and said there were others who were banging their feet and he asked that the handcuffs be loosened.

'Look here, they are cutting the hands off me,' said Mr Frayne.

> Judge Pattwell told him it was not his job to loosen handcuffs, that task fell to the prison officers.

The Corkman

The 19-year-old received a ten-month sentence, which was later suspended on appeal to the Circuit Court, for being the passenger in a stolen car which was crashed at Castlecor, Mallow, on 7 September 2006. The charge of contempt was adjourned.

Neighbours Up in Arms over All-Night Hooleys

Cathy Hanratty's home on the June bank holiday was the setting for the mother of all all-night parties. But neighbours, who had long since lost patience with the hooleys in Hanratty's, were not enjoying the deafening racket.

Cathy, who lives in Dunboyne, County Meath, was summonsed after her neighbours complained about noise pollution due to all-night parties. She appeared at Dunshaughlin Court for 'allowing music to be played at consistent, loud, repetitive volumes' all day and all night, and for allowing shouting and screaming in the rear garden of her house at Old Fair Green. The court also heard that all-night parties would often be held when she was away.

Paul Dalton, who has a two-year-old child and a newborn baby, said he lived next door to the house and that they [the parties] had been going on for over two years. Numerous parties went on from 7 pm to 7 am but the bash on the June bank holiday weekend was the 'straw that broke the camel's back'. So he and other neighbours then complained under the Nuisance Act.

According to defence solicitor Adrian Shanley, Cathy had instructed her son to keep the noise down and she said her son no longer lived in the house. Judge Brophy adjourned the case until September and warned Cathy that if there was any noise in the meantime he would hold her in contempt.

> He [Judge Brophy] said there were to be no late parties and that if her sons or daughters couldn't comply with this, to 'give them a kick up the backside'.
>
> *The Meath Chronicle*

Meanwhile, piped music has got a completely new meaning in Newbridge, County Kildare. A person living near the Riverbank Arts Centre can hear performances at the centre from their own home so well that they might as well have a front row seat – even though the auditorium is heavily sound proofed.

The case baffled staff for some time. Manager John O'Brien commented that on the night of a concert he could barely hear the music while sitting in the reception area. But a nearby resident rang up and as he was chatting to her he could hear the music better over the phone than he could hear it in the foyer. And the music did not have to be very loud to make its way to the house in question.

> As a result, John guessed that the music may be going through an underground metal pipe that travelled under both the centre and the house in question. He explained that he had had a similar situation in an apartment he rented in London where music had travelled along the plumbing to him, apparently bypassing other apartments.
>
> *Leinster Leader*

If the pipe theory is found to be correct, the centre's management have indicated they will install a false floor to stop any 'piped music' from travelling out of the building in future.

Mayor in Jail Cell over Mobile Phone

When Mayor of Fermoy William Hughes switched on his mobile phone on the morning of 13 July 2007, little did he think it would land him in the clink: in his case Friday the 13th lived up to its reputation for being an unlucky day.

First citizen William was in the local district court as a character witness for his nephew when his phone rang. Judge Michael Pattwell – dreaded for his tough stance on mobile phone usage in his courtroom – ordered that the red-faced mayor be taken to one of the cells.

Judge Pattwell then told the court that he would make a decision on the matter at the end of the hearing, leaving William to ponder his fate while a guest of the nation. Two hours later, Mayor Hughes was ordered back into the courtroom and his solicitor apologised for the incident.

Satisfied that the mayor had purged his contempt, the man on the bench decreed that two hours in a jail cell was sufficient punishment. 'Hopefully, I won't be in court again but, if I am, I will not be taking my phone in with me,' the chastened mayor pledged afterwards, having learnt his lesson the hard way.

> The mayor reported at the weekend that he regretted the incident but continued that he was upset at the time as he had just heard that his sister had been involved in a motor accident earlier in the day which, luckily, turned out to be slight.
>
> *The Corkman*

The mayor admitted being embarrassed by the incident. 'I wasn't best pleased at Friday's events and personally feel that the whole thing was blown out of proportion,' he said.

Several other judges have outlawed mobile phones in their courtrooms and Judge Patrick Clyne, who dispenses justice in Carlow, also includes infernal chewing gum among his pet hates.

'If anyone has a mobile phone that goes off during a case, they'll get thrown out without ceremony and their case will go to the end of the list. So get the message – mobile phones off!' he warned.

> Later on in the proceedings, Judge Clyne spelt out his distaste of chewing gum: 'One thing I have a thing about is chewing gum in court. You would not do it in church so why would you do it here? It shows a complete lack of respect. Not that I'm the Archbishop of Canterbury. I might be higher.'
>
> *Carlow Nationalist*

On the same day at Carlow District Court, one mobile phone was confiscated from a person but was later returned.

Knife Man Clapping like a Seal

Mark Power appeared at the door of his home in Fair Street, Mallow, with a bread knife in his hand when two gardaí came calling. When they asked him to put down the knife, he started to 'clap and make noises like a seal', the local court heard from one of the gardaí.

They said he was aggressive and smelt of drink. They shouted at him twice to put the knife away and he claimed he threw it two to three metres behind him when asked to do so.

Mark's solicitor, Philip Comyn, argued that his client was in his own private home when the gardaí knocked on his door. The solicitor also said Mark would not have moved onto the street if the gardaí had not asked him to.

> Superintendent Pat McCarthy put it to the defendant that he was acting a 'bit smart alecky' with the guards. 'What was all the clapping of your hands about the place for?' he asked.
> Mr Power said he 'started laughing but not clapping'.
>
> *The Corkman*

Judge Michael Pattwell threw out charges against Mark of being drunk in a public place and possessing a knife. Mark admitted having consumed five cans of beer on the occasion.

Sausage Row Sizzles at Breakfast

Breakfast cook Hannah Moran was in the kitchen of a Ballybunion hotel drumming up tasty sausages in the deep fat fryer. According to Hannah, the general manager stormed in and banged his fist on the counter, saying, 'It's no f***ing good talking to you, I'll do the rest of the cooking myself!'

She said he roared at her, came towards her with his fists flying, called her stupid and told her to get out of his hotel. 'He was acting like a madman. I don't know what happened. He attacked me for no reason,' she said.

Rugby fans waiting in the dining room for an early morning match and breakfast were unaware of the verbal maul taking place in the kitchen.

Her boss's side of the story was that he had told Hannah several times not to cook the sausages in a deep fat fryer but in an oven, as many of his guests were health conscious. However, she continued using the fryer that morning even though he had asked her three times to use the oven.

Hannah, from Ballybunion, brought an unfair dismissal case against the Cliff House Hotel in Ballybunion to an Employment Appeals Tribunal. The general manager, who said his family ran two hotels in north Kerry, was not named in the report of the tribunal's findings.

> She said he told her customers complained about fat on their plate and asked her to cook them in the oven instead of frying them. She said when cooked in the oven they were not well cooked and people were left waiting as the door of the oven was faulty.
>
> *Kerry's Eye*

Nobody had ever complained about her breakfasts, she said, and she often got compliments as well as gifts of money and sweets. She often started working at 5.30am but felt the general manager wanted her out and wished to give her job to someone else. Hannah had worked in the hotel since 1995 and was almost 61 when her employment ended there in July 2005.

The general manager denied being abusive and said he was surprised when she grabbed her coat and walked out. He expected her back in a few days but she never returned. He had never fired an employee and denied firing her.

Hannah won her case, however, with the tribunal ruling she was sacked unjustly and awarding her €3,500 in compensation.

Driver Caught Shaving Leads Gardaí on Slow Car Chase

When the gardaí spotted a car being driven in a swaying manner near Castleisland they decided to follow it. The driver showed no signs of slowing down until they pulled alongside him in the patrol car. They noticed he had his hand to his face initially and, eventually seeing them, he pulled his car in.

> The driver Adrian Ryan was in the process of having his morning shave behind the wheel of his car and was too engrossed in the act to notice the patrol car behind.
>
> *The Kerryman*

'Shaving whilst driving!' exclaimed a surprised Judge James O'Connor when the story was related to him at Castleisland Court.

He was also told how Adrian, a self-employed salesman from Monaleen in Limerick city, managed to maintain a legal speed during the brief 'chase'. The court was told Adrian drove constantly. But this was his closest shave with the law and he received the benefit of the Probation Act.

Private Detective Watches Man Who Had Fallen into Hole

On his way home early one morning in Waterford city, David de Courcey fell into a hole and split his heel 'in two'. The slip and fall happened on a footpath that was being repaired.

At first, David, from Larchville, thought he had sprained his left ankle, but x-rays later that morning at Waterford Regional Hospital confirmed that the ankle was actually fractured. He then brought a personal injuries action against the city council.

He told Waterford Circuit Court he was in plaster for up to three months and had to use crutches. Since the accident, he had a limp and his balance was affected, he claimed. The roofer denied being drunk and said he could no longer work or dig his garden because of his injury.

But the 'corpo' engaged a private detective, James Gaulsworthy, to work on the case. He told the court he carried out surveillance on David and watched him digging a garden for about an hour, adding:

> He appeared to have no trouble digging the garden plot. After that he swept and cleaned up with a brush.
>
> *Waterford News and Star*

Pointing out that the accident had taken place under a light and there had been some hoarding nearby, Judge Olive Buttimer ruled the blame was 50/50. She assessed damages at €15,000 and awarded David €7,500.

Baseball Bat from Santa Ponza Lands Man in Court

Cornelius Murphy was stopped by a garda who had seen him drive with a mobile phone in his hand. But it was a brightly painted baseball bat sticking out from under the car seat that aroused the garda's curiosity.

Asked what he was doing with the bat, Cornelius replied it was a present for a friend which he brought home from his holidays in Santa Ponza. However, the garda wasn't satisfied that he had offered a 'valid' explanation and took away the bat.

Cornelius, from Dan Murphy Place in Macroom, later appeared in the local court on a charge of possessing a weapon that could be regarded as offensive. He was stoutly defended by solicitor John Kenneally who described the so-called weapon as a 'novelty toy' and ornamental bat. The solicitor went on, 'I have two hurleys in the back of my car. Can I then be accused of having a hurley with intent to injure someone?'

> Superintendent Vincent Duggan said such items may constitute a 'novelty toy' when hanging on a tourist rack, but the item could move from being a toy to a weapon depending on the use intended for it.
>
> *The Corkman*

The Superintendent said there were scratches and a mark on the bat which he then handed to Judge James McNulty for a close look. Solicitor Kenneally chimed in, 'These items were hanging on two racks in a tourist shop knocking against each other.'

A number of legal points were thrashed out in detail including what 'intent' to use a weapon meant and how it could be proved. The judge dismissed an 'intent' charge but convicted on a charge of possessing a weapon.

Judge McNulty concluded: 'Given all the surrounding facts, the item, while described as a baseball bat, also has all the appearance of a baton. Even if baseball was played in the area there might be some excuse, but I doubt this is the case. The court is satisfied to convict the accused because he offered no reasonable excuse as to why he had this item in his car.'

He deferred imposing a penalty in the case.

'Send Them Back Home' – Deputy on Law-Breaking Foreign Nationals

People sleeping peacefully in their beds early on a Sunday morning awoke to a cacophony of sirens blaring across the tranquil Tipperary countryside. Patrol cars carrying gardaí from Cashel, Cahir and Thurles were rushing to a riot in Tipperary town.

The gardaí in Tipperary town had been attacked as they tried to arrest a foreign national outside a nightclub. Other men interfered and the gardaí were soon outnumbered. Five Polish men were arrested following the row. All were in their twenties and thirties and working and living in the area. The all-action flare up attracted a huge audience lustily cheering on the men involved. Footage was filmed on mobile phones and hastily posted on the YouTube website.

Four gardaí were injured in the fracas, following which local Fine Gael TD Tom Hayes called for tough action against foreign nationals or anybody else engaged in street violence late at night. He then went much further by calling for foreign nationals involved in such trouble to be sent back to where they came from rather than spending time in jail here at the taxpayer's expense.

> 'This State should not have to take up the bill for foreign nationals who are sent to jail for their involvement in such violent crimes. If they are living in this community they have to abide by the laws and regulations of the country. They should be sent home rather than be sent to jail in this country. If they are creating trouble, fighting, taking on the gardaí, that should not be tolerated. Most of them are working here and getting the benefits of living in a thriving economy, they should respect that,' said Deputy Hayes.
>
> *Clonmel Nationalist*

Foreign nationals involved in a variety of crimes including scams, larcenies, assaults and driving offences are increasingly taking up more time in courts around the country. Translation services provided at the expense of the State are now among the country's growth industries as many of these people have little English.

One of the most shocking cases arose from the blackmailing of a priest in Galway by a couple who claimed they had a videotape of him in a sexually compromising situation. Former Romanian Olympic boxer Petre Zsiga, aged 42, of Knocknacarra, Galway, and his Irish wife, Margaret Zsiga, aged 30, admitted at Galway Circuit Criminal Court to blackmailing Fr Brendan Lawless, parish priest of Portumna, by demanding €24,500 from him with menaces over a two-year period.

Judge Raymond Groarke sentenced Petre Zsiga to four years in prison with the last two years suspended. He sentenced Margaret Zsiga to four years also but suspended the sentence because, he said, one parent had to mind their five young children or otherwise the State would have to do so.

Passing sentence, Judge Groarke said crimes involving blackmail, extortion and demanding money with menaces were extremely rare because victims of such crimes rarely came forward to 'blow the whistle' on their blackmailers. He said victims were usually very vulnerable people in vulnerable positions and that is what Fr Lawless was.

> 'Notwithstanding the innuendo that may be drawn from the allegations made against him, he is to be commended for doing what he did. He was extremely brave to do what he did, knowing the efforts being made to pillory his good name,' Judge Groarke said of the victim.
>
> *The Connacht Tribune*

Judge Groarke said he was utterly convinced there had been no sexual relationship between Margaret Zsiga and Fr Lawless and he told her not to be hiding behind the ruse of her children. He reminded her that Fr Lawless was the innocent victim at all times in the case and, as a person convicted before the court, she had no credibility whatsoever.

Flamboyant Hotelier Not Amused but Has Last Laugh

All eyes turned towards a statesman-like figure as he stepped smartly from the Four Courts in his long, dark coat and black hat. Vincent O'Toole, a Waterford hotelier of longstanding, had just been awarded €50,000 damages and costs in his High Court libel case against the *Sunday World*.

A jury found that a reference in the newspaper to his Maryland Hotel wrongly meant he was a brothel-keeper. The former master mariner and successful horse breeder was delighted to have won his case, but not with the award. Asked what he thought of the money, the sprightly 80-year-old replied, 'You'd put that on a horse.'

Vincent had told the court that he was a man so conservative as to be boring and the offending article, published on 1 August 2004, under the headline *Suir You Couldn't Make Out A Word*, left him appalled. He did not regard it as a joke.

It referred to people in Waterford speaking a foreign language and to a website having come up with the 'first ever Waterford dictionary'. An entry described Maryland as an infamous small hotel in the red light district of Waterford and a colloquial term for a brothel.

But any suggestion that Maryland was Waterford city slang for a brothel was verging on madness, according to Vincent. It had been named Maryland in 1959 after his wife and the American state of the same name. The premises operated initially as a bed and breakfast before becoming a hotel in the 1960s, attracting all sorts of guests including judges and opera-goers.

> He got a phone call when the article appeared saying his hotel was being called 'a whorehouse'. He bought the paper and was absolutely appalled.
>
> *Munster Express*

Prior to the court case, Vincent had strongly attacked a book of Waterford slang and the *Up The Déise* website which, he claimed, gave the impression Waterford people were inarticulate and retarded. He dismissed the book by Cian Foley as 'crude trash'.

'The instigator of this crude booklet maintains that whenever visitors to Waterford meet the natives, they will need the help of this pathetic so-called dictionary to understand what language the Waterfordians are trying to speak,' Vincent declared.

Cian, however, described his book as a bit of 'cheeky humour' appealing to the Podge and Rodge generation. The entries were real words used by Waterford people and described in a humorous way, he maintained.

> 'The expressions were used where I went to school (Mount Sion), where I lived (Lismore Park/Lawn) and pretty much by anyone I've ever spoken to from Waterford, the likes of "lack", "gallybander", "blaa", "stawl", "well boy" etc. Rather than stigmatising Waterford, I feel it shows that Waterford people have a unique identity and I, for one, am proud of that identity. I am proud of my accent, the fact that I finish every sentence with "boy", and that I love washing down "red lead blaas" with a few "layarge bohhels offa de shellef"!'

> Waterford News and Star

The pocket-sized guide to Waterford slang contains over 170 entries including terms such as 'galavantin', 'jaynee mack', 'shellaky-booky' and 'well boy'.

It Wasn't Drink the Gardaí Smelt from the Driver – Just a Fisherman's Friend!

Sean Tanniane claimed he hadn't taken a drink for four and a half years, but he showed the classic symptoms of having consumed alcohol when stopped by the gardaí in Tuam.

They had seen him 'taking both sides of the road' as he drove along a one-way street at half past four on 12 February 2007. He was arrested by Garda Paul Agnew who observed Tanniane's speech was slurred, his eyes were glazed and he was unsteady on his feet.

Two gardaí also swore they got a strong whiff of booze from his breath after they had signalled him to stop his car in Bishop Street. Sean, from Polleighter, Kilkerrin, suggested the reason his speech sounded slurred was that he didn't have his dentures in at the time.

When he denied at Tuam Court that he had been drinking on the night, Judge Mary Fahy asked him how then the gardaí could have smelt drink from him. He replied that he had been sucking a cherry-flavoured Fisherman's Friend sweet.

Asked why he could not blow into the intoxalyser so as to give a breath sample, he said he had a bad chest. But Judge Mary Fahy, remarking that Sean's evidence was 'most perturbing', felt he was not telling the truth in court.

> 'When a mature man comes into court and swears on the Bible that he had no drink, it is very serious when the evidence is that he did have a smell of drink off him. It is a serious offence to refuse to give a sample but it is compounded by the fact that he came to court and told lies,' said Judge Fahy.
>
> *The Connacht Tribune*

She said she had a major difficulty with a defendant who swore to tell the truth but then gave 'nonsense about a sweet'. She fined him €1,000 and banned him from driving for two years.

Thief Bolts from Wardrobe and Escapes with a Kiss

It was around ten o'clock at night when a woman sitting down for something to eat in her city centre home in Limerick heard an unexpected noise from upstairs.

Bravely deciding to investigate, she picked her way gingerly up the steps. Entering her bedroom, she opened the wardrobe and found a youth wearing a hoodie inside. Obviously shocked, she screamed at the youth before hitting him with the door of the wardrobe a few times.

After she roared at him to remove himself pronto, the trapped burglar pleaded with her to, 'Just let me out'. He then ran down the stairs in a bid to escape, only to find the doors and windows had been locked. But the incident then took an unusual turn when the woman, who was in her twenties and the only tenant of the house, helped the bungling intruder to get free.

> 'The tenant then unlocked the front door to let him out and as she did, the burglar put his arms around her and gave her a hug before running off,' explained Sergeant Seamus O'Neill of Henry Street station.
>
> *Limerick Leader*

Having thanked the woman with a glancing peck, the grateful thief, who was 15 to 16 years of age and lightly built, fled into the night. Said to have 'narrow, slanty' eyes, he certainly left the house in Lord Edward Street in a big hurry – and empty-handed.

Meanwhile, two homeowners in Loughrea, County Galway, very kindly obliged an opportunistic burglar by leaving their doors unlocked on the night of 13 November 2006. The burglar hit both houses by simply walking through the front doors. The gardaí were alerted by one of the homeowners whose sleep was disturbed at around 3.40am.

But Garda Ciaran Whelan didn't have far to look. Soon afterwards, he found Jonathan Lynch, who later appeared before Galway Circuit Court, hiding behind a wheelie bin about 80 yards from one of the houses. Jonathan was wearing a jacket he had stolen earlier that night and had a rucksack loaded with items such as mobile phones, cameras, an MP3 player, a camcorder and a necklace, all of which had been stolen from the premises.

Hearing the doors had been left unlocked, Judge Raymond

Groarke said: 'It was always a pleasant feature in this country that people could go to bed leaving their front doors unlocked, but that is a little bit of ancient Ireland that is certainly gone and people should "cop on" and check that their windows and doors are locked before retiring each night.'

The Connacht Tribune

Jonathan Lynch, aged 21 and with addresses in Ballinasloe and Athlone, pleaded guilty to burglary and to having a knife. He received a three-year jail sentence, with the final 18 months suspended. The court was told he was addicted to prescription drugs and alcohol and had spent most of his life in prison since he was 15.

Where to Pee at Fleadh?

The gardaí were happy enough with 'facilities' at the main venue for the week-long World Fleadh in Portlaoise, but Judge Mary Martin had questions to ask.

Having allowed extensions to the town's 22 pubs to open until 2am each morning, she then dealt with another application to sell alcohol at the main Fleadh venue in the grounds of the CBS secondary school. She asked Inspector Tom Mooney if satisfactory toilet facilities would be put in place. And while the Inspector raised no concerns, she did.

'I hope they won't be peeing up against neighbour's doors. It is a reality and we won't shy away from reality,' she said while granting the extension. Portaloos would be on site, she was assured.

> The credentials of the Fleadh also came in for some judicial scrutiny at Portlaoise Court with Judge Martin remarking that she could see very little Irish music on the programme. Fleadh chief organiser Michael Carr explained to her that 'fleadh' was

the Irish word for feast.

Judge Martin interjected, saying she knew that. She pushed him on the use of the term 'fleadh'. 'Are you not encroaching on somebody else's territory?' she asked.

Mr Carr disagreed and said there are now fleadhs in Glasgow, Milwaukee and Lorient in France. 'Did you ask permission to use the name?' Judge Martin asked the organiser.

Mr Carr answered, 'No.'

Leinster Express

Young and Wild

Boy Racers Jailed – to Send out a Message

The spectre of two boy racers racing each other along the busy Galway to Tuam road at 11pm terrified gardaí and other people using the road. Two people walking on the hard shoulder had to jump out of the way as the young drivers overtook each other at speeds of up to 140 kilometres per hour.

One of the cars swerved onto the hard shoulder in front of the pedestrians, but swerved back onto the road again before driving off at speed.

Judge Mary Fahy imposed jail sentences on the drivers, sending out a message that such behaviour would not be tolerated by the courts.

Robert Browne, aged 20 and a welder from Turloughmore, and Mark Barry, a 19-year-old steel fixer from Oranmore, were each given four-month jail sentences and put off the road for two years when they pleaded guilty to dangerous driving. Leave to appeal was granted. Each had a previous driving conviction.

> Judge Fahy said most drivers would have got a shock at the thought of narrowly missing a person and would have pulled in

but Browne, she said, had carried on at speed as if nothing had happened.

The Connacht Tribune

On being told by Browne's solicitor that his parents had since restricted his use of their car to get to and from work in Athenry only, Judge Fahy remarked: 'On what planet are he and his parents living? Do they not watch the news and read the newspapers and see the devastation that the likes of their son is causing in this country? Do they not see or hear of the carnage that is going on every day on our roads?'

In Kerry, however, the parents of an 18-year-old car enthusiast, who died in a crash outside Castleisland along with two other young men, believe young drivers' love of motorsport should be respected.

Wayne and Kathy Toolan of Kilmorna, Listowel, who lost their son Jason in the crash, called for dedicated facilities to allow motoring enthusiasts do manoeuvres such as 'donuts' and handbrake turns in safety.

Meanwhile, boy racers continue to leave their mark on roads all over the country, with 'donuts', figures of eight and other signs of burning rubber caused by hard braking to be widely seen.

> The practice of 'donutting' refers to 360 degree wheel spins or driving in a manner that causes the car to lose traction. Once a favourite of boy racers at roundabouts, in recent weeks the evidence of this dangerous manner of driving is appearing throughout the region.
>
> *Western People*

Boy racers seem to think they have the roads all to themselves and dozens of cars often assemble late at night, their engines revving loudly before travelling at crazy speeds.

Dromahair under Siege during Drunken Teenage Rampage

Gangs of drunken teenagers who arrived in the sleepy village of Dromahair for a disco struck terror into the law-abiding citizenry. The normally peaceful County Leitrim village was under siege by large numbers of intoxicated young people who swarmed in on the night of 26 January 2007.

The young people went on a drunken rampage, according to the local garda sergeant who also said the real problem was the state some teenagers, many from Sligo, were in before they even got to Dromahair.

Youngsters themselves were also attacked and left in fear. Eyewitnesses told of cars from outside the area having been present in the village on the night and there were also attempts to push drugs on young people.

Youngsters were seen with litre bottles of vodka, beer and orange juice while there was 'an element carrying tablets' around for the night. 'It's well known who a lot of the people are who called out to Dromahair and caused this trouble. People were going around with their hands in their pockets with knuckledusters. There was threatening behaviour,' one speaker reported.

> Some young people were 'petrified' by what had happened and sought refuge in pubs while others were seen jumping over walls, allegedly to avoid being run over by cars.
>
> *The Sligo Champion*

A public meeting was later called in a bid to prevent further disorder. It was told how youngsters, described as children by some, were openly drinking and falling all over the place. One girl, aged about 13, was seen with her underwear around her ankles. 'If parents saw those kids, they

would be shocked. It was outrageous. There was complete pandemonium in the streets,' a speaker told the meeting.

The gardaí in Sligo confirmed they got a call for assistance just before midnight. However, no arrests were made.

One mother told the meeting: 'A lot of children are signed up to Bebo and if we looked up Bebo we would have learned a lot.'

Sergeant Conroy appealed for public co-operation but, ominously, some local people who might know a few things were reluctant to tell the gardaí because of fear of intimidation, or a 'bullet in the back of the head'.

Young Thugs Shatter the Peace of Ballysloe

Time was when people could sleep all night without hearing a sound in the Tipperary village of Ballysloe, but not anymore. Young hooligans now being bussed in from other areas are terrorising law-abiding villagers. The out-of-control teenagers hold drinking parties, throw eggs at houses, shout obscenities at old people and damage property.

Up to 20 of the youngsters congregate in gangs on the main street in the night hours of Friday and Saturday. They have turned one disused house in the village into a drinking den, breaking down the back door and vandalising the house.

Some residents gave vivid accounts of the havoc wreaked by thugs in Ballysloe in the small hours. One man installed searchlights in his yard to ward off the vandals.

> 'They are all aged from 14 upwards. We used to be a very quiet village here but in the last 12 months they've started arriving by bus at night. They use a field at the back of the school to go drinking in up until 4am. They've broken windows in the

school's prefabs, and let off fire extinguishers in the building. They told one local man that "he'd want to keep the number of the Munster Joinery (a window-making factory) handy".'

The Nationalist and Tipperary Star

Elderly people are now afraid to leave their homes at night. Such people never previously experienced trouble, but must now try to deal with it.

Residents met with gardaí to explore the possibility of installing CCTV cameras, brighter lights and other security measures in the village.

They're Robbing Trócaire Boxes Now

Fr Leo McDonnell was saying mass in Abbeyfeale Church when cynical thieves arrived unnoticed on Easter Monday. After sneaking into the sacristy they made off with Trócaire collection boxes containing €6,000 that parishioners had contributed for poor countries. Some of the boxes were subsequently found near Killaloe, but all of the money was missing.

Also on Easter Monday, at Caherconlish Church in Limerick, thieves stole petty cash and caused criminal damage to the inside of the church.

While Limerick City is better known for more high-profile, serious crime, a large amount of thefts, vandalism, assaults and thuggery paint a picture of the breakdown of law and order in County Limerick. According to local media reports, crime has become a 'living nightmare' for thousands of people in the county.

In a seven-day period at Easter, there were raids on business premises, bogus tradesmen tried to con their way into houses in Bruff, there was a drugs find in Cappamore and a garda patrol car was attacked after a disco in Newcastle West.

An angry crowd tried to thwart a patrol of five gardaí who were arresting three young men for public order offences outside the disco. The gardaí had brought a grilled 'paddywagon' to the scene but it took all their strength to get those arrested into the van, as other people on the street were trying to take the prisoners from them.

Sergeant Kelly said that a pattern had developed lately whereby some people from the Rathkeale district came to Newcastle West at weekends intent on troublemaking inside and, more particularly, outside the disco. He described the situation as a form of faction fighting between young men from the two towns.

'Law and order is definitely breaking down,' he said. 'Our wagon might only be an old Transit van, but it is worth its weight in gold in dealing with such incidents.'

Three young men from the Rathkeale area were charged with a variety of public order offences arising from the fracas. In other incidents, two cars were vandalised and a shop window was broken in the early hours by what one witness claimed were 'boy racers'.

One of the most affluent areas near Limerick city is not escaping the upsurge in break-ins, vandalism and antisocial behaviour. Residents in fashionable Killaloe are concerned about crime in an area that has traditionally been regarded as relatively immune from the scourge of criminality.

An elderly woman in Killaloe awoke to find she was being robbed by an intruder. Other local people reported that both serious and low-level crime has become a frightening reality.

> A number of high-profile individuals such as Celia Larkin and Gay Byrne's daughter, Crona, have bases in the Killaloe area which boasts some of the most expensive properties in the Mid-West. Some time ago, Ms Byrne was the victim of a burglary.
>
> *Limerick Leader*

A large number of businesses were broken into and women working in the Killaloe area had to suffer verbal abuse. 'A place up the road was robbed a few nights ago and a place across the street was burgled. The list is endless. If women are leaving work on their own they will be hassled and leered at,' one local businessman said.

Vampire-Like Attacks as Parts of Ears Are Savagely Bitten Off

After a night of violent attacks in Galway City, Damien Moloney could still feel bits of flesh between his teeth – flesh from a student's ear that he had bitten off. The unemployed bouncer, who had a lot of alcohol taken, had bitten three students in separate attacks.

The spree of violence started when Moloney headbutted Peter Connolly in a pub in Woodquay, injuring Mr Connolly's nose and eyebrow. Not satisfied with that, Moloney then bit the student on the ear. However, the quick-thinking young man did not pull against Moloney but 'went with him' as he was pulled around the toilet area by his ear clamped between Moloney's teeth. Peter believed he would have lost his ear had he not moved with his assailant.

Moloney then moved on to Boo Radley's nightclub. When he bit another student there, Bryan O'Gara intervened but Moloney pulled Bryan down towards him and bit off a chunk of his ear too. He spat the piece of ear onto the dance floor and then left. Bryan lost most of his right ear, something that would have 'permanent and life-altering' effects on him, in the words of Judge Raymond Groarke.

Following this attack, Moloney slipped out of the nightclub and went to a house where he was staying for the night. He told the shocked occupant of the house that he still had bits of flesh stuck between his teeth and recounted how he had completely bitten off a young man's ear.

> Surgeons at University College Hospital, Galway, were
> unsuccessful in their efforts to re-attach the top of Bryan's ear.
> The young man has grown his hair to try and cover his ear and
> he wears a woollen cap whenever he is in public. His parents
> will have to spend a large amount of money for reconstructive
> surgery. He will need further plastic surgery, possibly in
> Canada, according to a medical report.
>
> *The Connacht Tribune*

All the aggression on 1 March 2006, was 'totally unprovoked' the gardaí
said.

At Galway Circuit Criminal Court, Judge Groarke was told Moloney,
aged 24 and from Hymany Park, Ballinasloe, had previous convictions
for assault and had jumped out the window of a two-storey building
before getting treatment for a drink problem in August.

Moloney, who pleaded guilty to the assaults, said he had consumed six
cans of beer and a half bottle of Wicked vodka before going out that
evening. He then drank more in a pub before hitting Boo Radley's night
club.

Before sentencing him to eight year's imprisonment, with the last
three suspended, the Judge described his conduct as 'sheer savagery'.
He also did not believe Moloney had so much drink consumed, saying
he would have been 'on the floor' if he had.

Judge Groarke told Bryan O'Gara and his friends they might have
grounds for a case against Boo Radley's nightclub which had let Moloney
into the premises knowing he was intoxicated.

The ear-biting phenomenon is being reported from Kerry to Donegal.
In another incident of this kind, a Tralee civil engineering student was
told by Judge Carroll Moran he must come up with €25,000
compensation or go to jail for two years.

Stephen Hannafin, aged 20, of Michael O'Regan Place, Tralee, admitted biting off the earlobe of Greg O'Brien during an unprovoked attack in Tralee on St Patrick's Day 2004. Surgeons at Cork University Hospital were unable to re-attach the earlobe. Greg's mother said he was very sensitive about the injury and it affected his school work.

> Judge Moran said it was a disastrous injury and Greg would be disfigured for the rest of his life. 'This type of assault of biting people's ears is becoming quite common. It was completely unknown 20 or 30 years ago.'
>
> *Kerry's Eye*

Similar attacks, described as 'bordering on savagery', are also being reported in Donegal, with two ear-biting incidents in Letterkenny and one in Gweedore during the Christmas/New Year period. Those involved were generally young people and the assaults were associated with drink and drug abuse, according to Superintendent Jim Gallagher.

Drunken Teenagers Cause 'Absolute Mayhem' in Castlerea

The mad night in Castlerea when gangs of drunken teenagers ran amok will not be easily forgotten by locals or by the gardaí who were grossly outnumbered on the occasion.

Peace reigned in the Roscommon town until buses began to arrive from as far away as Galway, Athlone and Carrick-on-Shannon. Around 800 teenagers flocked in for a disco. Many were drunk when they hit the venue as they had been drinking cans and bottles of alcohol while en route, according to the gardaí.

It soon became clear that the situation was getting out of hand and extra gardaí were drafted in from Roscommon town and surrounding areas.

Gangs of teenagers were involved in scuffles, with rows breaking out on the streets throughout the night. Five youths were arrested for being drunk and disorderly while one male teenager was arrested for having ecstasy. An ambulance was also called to the scene, as there were fears for the safety of two extremely drunk teenagers.

Up to 15 officers were on duty to deal with a volatile situation. However, the melée took a dangerous twist when the gardaí tried to break up two 'warring factions'. As officers intervened, some of the youths began throwing stones at the gardaí.

> A sergeant and a garda were both hit on the side of the head and suffered injuries. Local gardaí described the scene as 'absolute mayhem' and were fiercely critical of the actions of the teenagers, which resulted in a dangerous situation for those trying to bring about law and order.
>
> *Roscommon Herald*

Sergeant Mick Clesham said: 'It was a harrowing situation and, yes, it was frightening. We tried to isolate and separate rival factions when two members (gardaí) were hit on the head with rocks. Another member was directing traffic out of the area when a stone went flying past his head. If it had hit him it would have caused serious harm. If we hadn't managed to separate the groups it would have been a riotous situation and there would have been numerous casualties.'

Three people were arrested and questioned in relation to the stone-throwing incident. The gardaí eventually managed to get the teenagers back onto buses and out of the area.

According to Sergeant Clesham, there had been no prior consultation with the gardaí in relation to the scale of the disco that was taking place and they had no knowledge of what was happening until a very late stage.

'Only for the efforts of a number of gardaí, there would have been serious injuries. They managed to prevent a serious melée or serious casualties or injuries,' he maintained.

Boy Racers Take Over – Noise and Sleepless Nights Result

The revving engines could be heard on all approach roads to Killarney as the souped-up cars zoomed in for the Rally of the Lakes. It was the May bank holiday – the busiest weekend of the year in the throbbing tourist haven – and the boy racers took over.

Hundreds of youthful drivers came from all over the country in their modified cars. They wanted to show off by burning rubber and performing stunts – donuts, wheelies, figures of eight and handbrake turns. The organisers of the Rally of the Lakes and townspeople were not too pleased at the biggest ever influx of boy racers.

Killarney was 'black' with gardaí that weekend, as extra personnel were drafted in and the eye-in-the-sky helicopter hovered overhead. They tried to keep out the boy racers by blocking off public car parks, but the young drivers found other venues and moved to neighbouring towns before returning to Killarney again.

Some local people got no sleep that weekend as the boy racers sped around housing estates at all hours. 'It's a crazy situation that they can be allowed disturb people up to three or four o'clock in the morning,' said an angry local councillor, Michael Courtney.

The Rally secretary, Mike Marshall, called for a nationwide crackdown on boy racers who, he claimed, were outnumbering the gardaí.

'The number of boy racers is increasing around the country and we have to call a halt to these people. They are terrorising people. They are going into private ground and housing estates at night and the noise they are making is intolerable . . . the gardaí must be able to do something under disturbances for public order, or the blackening of the road from "doughnuts" . . . I want to see these cars seized,' he declared.

The Kerryman

Up to 60 arrests were made in Killarney during a troublesome weekend. When the boy racers had left, evidence of their presence was there for all to see – artistic-looking brake marks on the roads, junctions and tarmac surfaces.

Two cars blocked the Mallow-Killarney road on Sunday evening so that others could perform tricks and turns on their way home from the rally, but they were nabbed by an undercover garda.

At the other end of the country, residents of Sylvan Park in Letterkenny were taking a zero tolerance approach to boy racers following several late-night incidents in the area.

The no-nonsense approach followed two separate arrests after several boy racers were causing havoc in the area. In one incident, a man was arrested at ten o'clock in the morning after keeping residents awake from four o'clock until eight. Two houses in the estate are believed to be occupied by groups of the young men and, since the incident, a landlord has taken measures and evicted his tenants.

Donegal News

One upset Sylvan Park resident said people in the area were being 'terrorised' by the behaviour of some boy racers.

The residents started to report any speeding or noise to the gardaí and were hoping for prosecutions. Some residents claimed they were being intimidated, but were recording the drivers on digital camera or video. Following one of the incidents, a landlord evicted unruly tenants.

Gardaí Brake Hard to Avoid Crash with Motorists 'Racing' Each Other

It was half-past nine on a dry August night as two gardaí in a patrol car approached a bend near Buttevant, County Cork. They were travelling at about 50 kilometres per hour when two cars came towards them at high speed. One of the cars was on their side of the road.

The gardaí believed they would have been killed if they didn't brake quickly and bring their patrol car to a halt. Both gardaí were convinced the two cars were racing each other.

The driver of one of the cars, David O'Sullivan of Churchtown, Mallow, later appeared in court and pleaded not guilty to dangerous driving but admitted he was 'foolish to have sped' going round a bend.

The observer in the patrol car, Garda John F Horgan, told the court the defendant was driving a white car. The other car driver, who had a black car, had not yet been located.

> He went on: 'They appeared to be racing each other. Garda Doyle had to apply the brakes. We turned the patrol car around and followed them and put on the siren. The black car overtook the white one and, afterwards, the defendant pulled in. When cautioned, the defendant said: "I am sorry. I know I am wrong."
>
> 'He refused to give the name of the other driver. If we were driving any faster I have no doubt we would have been killed. I could not estimate the speed but they appeared to be jostling for position.'
>
> *The Corkman*

David O'Sullivan, aged 24, said his girlfriend was in the car with him on the occasion when a black car came up behind him. He 'stupidly sped up' but did not cross the white line. 'When I came around the bend, the garda car was pulled in. It wasn't moving at all. I was going at about 100 kilometres per hour,' he said, adding that he was travelling at speed only because the black car was behind him.

In evidence, the gardaí rejected suggestions that their patrol car was stopped at Paddy Mack's pub and were adamant they were in motion when the defendant came round the bend.

Replying to a claim that David was on his correct side of the road, Garda Horgan said he was being very selective with the truth.

After listening to lengthy deliberations from both sides, Judge Michael Pattwell, who said it was a 'great shame' on Mr O'Sullivan if he was racing, convicted him of dangerous driving, fined him €2,500 and endorsed his licence for one year.

'What it boils down to, Mr O'Sullivan, is that you were on the wrong side of the road. If you were racing you should never drive again, and if you allowed yourself to be pushed into speeding it shows a lack of character,' said Judge Pattwell.

Horse Tranquiliser Drug Hits Party Scene

The ultimate accolade for a great Kerry footballer is to have a reputation for being a 'horse of a man' but that could yet have a new resonance. A prescription horse tranquiliser, ketamine, is the latest recreational drug on the Kerry social scene. While it doesn't claim to be capable of bestowing equine qualities on consumers, it can have striking effects.

Generally known as Special K, it's certainly not recommended for footballers. Its effects, often compared to PCP or angel dust, include hallucinations, numbness and out-of-body experiences. Users can enter a trance-like state where their bodies are virtually paralysed until the drug wears off about two hours later.

Administered as a horse anaesthetic by vets, its use on people was discontinued in Ireland in 2005 after some negative experiences including hallucinations, strong outbursts and extreme violence, among those taking the drug.

Illicitly-sold ketamine often comes from diverted, legitimate supplies or theft, primarily from veterinary clinics, and is sold in either powdered, tablet or liquid form. In powdered form, its appearance is similar to that of pharmaceutical grade cocaine and it can be swallowed, injected or placed in beverages.

> Many users' first contact with ketamine is accidental, from a pill sold as something else, commonly ecstasy. Its ease of availability and manufacture means it is one of the cheapest drugs on the Irish market with a hit of the drug usually costing no more than €5.
>
> *The Kerryman*

According to the gardaí in Tralee, ketamine is freely available on the streets of the town but is not yet as popular as ecstasy. The gardaí seized the drug from local dealers selling it as ecstasy and it was only revealed to be ketamine following forensic analysis.

Man Lying on Railway Tracks as Train Passed over Him

There it was for all to see on the YouTube and Bebo websites – a 20-year-old man filmed lying under railway tracks as a train sped over him at over 100 kilometres per hour. Two of his friends made the film and later uploaded it to the websites.

The lunatic incident happened close to Monasterevin railway station and locally-based garda, Sergeant Niall Lynch, confirmed that a formal complaint had been made by Iarnród Éireann. Three men had been identified and all three were to be interviewed with charges likely to follow.

The sergeant, who had investigated a similar incident at Portarlington four years previous, said: 'It is a ferociously dangerous practice. The unusual thing about this time, compared to four years ago, was that instead of scooping out the gravel under the tracks, the man lay down perpendicular with the railway under three wooden sleepers. It was stupid and ridiculous. They seem to be egged on by these Bebo and YouTube websites. What makes it more ridiculous is that these people are in their twenties.'

Barry Kenny of Iarnród Éireann described the incident as being 'moronic beyond words'. 'It was incredible that a person could have been so stupid to put himself in such clear danger,' he remarked.

> Mr Kenny said the entire track network in the area is walked twice weekly with continuous observations along it to ensure there was no danger to commuters in relation to the incident. 'The danger was to the individual and not to the commuters,' said Mr Kenny.
>
> *Laois Nationalist*

Sergeant Lynch was also in charge at Portarlington station at the time of the previous incident when a section of track was being used for a similarly dangerous practice by young children. Gravel filling was being removed from beneath the track to about a depth of 30 centimetres and cardboard was then put down so as to allow young children lie down along the tracks as trains travelled over them as a dare.

In confirming the incidents had occurred at that time, Iarnród Éireann said it was the first such case it had heard of. Works were then carried out to prevent children from the area gaining access to the tracks.

Bank Holiday Mayhem in Top Tourist Town

It was the August bank holiday in An Daingean (Dingle), a droll town best known for a confusing row about its name and for Fungi the playful dolphin. An Daingean is a place where people can relax and enjoy themselves most of the time, but its worst night of mayhem was about to erupt.

Clashes between some locals and a gang from Dublin ignited with a vicious brawl outside the Hillgrove nightclub car park. This was followed by a second melée in a housing estate.

And then the real drama started. Three of the 'Jackeens' hightailed it from the fight and found refuge in a jeep. The jeep was then driven into the group involved in the skirmish and others standing nearby were knocked to the ground. A few sober people around the place feared someone was going to get killed.

'People were jammed against a wall by the jeep. The jeep was driven at people five times and, in my opinion, it was attempted murder . . . Then all the Dubliners got into the jeep and drove away . . . It was like something you'd see in a film from a war zone. There was blood everywhere and people were being brought in the whole time,' one witness said.

One father said of his injured son, 'He was attacked and doesn't remember anything about it. Two strangers picked him up and brought him to the medical centre. Thanks be to God we're not going to his funeral or seeing him on a life support machine.'

Twenty people were injured and doctors at the An Daingean medical centre had a busy night stitching wounds, looking at black eyes and examining broken bones. Rumours were flying that the fleeing 'Jackeens' had links with a notorious Dublin drugs gang.

> The bank holiday weekend marked the most violent and savage night of mayhem ever witnessed in Dingle . . . Dingle man Pat Hanafin, who is Chairman of the Ambulance Association of Ireland, described it as one of the worst nights ever experienced by his members in Dingle. 'It seems that a lot of people were injured when they went to help their friends who were being attacked. It was lucky that nobody was killed,' he said.
>
> *The Kerryman*

Some people visiting the town for the weekend said they were shocked and they had never seen anything like it. They also said they would never return, according to the newspaper.

Youngsters' Fights Broadcast on Internet

Staged fights from the western town and county of Sligo are being broadcast on the internet for the world to see.

One five-minute video, recorded on a mobile phone, showed barefisted teenagers scrapping in a basketball court in Sligo watched by a cheering crowd of up to 20 other youngsters. The fight was stopped twice as the pair involved took rests before resuming hostilities.

One of the pugilists was holding his bloodied hand in pain. They punched, kicked and pushed each other repeatedly during the course of the footage. A spectator, also a youngster, could be seen lying across one of the basketball hoops enjoying the best view from his vantage point.

Afterwards, both fighters received rounds of applause from their audience. The fight had been viewed by over 1,000 internet users a short time after it was uploaded onto the YouTube website. Many of those that viewed the footage offered comments on the action with some awarding it a four-star rating.

> Yet this isn't the only video on this website showing Sligo youngsters fighting. Another one showed two boys fighting in the grounds of a well-known Sligo building. This footage was on the website up until Friday evening but has now been taken off. The footage was titled 'Summerhill fight' and it showed students in Summerhill College uniform, along with other youngsters, cheering on the two fighters. This particular footage had over 100 viewers before it was suddenly taken off some time over the weekend.
>
> *Sligo Weekender*

One Summerhill College student said, 'These fights take place every couple of months. And it is a regular thing for two boys to fight each other if they have had a disagreement. They sometimes take place at lunchtime and they take place in different venues. But they mostly take place after school. And they are nearly always recorded on mobile phones. There could be a few people recording the fight on their phone so they can show their friends.'

Eggs and Stinkbombs Thrown at Roses

The delicate scent of roses should have perfumed the air in Tralee but it was the odour of stinkbombs that assailed no strils at the start of the town's famous festival.

The opening Rose of Tralee parade had gone only a short distance when 'gurriers' began to hurl eggs and stinkbombs at a float carrying the girls from Darwin, Cork, Boston and London. Luckily for the Roses, none ended up with egg on their stylish dresses but some children from Chernobyl, who were also on the float, were hit.

The targeted second float was in a long line travelling just behind RTÉ's Ray D'Arcy, the show's compère, and the reigning Rose of Tralee, Kathryn Feeney. On the float was Chernobyl Children's Project volunteer Anne Dempsey who said the first thing they noticed was an awful smell.

> 'We thought it was the sewers but we realised then people were throwing eggs and stinkbombs at us. It was disgusting. The ambulance was destroyed and there were eggs all over the float. There was a little girl from Chernobyl with us and she was very upset . . . People spent a lot of time preparing the float just to have it ruined by some little thugs. It shows the town in an awful light for the visiting roses,' she said.
>
> *The Kerryman*

In the festival's 48 years, nothing like this had ever happened during the colourful, opening-night parade through the streets. Approached some time afterwards, festival spokesman Ted Keane said he was unaware of anything untoward happening but described such an incident as 'scandalous' – if it happened.

However, the newspaper was in no doubt and didn't hold back when reporting that the Chernobyl float was 'pelted with a barrage of eggs from thugs hiding in the crowd'. Also, during festival week seven Roses had to be turned away from the Tralee Races after a hoax bomb alert that delayed the start of racing by 40 minutes.

On the streets, it was comedy singer Richie Kavanagh who had tongues wagging after he hit the wrong note with some parents who felt parts of his repertoire were not suitable for children. Richie, famous for his song 'Aon Focal Eile', is known for his innuendo-peppered lyrics and stage banter.

But the festival's entertainment organisers had the last 'focal'. They said they had received no official complaints and pointed out that lots of people had enjoyed Richie and queued for his autograph afterwards.

Drink and Debauchery

Pubs Almost Deserted by Drink Driving Crackdown

It just didn't feel like Christmas in Dromey's bar in the west Cork village of Kilmichael. High stools awaited bums, punters were scarce and conversation muted. So silent were some pubs that lifelong customers had the rare experience of hearing the soporific tick-tock of the house clock – something that never happened before when crowds of noisy revellers packed in to celebrate the festive season.

Who would ever have thought Irish pubs would be almost deserted at Christmas, of all times? An old way of life was passing. The enforcement of new regulations on random breath testing for alcohol went down worse than a dodgy pint, with some pubs reporting a 50 per cent drop in business.

Nicholas and Maureen Dromey run a typical country pub from which punters are now being turned away by the tough, new road safety legislation as well as changes in lifestyles and drinking habits.

'Rural life has been destroyed. The pub should be the focal point of the community now that the creamery and post office have closed, but it is not,' Nicholas complained.

Kilmichael was scene of a famous ambush during the War of Independence in which a large group of Auxiliaries and Black and Tans were wiped out by the IRA. There was a time, not too long ago, when people there also had a rebellious attitude to the drink-driving laws. Nicholas Dromey admitted that they would have one, two, three, or even more drinks before sitting into their cars and driving merrily homewards. But that happened no more, he stressed.

In nearby Newcestown, the festive spirit was also dampened severely. Cornelius O'Mahony was now welcoming only 10 to 15 customers per night to his pub, compared to 20 to 30 previously. He likened the ghostly scene to pubs in the grim 1950s. In O'Mahony's and thousands of other pubs, everyone spoke about breath testing. Most of all, they were afraid of being 'over the limit' the following morning and being caught while driving to work.

Ingrained attitudes of men and women who had routinely been drinking and driving for years were seriously challenged that Christmas. Many such people never had an accident. But gardaí were not impressed by such an argument and pointed out that road deaths had been reduced by 30 per cent since random testing had been introduced the previous July. Random testing had a greater impact than any previous measure to eradicate drink driving. Rumours abounded and there were plenty of tall tales, such as the one about the teetotaller publican from a village in County Limerick who failed the breath test after eating sherry trifle!

Local councillors and a number of Dáil deputies were quick to jump on the bandwagon: some, including Cork North East Fianna Fáil TD Ned O'Keeffe, called for a separate law on drink driving for rural dwellers. Some regional newspapers saw the rigorous enforcement of random testing as yet another attack on rural Ireland.

It is all very well to pontificate about road deaths, but to forget that rural Ireland itself is beginning to die and that government policies make it less attractive for people of all ages to live in isolated rural communities cannot be ignored. When it comes to General Election 2007, the politicians will certainly be getting it on the doorsteps.

The 'overkill' policy on drink and driving is, unfortunately, supported by daily newspapers based in our two major cities where populations have the advantage of readily available taxis, a level of service not applicable to isolated rural regions.

The Southern Star

Healy-Raes Hit Minister O'Donoghue for a Double

Always ready to pounce on a populist line, the Healy-Raes were quick to capitalise politically on publican/drinker resentment of random breath testing in Kerry. They even went one better by blaming Fianna Fáil Cabinet Minister John O'Donoghue for bringing too many gardaí to the constituency. That was the spin the Independent Healy-Rae dynasty put on the controversy so as to score a double-whammy at the expense of O'Donoghue, their arch rival.

Michael Healy-Rae, a councillor and heir apparent to his father Jackie, claimed that the Caherciveen (O'Donoghue's home town) and Valentia areas were 'totally overpoliced' since the days when O'Donoghue was Minister for Justice between 1997 and 2002. He said large numbers of recruits coming out of the Garda Training College had been sent to Caherciveen during O'Donoghue's time in Justice.

'There's an unbelieveable number of checkpoints at the moment and people are getting fed up of it. You could get stopped and bagged in one end of Caherciveen and be stopped again down at the other side of the town,' he moaned.

The situation had become so ridiculous, he declared, that two parish priests, both teetotallers, had been stopped and breath tested.

Gardaí were clearly upsetting publicans and some voters in Healy-Rae strongholds around the Ring of Kerry. Rather than deploying too many gardaí around the Ring, Michael Healy-Rae maintained they could be better used in bigger towns such as Tralee and Killarney where there was plenty of trouble to be dealt with, especially at weekends.

He also grumbled that the pub trade in the constituency was being seriously hit, and he ought to know as he held 35 monthly clinics in pubs. Pub closures were also on the way, he warned.

> Older people driving home after a few pints were seldom, if ever, the cause of accidents, he believed, and mounting too many checkpoints in rural areas was not the solution to ongoing road carnage. Healy-Rae, himself a very moderate drinker, went on: 'Gardai should be able to use their own discretion about who to stop and use their own commonsense. Stopping and bagging life-long pioneers makes no sense.'
>
> *The Kerryman*

Morning-After Breath Testing a Reality

The truck driver who was 'bagged' at Tinahely at five o'clock in the morning got a shock and knew all of a sudden that life had changed. Breath testing the 'morning after' had become a reality for drivers who would now have to be careful about how much alcohol they consumed the previous night. All around the country gardaí were relentless – day and night.

Sergeant Joe Ellis of Carlow said drinking the previous night might be a particular issue for truck drivers. 'We were in an area outside Tinahely last week and a lorry driver I was testing said to me that he'd never thought he'd see the day where he'd be breathalysed at 5am in Tinahely,' Sergeant Ellis said, also urging drivers to take adequate rest and a proper sleep following a night out.

Gardaí in the Carlow/Kildare/West Wicklow division were also mindful of other aspects of road safety. These included driving while under the influence of drugs and a large number of cases of drink driving among foreign nationals.

> Gardaí said many foreign nationals came from a culture we had 30 years ago when drink driving was tolerated in the public mind. Drink driving among foreign nationals is very high, according to gardaí.
>
> *Carlow Nationalist*

Arrests for drink driving offences in the Louth/Meath Garda Division, one of the worst in the country for road deaths, soared – up by 20.5 per cent in a year.

> There is still a hardcore of people driving with excess alcohol in their blood and ignoring the new climate of intolerance on drink driving aimed at reducing road accidents, gardai pointed out.
>
> *The Meath Chronicle*

Chief Superintendent Pat McGee commented that gardaí were surprised at the increase in drink driving detections because they thought people had 'got the message by now'. He warned that people who continued to drink and drive would be caught.

A point also being made was that while people with excess alcohol consumed were being easily detected by the gardaí, drivers who had taken other substances were getting away. Waterford Fianna Fáil TD Ollie Wilkinson, a member of the Dáil Transport Committee, called on the government to press ahead with plans for mobile drug-testing clinics which were working successfully in Victoria, Australia.

It's planned that specially-equipped buses, manned by gardaí, a doctor and a nurse, would be particularly visible at summer concerts and gigs where garda intelligence shows drugs are consumed in great quantities.

Munster Express

Priests and People at Risk in the West

Things were so bad in the west of Ireland that priests were running the risk of 'failing the bag' after consuming a little altar wine while saying mass. At least that's what Deputy Paddy McHugh had to say about the situation.

Worshippers were also afraid to drive to mass, he further suggested, as gardaí were throwing cordons around churches on Sundays and randomly breath testing any God-fearing soul that moved. The independent deputy, who earned himself the title 'Paddy the Liberator', maintained that soon only paid-up pioneers would be making it safely to church on Sunday mornings.

In a tongue-in-cheek piece in *The Tuam Herald*, reporter Tony Galvin referred to fears raised by Deputy McHugh about poor priests being dragged before the courts after a drop of altar wine put them over the limit.

So concerned is Deputy McHugh over the impact of this draconian policy that he has issued a hard-hitting statement which basically tells the gardaí to find something better to do with their time than persecute Massgoers, who may or may not have had a few pints on Saturday night. He says the fear of the early morning alco-dragnet is inhibiting people on their way to morning Mass.

'People on their way to Mass are not known for their propensity to cause carnage on our roads and statistics would not suggest that Massgoers are the cohort of people who drive at dangerous speeds.' Deputy McHugh goes on to say the gardaí are under-resourced, particularly in terms of manpower, and it seems a waste of scarce garda manpower to have checkpoints at morning time when in many cases people are not engaged in any more offensive behaviour than attempting to get to Mass on time.

The Herald could not establish when going to Mass became offensive behaviour since the Penal Laws were repealed, thanks to that other great Independent TD Daniel O'Connell, but our lawyers are checking it out.

The Tuam Herald

Any Chance of a Lift?

Images of blacked-out, almost eerie villages were enough to force anyone to stay away from sepulchral pubs. There were calls for rural transport schemes and a transport initiative mooted by Gaeltacht and Rural Affairs Minister Éamon Ó Cuív received mixed reaction. Desperate drinkers would be happy to take any kind of a lift to their locals. But some publicans, including Nicholas Dromey of Kilmichael in West Cork, were sceptical about the Ó Cuív proposal and did not believe it would work. Nicholas felt this was an election ploy and asked who was going to pay for the operation.

A more enthusiastic advocate was Kerry Fianna Fáil councillor and election candidate Tom Fleming, who is also a publican. He felt the drinks companies, publicans, drinkers and the government should all contribute to the cost of a transport scheme.

All the vested interests were looking at ways of keeping pub cash registers tinkling and ensuring the survival of many struggling premises. There were warnings that many pubs would be sold. But, given the depressed outlook being voiced by the trade itself, who in their right senses would buy them? The mood in publand was downbeat.

> A drive through the north Galway area on the night before New Year's Eve showed pub after pub in total darkness at 8pm – proof that even the so-called big venues of old are dying on their feet.
>
> *The Connacht Tribune*

Hope radiated from west Cork, however, signalled by the success of a 'booze bus' – a phenomenon that could be the answer to drinkers' prayers in country districts across the land. The bus was a big hit in a scattered area from Dunbeacon to Mizen Head. It took people to the pubs of their choice in places such as Goleen or Crookhaven and collected them again at 12.30am, free *gratis*. Provided under a pilot scheme funded by a community council, the service was a gesture of thanks for people's support for a local fundraising lotto.

> All we ask the users to do is to enjoy it (the bus) as it's not often you get something for nothing . . . remember, if you're a man who likes his porter make sure you use Betty's bus.
>
> *The Southern Star*

Dropped Trousers on Stag Night

Groom-to-be Jimmy Maloney may have reason to remember his stag night much longer than his actual wedding. After having too much to drink at his last bash as a bachelor, he lost the run of himself. He decided to drop his trousers for a lark and rub his backside on a female singer's legs.

Several of Jimmy's friends from Kildare were enjoying themselves in

The Wooden House, Kilmore Quay, County Wexford, on 29 April 2005, when the shenanigans started.

The band Jigsaw was playing on the night with singer Emma Sutherland. She was sitting in front of the stage close to where the people at the stag party were. Some members of the stag party interfered with and obstructed the performance. But the fun landed Jimmy before Wexford District Court.

The court was told Jimmy pulled down his trousers and rubbed his backside on Emma's legs on a number of occasions. Emma was very upset. She had been due to sing until 12.30 am, but called off the show at 11.45 pm because of what had happened.

Jimmy was mortified and very embarrassed to be in court according to his solicitor, Helen Redmond. 'He has since got married, regrets this behaviour very seriously and wishes to apologise sincerely,' she said.

> Ms Redmond described what happened as totally out of character and said Jimmy, who admitted the charge of indecency, was 'incredulous' as to his behaviour. 'He doesn't wish to make any excuses, and does not want to use drink as an excuse. He comes before the court fairly and squarely.'
>
> *Wexford People*

Judge William Early said that no-one should have to suffer from the kind of crass and crude behaviour displayed by Jimmy Maloney, whose address was given as Kilmege, County Kildare. He was fined €350.

In Killarney, meanwhile, one well-known hotel is turning away accommodation bookings for stag and hen parties. Sean Buckley, owner of the Arbutus Hotel, said such parties were 'particularly boisterous' in a family-run establishment. 'Out of respect for our other guests, we don't accept this kind of business. Do we discriminate? Yes we do,' he admitted.

But, sometimes, stag groups try to get in by pretending they are parties of golfers.

Killarney is like a magnet for stag and hen parties on weekends and many other hotels in the leading tourist town, always reluctant to turn away any form of tourist business, welcome their custom. One unnamed hotelier said they bring good business and are big spenders. 'There is no anti-stag party agenda in Killarney and we don't want that message going out,' he emphasised.

The Kingdom

Vodka Drinker Forgot Where He Lived in Estate

Show me the way to go home – a problem confronting a Kerryman who had a 'few too many'.

It was 2.40am on 27 August 2006 when the gardaí in Killarney got a phone call saying a man was banging on the doors of houses in the Ballydribbeen estate and that he was waking people up.

Thomas O'Brien, a building contractor, had been out partying with a number of Polish men who had been working with him and were leaving the country.

> His solicitor explained: 'On this night, he drank vodka which is not his usual drink. He didn't know where he lived and began banging on the doors in the estate trying to find the house.'
>
> Judge James O'Connor commented: 'By process of elimination.'
>
> The Kingdom

O'Brien pleaded guilty to disorderly conduct and was fined €300. Having been told he had 22 previous convictions, Judge O'Connor warned him that he would be sent to jail if he came before the court again.

Clash of Hooks Rings in New Year in Waterford

The peal of bells ringing in the New Year in Waterford was drowned out by the sound of clashing slash hooks during a violent fracas in a housing estate in the city.

After responding to a number of 999 calls on New Year's morning, the gardaí came across a brawl involving a number of people, many of whom scarpered on the arrival of the authorities. Two men were arrested. One of these was subsequently taken to hospital for treatment of injuries sustained during the altercation at Ardmore Park. The official report was that while his injuries were thought to be serious, they were not life-threatening.

Machetes were also among the array of weapons used in disturbances in the Ardmore Park area of Ballybeg. The gardaí in Waterford certainly earned their New Year overtime in dealing with numerous other drink-fuelled incidents around the city during which several cars and motorcycles were burned.

> Later that day, at about 1.20pm, gardaí returned to the house that had been at the centre of the initial dispute and encountered another clash which involved some 20 people, a number of whom were in possession of weapons such as machetes, golf clubs and slash hooks. Four local men were arrested and brought before Waterford District Court.
>
> *Munster Express*

Foreign National Ends Up in Hospital after Enjoying a 'Good Irish Christmas'

It was his first night out in Ireland and Slawomir Nowak's friends wanted him to experience what a 'good Irish Christmas' was like. He joined his work colleagues from a local building company in Caherciveen for the Christmas work party, supped well, if not wisely, and ended up in hospital.

A great night was had by all, but Slawomir was unable to stay the course with his more seasoned Irish buddies. At 3.30 on the morning of 17 December, the gardaí found him on the street in Caherciveen.

He was so drunk that they failed to rouse him, so an ambulance was called and he was taken to Kerry General Hospital, 60 kilometres away. That journey cost the State €440 and left south Kerry without an ambulance service for three hours.

> His solicitor later told Caherciveen Court that Slawomir was not used to drink, adding: 'His workmates wanted to show him a good Irish Christmas.'
>
> *The Kerryman*

Judge James O'Connor gave him the benefit of the Probation Act provided he paid €300 into the poor box.

A Shock for Drinkers in 'Samurai' Lounge

Customers having a civilised drink in Keane's pub in Listowel nearly choked on their pints when a man burst in without warning, clutching a sword under his jacket. It was a scene that the late playwright John B Keane could easily have penned himself.

The intruder was accompanied by another man. Both looked frightened, but not nearly as frightened as the drinkers who were witnessing a local gang feud – real-life drama in Keane's for a change.

John B's son, Billy, who now runs the premises, quickly banged the doors shut, but a rival faction then arrived on the street outside. Obviously pursuing the two intruders, they started knocking frantically on the windows. The men being chased asked to be let out the back door of the bar, but were refused and then went into the toilets at the rear of the premises.

Within minutes the men were ejected from the bar by which time their assailants had fled. Customers needed stiff drinks to recover from the trauma. The gardaí were already on the trail of the feuding gang after being alerted to a smashed-up car in the middle of the road, further up the town, a short time earlier.

> It is now thought that the two men who entered the bar were the occupants of this car when it was set upon by a gang armed with baseball bats and other heavy implements. They are thought to have begun smashing up the car with the two men inside. Both occupants somehow escaped and were chased down Market Street where they took shelter in John B's.
>
> *The Kerryman*

A neighbour of Billy Keane, Listowel Councillor Ned O'Sullivan, was also upset by the incident. 'This is one of the best run bars in the country and I don't believe there has ever been such an incident in the history of the premises. I'm very disappointed that it would be targeted in this manner. It seems young people today are doing what they want to and getting away with it, and Listowel, I'm afraid, seems to be no exception.'

Local wags afterwards christened the bar the Samurai Lounge.

A Case of Costly Exposure by Young Plumber

Drink was flowing and the craic was mighty in an Ennis hotel, but the air of bonhomie got the better of a few young men. They decided to drop their pants in the full glare of all present in a Limerick Road establishment.

One of the lads, Mark O'Loughlin of Showgrounds Roads, Ennis, also became very abusive to other people in the hotel. He later admitted to being intoxicated, abusive and insulting when he came before Judge Aeneas McCarthy, who was not amused.

The solicitor acting for the 24-year-old told the court he was excessively drunk on the night and was 'mortified' when he sobered up.

> He did take down his pants, she admitted, and came to court to answer for that. She asked for an adjournment of the case for a professional report on O'Loughlin. 'It was a moment of madness gone wrong,' she added.
>
> *The Clare Champion*

Judge McCarthy replied: 'I don't need a report for someone who pulls his pants down in public. It's an outrageous thing to do.' He ordered O'Loughlin to pay €500 to the poor box and described it as a case of costly exposure.

Drunkenness and Debauchery in Hen and Stag capital

It's the small hours of a Sunday morning in Kilkenny and hordes of intoxicated revellers are on the streets. Throngs of people – some would say thousands – descend on the marble city at weekends for stag and hen parties or plain drunkenness and debauchery.

They leave a trail of destruction in their wake and one High Street trader, Anne Ryan, claimed her business is being affected on an ongoing basis by this yobbish behaviour. 'Every Monday morning you can see the aftermath of what is going on in our streets at the weekend. This includes vomit outside the front door, broken glass and beer spilled outside the shop. People also urinate in the doorways and this has to be cleaned,' she said.

One young man from Mitchelstown, County Cork, who was attacked coming out of a disco during the May bank holiday weekend could easily have been killed according to the gardaí. He had to be put on a life support machine while another visitor to the city was seriously injured when he was attacked with a glass. Kilkenny's most senior garda, Superintendent Pat Mangan, successfully prevented pubs from opening after 1.30am for the Cat Laughs Festival during the June bank holiday weekend. Pubs had previously been allowed to open until 2am for the comedy festival.

The local court was told the city was out of control at weekends. The debate was aired on national radio with several callers ringing Joe Duffy's *Liveline* to voice their disgust at the mayhem they had witnessed on Kilkenny streets.

Limerick-born comedian Karl Spain, who was performing at the festival, heard the conversation about Kilkenny crime on the radio and couldn't resist the quip: 'I'm from Limerick; this is the best thing that's ever happened!'

The head of tourism in Kilkenny, Declan Murphy, rowed in behind the guards saying it was time to tackle the city's public order problems. 'There is no doubt that the influx of hens and stags into the city cuts across the image of Kilkenny as a medieval city. We have reached a watershed in terms of what direction we are going to take and our strategic approach to tourism, and it is incumbent on everyone to look at the problems which exist and chart a new way forward,' he said.

Kilkenny People

Judge William Harnett told the court that there was a high possibility that a 'lunatic fringe' would attend the festival and agreed that the closing times should be extended only to 1.30am.

Also, there are plans to install a closed-circuit television system (CCTV) in the city in the hope of identifying people involved in assaults, damage to property, intimidation, littering, urinating on the street and anti-social behaviour in general.

However, some local councillors pointed out that there were 'certain sectors' in Kilkenny who didn't want to focus attention on what goes on late at night on the city's streets. 'The offences that are being committed on our streets must end up in the courts if we are to have a civilised society and streets that we can all feel safe in,' Councillor Betty Manning said.

Cider and Graveyard Drinking Parties

From listening to some local politicians you'd think that cider is the only alcohol consumed by teenagers at late night drinking parties. For some macabre reason graveyards appear to be popular locations for these youthful get togethers, as well as derelict houses, town parks and children's playgrounds.

In south-east Clare, a 300-year-old graveyard was the venue for a bash which involved 'debauchery and vandalism' with rocks being hurled at a headstone, according to Clare county councillor Cathal Crowe.

But cider producers are getting tired of being blamed for all the trouble. Paula Pegman, of the Cider Industry Council, took the councillor to task after he claimed Kilavoher cemetery had been the scene of cider parties.

Paula, however, was anxious to learn if cider was a contributory factor to the disturbances. Her council, she stated in a letter, wanted to address underage drinking and promote responsible attitudes to alcohol. Independent research had shown that when outdoor drinking took place, cider, if used at all, was only one of a number of types of alcohol being abused.

'I would be grateful if you could clarify if it is cider, or other types of alcohol generally, that are being abused,' she asked Councillor Crowe.

But he couldn't provide such data that would back up his assertion. And neither was he in the mood to poke among the cans and bottles in the graveyard to find evidence that cider was the beverage of choice. He said he did not want to single out any company and felt responsibility lay with a number of interests.

Local curate Fr Fred McDonnell condemned the desecration of the graveyard which followed a major clean-up 18 months previously when 12 bags of drink bottles and cans were removed.

> 'I believe teenagers are going into this holy, sacred ground at ten or eleven o'clock at night for drinking purposes. I can't understand why they are going into this graveyard at night. They have no right to be there, [they] are not going there to say prayers and are trespassing,' he said.
>
> *The Clare Champion*

Priests in other parts of the country have to lock up graveyards and, in some cases, erect floodlights to stop late night drinking parties and vandalism in such grounds.

Even a cursory perusal of the 'evidence' left behind invariably shows that cider is not the only form of booze involved – beer, lager and spirits are also popular with the rising generation which is obviously intent on ensuring that a national drinking culture not only survives but also thrives.

Sherry Trifle Puts 'Pioneer' Publican on the Spot

He's a publican in a village just outside Limerick City where he's known as a teetotaller. But he failed a roadside breath test for alcohol after being stopped by the gardaí one night while driving customers home from his premises.

The man has a liking for sherry trifle, which he ate that day, adding that he has it several times a week.

> But he also added, 'I don't normally drink,' leading the community to speculate whether he simply fell off the wagon and landed into this comical spotlight. For over a month now the incident has continued to cause questioning in a village just outside Limerick, where the well-known publican is regarded as a steadfast pioneer.
>
> *Limerick Leader*

But, after failing the initial breath test, the blood sample taken later from the publican, who is in his mid-thirties, is believed to have shown that he was under the allowed limit for drink driving.

The local gardaí would not comment on the intricacies of such a unique case. 'As it will not be brought to court, the details of the case cannot be made public,' was the sober and easy comment from one garda.

A spokesperson from the Garda Press Office was just a little more forthcoming. She doubted a person could fail the initial drink-driving test after a slice of sherry trifle but did not rule it out. 'It's possible but I would doubt it. I wouldn't imagine the alcometer [testing gear] is that sensitive unless the trifle is laced with alcohol,' she remarked.

For weeks, the story was the talk of a stretch of countryside around Limerick and it led some people to question the reliability of the breath-testing apparatus which continues to terrorise drinking drivers.

The gardaí, however, were quick to dismiss any theories that alcometers were faulty. 'The alcometer is only supposed to act as an indicator that a person may have been drinking. It just measures alcohol on the breath,' the spokesperson explained.

The blood and urine specimens taken in the station are said to be 17 per cent more accurate than the roadside breath test. But even the gardaí admit there is a fine line in this matter. A big man who has consumed quite a lot could be under the legal limit depending on his body mass, and vice versa for a skinny man. 'There are a lot of factors to take into account,' said the spokesperson.

Can Smoke but not Drink outside Pubs

It can be a sad enough spectacle, especially in the rain – nicotine addicts standing, hands in pockets, outside pubs in towns all over Ireland having a puff before returning to the warmth and shelter inside.

Some smokers like to take their drink out with them in summertime, but they run the risk of being prosecuted for breaking new by-laws which ban drinking in public places. It's an issue that's coming up in local councils countrywide, some of which are having problems coming to terms with it.

Up to now at least, we don't have a tradition of drinking outdoors but many of our immigrants come from countries where this practice is accepted. After much grappling with the issue, Kilkee Town Council in County Clare eventually decided to adopt by-laws.

> All councillors backed the idea of banning drinking at the bandstand, in public parks and on Kilkee beach, yet a number were fearful that people caught drinking outside a public house while smoking may be contravening the new bylaws.
>
> *The Clare Champion*

Some councillors felt the council should proceed even more slowly on the matter while others warned against inflicting 'another surprise' on townsfolk. This was a reference to consternation caused locally by a decision to have double yellow lines in parts of Kilkee.

On smokers having a drink outside pub doors, however, the Mayor of Kilkee, PJ Lardener, said, 'No guard is going to stop someone having a glass in their hand outside a pub.'

It would all be down to the discretion of the gardaí who could turn a blind eye if they wished. 'Trust the gardaí for goodness sake. They're grown people,' Councillor Tom Nolan declared.

Music, Mud and More Mud at Rain-Lashed Oxegen '07

Only abandoned cars, tents and wellies remained stuck in the mud at Punchestown on the Monday morning. The thousands of music fans had all gone home from Oxegen '07 having taken the full brunt of the wettest month of June since Noah floated about in his ark. Getting soaked may not have been fun but some had a good laugh at seeing others splashing around in the mud.

In the veritable sea of mud, a small army of staff set about the massive clean-up operation. Dick O'Sullivan, manager of Punchestown Racecourse, proclaimed himself absolutely delighted to have got through the weekend given the horrendous weather conditions that had made pleasure so difficult.

As for rumours of Oxegen's move to Cork, he felt there wasn't another location in the country that would have been able to manage and complete the event in the circumstances. He apologised to local people for headaches caused by traffic delays and long tailbacks on the Friday night. 'This was caused by a chaotic day's weather and the car park getting jammed up. There will be plans in hand next year to ensure that doesn't occur again,' he quickly added.

Dick conceded that the aftermath of the festival was 'pretty horrendous' but the racing surface was almost perfect and would be ready for action later in the year.

Kildare County Council expressed itself generally satisfied with the event but would be checking to make sure the concert promoters, MCD, met all the planning conditions attached to their licence, especially in relation to litter and waste.

> The concert promoters were obliged to provide adequate litter bins at the shuttle points in Naas and at Goffs. However, it remains to be seen whether the removal of mud will be undertaken by MCD, Naas Town Council or simply left to the ever-obliging rain.
>
> *Leinster Leader*

Drugs were in plentiful supply. During the weekend a total of 405 drug seizures were made along with 52 arrests for public order offences. The gardaí reported 20 arrests for the possession of drugs for sale or supply, and over 20 people were arrested en route to the festival after searches were carried out on coaches and cars. Around €40,000 worth of cocaine and ecstasy was seized at the Curragh the previous week which, according to the gardaí, was almost certainly destined for Oxegen.

Cars were broken into and personal items stolen. Some fans had their tents slashed and others complained of being threatened with violence by gatecrashers who were in the market for wristbands and personal items.

Fifty-six people were taken to hospital but someone went to pains to show that, statistically, that was a miniscule figure – only 0.07 per cent of the 80,000 capacity attendance. But it's the mud most of them will remember long after Oxegen '07 itself is forgotten.

Nineteen-year-old Jonathan Cosgrove of Ard Easmuinn, Dundalk, didn't bring wellies or rain gear and described the site as a complete mudbath with the first night being horrific. He and his friend shivered as rain bucketed onto their tent.

> Jonathan paid €200 for his ticket, but spent Friday night walking around talking to people because it was too cold and wet to lie down . . . According to Emma O'Hare, Armagh Road, Dundalk, the rain was bad but it was funny watching everyone run around in the mud.
>
> *Dundalk Democrat*

Judge Refuses Booze Licence for Children's Event

The image was enough to get outspoken Judge Michael Pattwell up on one of his favourite hobby horses again. Little girls in ringlets and fake tans running around sipping coke and licking ice cream laced with alcohol; a surreal scene that stretched the imagination somewhat.

This judge is one of a minority of prominent people who believes strongly that every cockfight from birth till death, including children's events, should not be drowned in drink and seen through an alcoholic haze. Former GAA President and coroner for North Mayo, Dr Mick Loftus, is another who has often trod the lonely temperate, if not teetotal, path.

Judge Pattwell, who dispenses justice in much of County Cork, got the perfect opportunity to expound when a drinks application for a 'family fun day' was made before him at Mallow District Court.

Publican Nicholas Corkery applied for a licence for seven hours on the fun day to be held in Laharn Heritage Centre a few kilometres outside Mallow. The organisers saw nothing unusual in that as serving drink was 'traditional' on the same day each year and there had never been the slightest trouble before, the court heard.

> Taking the stand, Nicholas said the event included singing, dancing and story telling. Judge Pattwell questioned the monitoring of the alcohol and Mr Corkery told him that he would certainly be minding his licence.
>
> *The Corkman*

Judge Pattwell wanted to know what exactly a family fun day meant and also asked who would monitor the children at the event, should a licence be granted. 'Will there be ice-cream with wine running through it?' he mused.

Mallow gardaí did not object to the application and said there had never been any evidence of alcohol being served to a minor at the event.

Sheila Crowley, a voluntary committee member, said the event was very well manned. 'The children are always supervised and there has never been an ounce of trouble. An adult is with a child at all times and the group has 17 volunteers,' she explained.

But the judge refused the application saying it was totally

inappropriate. 'All the events described to me are children's events; Irish traditional dancing, face painting, bouncy castles. You do not need drink at a children's event,' he declared.

Could Hardly Stand but Tried to Drive Truck Away

A man was so drunk that he could hardly put his legs under himself after being thrown out of a pub in County Galway. But he still hopped into a truck parked outside and tried to drive it.

When Cathal Dervan was put out of The Beautiful Bird premises in Laurencetown, he went to the backyard and took the truck without the owner's permission, the local court was told. He attempted to drive the truck and damaged both it and a gate that stood in its path.

Cathal, aged 23 and from Oghilmore, had a record with convictions for assault and burglary. He had, however, made attempts to sort himself out while in jail in England, including attending English lessons.

> His solicitor, Ciara Macklin, admitted he had a very bad record as a result of a chronic alcohol problem. On this occasion, he was hardly able to stand up. She said he had been in custody since April 24 on these charges and had been 'on the dry' even though alcohol and drugs had been offered to him.
>
> *The Connacht Tribune*

Judge Michael Reilly, who said he had a longer term in mind, imposed a ten-month sentence and a ten-year driving ban for taking the truck without the owner's consent.

Old Heads, Young Hearts

Dan's Still the Man at 105

Never let the worries of life get to you – one of the secrets of longevity according to the fourth oldest man in Ireland. Dan Keating, who is remarkably sharp and alert for his years, treated himself to a 'little tipple', but no more than that, on his 105th birthday.

Born into a small farm in the foothills of the Tralee mountains on 2 January 1902, he worked as a barman for most of his life in The Comet, Swords Road, Dublin, and returned to his native Castlemaine 30 years ago.

Dan never touched a drop of alcohol until he sampled Benedictine liqueur at the age of 57.

An avid GAA fan, he attended 154 All-Ireland football and hurling finals and saw nearly all of Kerry's victories. A lifelong republican, he refused to attend the 2006 final on principle because he believes the GAA 'sold out' by allowing Croke Park to be used for soccer and rugby matches.

Dan spends a couple of hours walking each day, takes a shopping trip to Tralee by bus every Friday and makes an occasional train journey to

Dublin. The widower told friends attending his birthday party he was in perfect health for his age, but had no ready explanation for his long and robust life.

> I don't know. I was lucky all along. I had no troubles and no worries. I worked hard, I ate good wholesome food and never let the worries of life get to me. Life is good and, hopefully, it will stay that way for a little longer.
>
> *Kerry's Eye*

Jack Celebrates His 100th Birthday . . . Again!

A man from the Kerry gaeltacht celebrated his 100th birthday three times, but received only one cheque from the State to mark the events.

Jack Micilín Ó Cíobháin, from Ventry, is fully entitled to have three birthday parties every year, as can be proved by official records. He always celebrated his birthday on 7 March but, according to his baptismal certificate, he was born on 27 March 1907. However, the Register of Births shows that he was born on 27 May 1907.

The State decided to accept the evidence of the baptismal cert and President Mary McAleese sent Jack a personal letter and a cheque for €2,540. He was the first resident of Dingle Community Hospital to hit the century. Jack's relations, friends and neighbours, along with hospital staff, gathered in the hospital dayroom for the celebrations.

The cheque was presented by An tAthair Eoghan Ó Cadhla who also read out the President's letter. And no sooner had Jack accepted the cheque than he gave it away. The money was donated to Fr Sean Cremin who is with the Kiltegan Fathers in southern Sudan.

Jack's wife, Brigid, died some 20 years ago and the couple had no children but there were plenty of relations around to help him celebrate, including his youngest relative, eight-week-old Cian MacGearailt.

The Kerryman

Jack has been a strong supporter of Gaelic football all his life and attended his first All-Ireland final in Croke Park in 1929. The Gaeltacht football club presented him with a framed jersey for his birthday. Other groups also made presentations and a memorable time was had by one and all.

Unique Treble for Bailieboro Family

It's the kind of happening that would attract outlandish odds, maybe even a million to one. What bookie could refuse a wager that three generations in the same family would end up with the same birthdays?

A Cavan baby, Nicole Carolan, came into the world on the very same date as her mother and her grandmother – 12 February – a date that will never be the same again for the family.

Nicole's mother, Marian Carolan, was born on 12 February 1974, and her grandmother, Bernadette Gorman, was born on 12 February1949, making it a remarkable hat-trick that defies all odds.

Marian was more than a week overdue and the unusual coincidence became likely when her husband, Philip, was told that the birth was likely to take place inside 24 hours.

The Anglo-Celt

Nicole, the couple's first child, was born in Cavan General Hospital at eight o'clock on the morning of 12 February 2007.

'As the day came closer, we were thinking it would be something else if the child happened to be born on 12 February and another coincidence if it happened to be a girl. We just can't believe it. That's three generations of girls all born on the same date. You wouldn't think something like that could happen,' said Nicole's uncle, Noel Gorman.

Her overjoyed grandmother, Bernadette, who lives in England, was looking forward to the meeting of three unique generations, and that special photograph of all three together.

False Fact about 'Boy Soldier' Becomes an Established Truth

Ever since John Condon fell mortally wounded in the killing fields of Belgium in 1915, people have believed he was the youngest soldier to die in the Great War. The Waterford City lad was said to be only 14 at the time but official records now show he was, in fact, 19.

According to popular legend, he gave a false age when he joined the Royal Irish Regiment in Clonmel as a private. However, research by Michael O'Connor, the director of Waterford's Heritage Services, refutes this accepted wisdom.

Having checked census, birth and baptism records, Michael believes inadequate research was carried out in 1923 when John Condon's remains and effects were discovered. At that time, people came to the conclusion that he was only 14 when killed. That notion became established and every effort has since been made to justify and explain it.

The Civil Registration Record of Births shows that John Condon was born on 16 October 1896. The baptismal record lists 5 October 1896 as his date of birth and 11 October as his date of baptism. Often, discrepancies occur between these sources but they provide reasonably accurate confirmation of when someone was born, according to Michael O'Connor.

The 1911 Census shows that John Condon was aged 15 and lived with his parents John and Catherine Condon and siblings at Wheelbarrow Lane.

Michael states: 'He (Condon) has become a symbol and there is nothing wrong with that in any way. There were hundreds of thousands of other young lads (of 19) killed in that war. He has become the individual symbol but the fact is that he is only of media interest because he was supposed to be 14. That is a very interesting [example of the] way a false fact becomes established truth.'

> There is no John Condon recorded as born in Waterford city in 1901. Nevertheless, a local committee is going ahead with plans for a memorial to someone who was always known as a boy soldier – on the basis that he is still a potent symbol of Irish people killed in the conflict.
>
> *Waterford News and Star*

Former Mayor of Waterford Pat Hayes, who chairs the John Condon Memorial Committee, points out that John Condon is still internationally recognised as the youngest Allied soldier to die in the Great War. His grave in Poelkapelle Cemetery, near Ypres, lists his age as 14 and members of his family in Waterford also maintain he was that age when killed in battle.

'People use John Condon as an example of all those who died in that conflict. I don't care if he was 14 or 19. He and others of that age who died in the Great War were still only children and had no place being butchered out there. To be honest, as far as I am concerned, it's what John Condon represents that's important.'

A sum of €180,000 is being collected in Waterford for the memorial which will also commemorate all other Irish men and women who died in the Great War.

Jack the 'Miracle Boy' Gives to the Doctor Who Saved His Life

Jack Young was just two years old when he suffered two strokes and doctors didn't expect him to live. But he was nursed back to health at Temple Street Children's Hospital in Dublin. Now aged five, he's attending school in County Sligo.

Dr Brian Lynch, the neurologist at Temple Street who helped bring him back to good health, described Jack as a 'miracle boy' whose story is inspirational.

Jack and his mother, Ann, wanted to give something back to the hospital so they raised almost €8,000 through their friends and some events they organised in the local community, including a leg-waxing night.

'We spent over two months in Temple Street Hospital and they were so great to us. It was like a home from home. I wanted to thank the hospital for what they did for Jack and I decided to raise money for much-needed equipment,' said Ann.

Dr Lynch travelled to Sligo to congratulate Jack on his progress, to commend his mother and, of course, to accept the cheque on behalf of the hospital.

'It was a great day for us because Jack was very sick for a long time and it was something that we could do to say thanks,' said Ann.

Sligo Weekender

Jack is now a happy pupil at St Brendan's National School in Cartron. The money raised will go towards funding equipment for the Temple Street's neurology department.

Amanda's Death Inspires Young People's Road Safety Campaign

Amanda Fahey was a popular girl with her peers in south Tipperary. Her death in a road accident had such a traumatic impact on other secondary school pupils in the area that it prompted them to do something positive to prevent more road deaths. A chilling statistic was that 16 secondary students from the area had lost their lives in similar accidents in the previous 20 years.

Transition Year and Applied Leaving Cert Students in Coláiste Dún Íascaigh, Cahir, were shown a list of the names of the dead by teacher Seamus Lahart and school chaplain Fr Matthew Knight before they started a project to promote road safety among young people.

All the students who worked on the project would have known Amanda, who had died in an accident in Clonmel. She would have been doing her Leaving Certificate in Cahir the following year and her death caused a huge amount of sorrow and distress among all her school friends.

> 'We always think of the last person who died. We always think of it as a once-off tragedy but that is not the case. It is hard to believe that 16 secondary pupils from Cahir died on the roads in the last 20 years,' said Seamus Lahart.
>
> *Clonmel Nationalist*

Students working on the project had first-hand knowledge of the grief and heartbreak that the death of somebody so young and full of life causes. Just looking at the list of all those who had died had a powerful effect on everybody, according to Seamus.

South Tipperary County Council agreed to erect a sign designed by the students on the approach roads to all main towns in the area. The hope now is that the strong message sent out by the sign – *Speed Thrills* . . . *Speed Kills* – may help save lives that would otherwise be lost.

Baby Nicholas Remembered in Cliffs of Moher Centre

In the summer of 2006, an American couple, Kelly and Delia Stokes, were on holiday in Ireland. During a visit to the Cliffs of Moher, Delia went into premature labour and gave birth on the cliff site but lost her baby, Nicholas, who was buried in Ennis.

After her traumatic experience, the couple decided to do something that would both honour the memory of their child and improve emergency services in County Clare. Within a few months, they donated US$86,000 towards the building of a modern first aid facility at the new Cliffs of Moher Visitor Centre.

Named the Nicholas Room, it was officially opened by the Taoiseach, Bertie Ahern, in February 2007. It has high-tech equipment and is directly linked to the Mid-West Regional Hospital in Ennis.

The Stokes also did their bit for tourism in Clare, bringing family and friends over with them from Arizona later in the year. Their story was described as 'amazing' by Ger Dollard of the Cliffs of Moher Visitor Centre.

> 'It's not just the Nicholas Room that they are interested in, their interest is much wider. Their interest really is in developing and improving the emergency services in Clare and the region. I think in terms of the Nicholas Room, while we have it kitted out and Kelly and Delia are very happy with it, we will work with them on the finer details; though I wouldn't see much more improvement in the room itself.'
>
> *The Clare Champion*

The Stokes also met health service managers in Clare. Exchange visits are planned between the emergency authorities in Arizona and Clare with a view to learning from one another. In April, for example, the Deputy City Manager for emergency services in Arizona came to the Banner County.

As the Stokes see it, the project goes beyond the Nicholas Room. They want to become more involved so that they can help develop overall emergency services, including areas such as water safety and health, according to Ger Dollard.

Anna Still Loves Her Smoke after All These Years

Not many smokers see the century, but Anna Burke has defied medical science more than once in her long life. Anna is 100 and still enjoys her cigarette. She saw a lot of tough times and believes it's the little comforts, including her fag and glass of whiskey, that have kept her going.

Though admitting that cigarettes are not good for her, she says it would kill her if she tried to give them up now. 'I'm trying to cut down,' she concedes with a roguish twinkle in her eye. 'I won't tell you how many I used to smoke!'

A widow since 1960, Anna has spent nearly all her life on the farm she married into in Whitegate, County Clare. She and her late husband, James, had ten children, three of whom have died.

When her children were growing up, she spent very little money on herself, but later enjoyed shopping for designer label clothes and expensive shoes. Anna has experienced lots of changes, especially in regard to money and work. When she was younger, for instance, people did not expect to be paid for small jobs.

'That has changed completely. People expect payment to do the smallest things now. I think that the youth have too much money, it's too easy to earn it now. Some of them can't handle it. It's only leading to trouble.'

The Clare Champion

In recent times, Anna has been dogged by ill-health. Many had given up hope for her when she suffered total kidney failure, was in a coma and also had other complaints. Doctors thought she had only minutes to live and she was anointed. But she bounced back and was home again to celebrate her 100th birthday with her children, 15 grandchildren, 11 great-grandchildren and many friends.

Longevity is in the centenarian's genes, for her mother made it to 101 and four of her siblings survived to well over 90. So, what's the secret for a long life? 'No secret, just lots of hard work,' she says with a smile and another deep puff from her cigarette.

Close Shaves from Tomás, the Story-Telling Barber

Few indeed are the barbers without a legion of stories to tell and memories to share. But not many can claim to have shaken hands with Pope John Paul II, gone to school with the playwright John B Keane or to have met the iconic American actor, John 'The Duke' Wayne.

Tomás O'Quigley, now retired, practised the tonsorial arts for about 60 years. He started in his native Listowel, Co Kerry, then moved to Galway city and, finally, to Gort, where he spent most of his life.

When he started in the trade in 1943, the style was definitely short back and sides. Shaving was also a big thing – they used the trademark open (cut-throat) razors – accounting for about half of a barber's business. The 'cut-throat' was a risky weapon, especially when men, still half drunk, came in for a refreshing shave on mornings of the Galway Races.

'You had an open razor, which was very sharp, and these fellas would have been very fidgety from having been on the drink the night before. While they wouldn't be falling around the place drunk, they would be giddy and shaving them was very difficult. They never realised the danger of an open razor,' Tomás recalled.

A hot-towel shave might be regarded as a 'very yuppie thing' to do now, especially for grooms and bestmen on the day of a wedding. Tomás, however, remembers a time when it was anything but that. 'They pay well for a hot-towel shave now. When I started, a shave cost four pennies.'

> When long hair became fashionable for men in the 1960s, some barbers went out of business but Tomás did a course on how to style long hair and survived. After that, he opened a unisex business, with men coming in for washes, blow-dries and layered haircuts and women for perms and sets.
>
> *The Clare Champion*

Celebrities such as David Beckham set the trend for young fellows nowadays, but in Tomás's early days every fellow had the same haircut. Any chap with long hair would be considered unusual, if not eccentric.

His wife, Patsy, was also a hairdresser and the couple ran a salon that was an institution in Gort for generations. Patsy has sadly died, but Tomás is left with many happy memories.

He shook the hand of the Pope in Knock in 1979, and loves to tell the story of the day John Wayne strode into the small barber's shop where he was then working in Galway. 'The Duke' was in the west for the making of *The Quiet Man* (1952). Wayne gave a dollar tip to each of the barbers in the shop. 'Wayne was a very nice and pleasant man . . . I said I'd never spend that dollar, but I have to admit it didn't last long.'

Kidney Joy Gives New Life to Teenager Jaydon

Jaydon Brittion Mullen wanted a new kidney so badly that he couldn't wait to get into the operating theatre at Temple Street Children's Hospital in Dublin. No question of Jaydon taking a trolley to the theatre – he practically bounced down the hallway on the day of his surgery.

The 15-year-old was born with just one kidney, but worse news was to come for his parents when they discovered some years ago that the solo kidney was functioning at just 20 per cent. Jaydon was placed on the kidney donor list and so began the anxious wait for a compatible donor.

For two years and four months he was on full-time dialysis, ten hours per day, six days a week. This severely curtailed what would, normally, be an active young life.

Life for Jaydon, from Tullow, Co Carlow, was hugely restricted, including his diet. Out were burgers and chips, chocolate and sweets – all the things teenagers love and the things he wanted most.

At six o'clock on the morning of 17 April 2007 the call the family had been eagerly waiting for finally came. A suitable kidney had become available and, by half-past four that afternoon, Jaydon was being brought to theatre for his four-hour operation. The surgery was a success and he was up and walking around the following day.

> 'Now he has 20 per cent function in one kidney and 100 per cent in this new normal kidney. It's fantastic. For the first time, his life is normal. He's doing really well and so far everything

is great,' said his delighted mum, Sharon.

Carlow Nationalist

It was the beginning of a new life for Jaydon, who had been connected to a machine every evening, unable to do anything, unable to do normal things like go out and meet his friends.

Jaydon, his parents and sisters have written letters to the donor's family letting them know how their generosity has changed the lives of the Brittion Mullen family. They don't know who the donor is, but asked the Kidney Association to pass on their letters. They also urged people to carry organ donor cards.

'It's so very important for people to carry donor cards . . . people should know that you really can change someone's life,' Sharon emphasised.

Brotherly Love Transforms Life for Karl Kearins

In January 2005, Karl Kearins, a member of a famous sporting family, was diagnosed as having acute kidney failure. The former Sligo footballer, aged 34, started regular dialysis treatment three days a week, but realised the only long-term solution to his illness was a kidney transplant.

'The way you'd feel after dialysis was a bit like a heavy hang-over and I've had plenty of those,' Karl, a Dublin-based detective, laughed.

Tests on his brother, Adrian, and sister, Valerie, showed both were a match as donors. So which one of them would it be? Karl did not try to influence his willing siblings in any way, but Adrian decided himself that he wanted to do it.

The brothers – sons of the man regarded by most experts as Sligo's greatest ever Gaelic footballer, Mickey Kearins from Dromard – underwent a transplant operation at Dublin's Beaumont Hospital.

The unique, seven-hour operation was the first live donor transplant to be carried out in Ireland in 2007. 'It's a miracle. I'm very proud and relieved. Karl's life has been transformed,' their mother, Frances, said afterwards.

> Adrian, who is also a guard, based in Co Mayo, was playing down all talk of heroism. 'It was just something I decided I wanted to do. I had to give it some thought, but it wasn't a hard decision. I will still be able to lead a normal life, but the difference is that so will my brother from now on,' he said.
>
> *The Sligo Champion*

Karl, however, saw it as a very brave decision which helped transform his life.

Normally, a donor's recovery is expected to be slower than the recipient, but Adrian reported: 'The first day or two after the operation was tough but I'm feeling fine now, well on the road to recovery. Up to the very last minute, they were giving me the option of pulling out but it never crossed my mind. I'm just glad that it's over and that it has been such a success.'

First Communion a Tsunami of Commercialism, but not for Galway Family

There was no sign of a chopper, a stretch limo or even a modest family car as the Codyre triplets prepared to leave their home in south Galway to make their First Holy Communion.

But the seven-year-olds did make it to St Teresa's Church in Killure in some style. Their father, Tim, insisted on dusting down the family trap and tackling Victor the pony to take them the few miles from their home near Ahascragh, Ballinasloe, to the church.

The non-identical triplets – Georgia, Taidhge and Barry – were the only children from their tiny, 22-pupil school to receive on the day and were very excited about the occasion.

> At a time when limousines, helicopters and holidays abroad are commonplace for Communions, the Codyres insisted on making the children the focus of the day. After Mass, celebrated by Fr Christy McCormack, they had a surprise breakfast laid on by the school and then returned home for a slap-up meal with the extended family.
>
> *The Connacht Tribune*

First Communions and Confirmations have become hugely expensive splash-outs for many families. Hand-dyed silk shoes, designer dresses from Paris and Milan, hairdos and French manicures have, at least for well-off folk, given such occasions a Hollywood aura.

Some little girls are turned out in €500, raw silk dresses brought in from Italy, have special suntan holidays beforehand, wear flickering tiaras and have purses stuffed with money. And that's saying nothing about the restaurants and the parties that follow.

In the vulgar rush to show off what parents can afford, old values are forgotten and the spiritual element of the event overlooked. Some priests say that only for teachers, the children wouldn't have learnt their prayers as the sacramental side of things is all swept away in a tsunami of commercialism.

Marilyn Barrett of Listowel believes it's all about money and keeping up with the Joneses these days.

'It's definitely gotten out of hand. You ask a child about the religious side of it now and they haven't a clue . . . Communion and Confirmation both seem equally costly these days, although the cost of dresses for girls at Communion time seems scandalous,' Marilyn said.

The Kerryman

The days of hand-me-down Communion dresses in families have long since past and low-income families are being forced to join the rat race. Some fashion house owners now say Communions have become like mini-weddings.

Tim and Marie Codyre hit the January sales to keep the expense to a minimum and kitted out their triplets in one go. And, of course, only one party was needed. They had a comparatively simple but highly enjoyable First Communion day, blessed by a beaming sun. 'It was perfect, absolutely perfect,' a proud Marie said.

Impassioned Plea from Priest to Young People Thinking of Suicide

An eerie silence came over the congregation when the local parish priest began his homily at a particularly sad funeral mass in Bunclody.

Fr Aidan Jones was unusually forthright about a subject many other people in authority tend to fudge, or completely shy away from – suicide among young people. Jason Tobin was only 14 when he died tragically a few days before at his home in Kilbrannish on the Carlow/Wexford border.

The untimely passing of the popular first-year student resulted in deeply-felt grief among his family and friends. Jason had many hobbies and interests, had a passion for quad bikes, was into hurling and was a huge Manchester United fan which was reflected by the numerous pieces of memorabilia from the Reds surrounding his coffin.

He also loved the countryside and, to all appearances, had an idyllic boyhood in the foothills of Mount Leinster.

The Holy Trinity Church was full to overflowing for Jason's farewell mass. Sitting in the pews were hundreds of young people, including his shattered school pals from Bunclody, and Fr Jones started his homily by speaking to them directly:

> 'With all the pressures you face, it may sometimes seem that life is bleak and not worth living, especially if you are having trouble at home or in school, or you feel that no-one understands you. If this is how you feel, talk to someone. If that someone you choose will not, or cannot listen, talk to someone else.
>
> 'Very few people can read minds. Your parents, teachers, friends may think they know what is going on but they can't really know unless you tell them. If you have considered suicide, please talk to someone soon. Talking about it will not make it happen and it can prevent it.'
>
> *Carlow Nationalist*

Fr Jones then turned to parents and people working with the young, urging them to be aware of changes in mood or behaviour and to be available to talk and listen to young people.

The priest also pointed out that suicide has struck a number of times in the community over the past ten years.

'We cannot continue in denial. To die by one's own hand is a momentary sickness, not a sin. Every unexpected, tragic and traumatic death such as this creates deep wounds, but familiarity with the recurring tragedy runs the risk of dulling the collective anguish,' he said.

'The danger is that the community will grow less sensitive to personal despair and come to regard this way as a normal, or relatively acceptable, method of solving personal crisis.

'No family tiffs, no school rows, no lovers' quarrels ever justifies suicide – it is not cool, it is not brave. It is a non-runner, full stop,' Fr Jones concluded.

Elderly Becoming 'Almost Too Secure' in their Homes because of Fear

The garda sent to check the home of an 89-year-old man who had not been seen for over a week looked through the letterbox and saw the body of a man lying in the hallway. Joseph Connaughton lived alone in Ballina, County Mayo, in a house that he had so well secured that even the most skilful burglar would have found it hard to enter.

Joseph had stayed in Galway with his niece, Brid Henderson, for a number of days before getting the bus back to Ballina on 1 December 2006. Brid tried to call him on 17 December but his phone was engaged. Her concerns rose after she spoke to his neighbour in Marian Crescent and learned that her uncle had not been seen for about a week. She then contacted the gardaí in Ballina.

However, when Garda Gerard Taheny called to the house, he was faced with a Fort Knox-like scenario. His first problem was how to get into the house. He broke a small pane of glass in the sitting room window and stepped inside, but the door leading to the hallway from the sitting room was locked.

He then tried to get in the back door but there seemed to be something firmly placed against it and it would not budge. He later found a plank of timber wedged against the door. The front door of the house had two locks so he broke the glass on the door. Luckily, the key for the door was still in the lock and the guard was finally able to get in.

At an inquest later in Ballina, the coroner, Dr Eleanor Fitzgerald, noted the difficulty Garda Taheny experienced in getting into the house.

> She commented: 'Mr Connaughton's house was secure, almost too secure. I worry about this as many elderly people live alone and may not be able to get help in an emergency. It is fear that is causing this.'
>
> *Western People*

Like thousands of other old people, Joseph Connaughton obviously lived in fear of his home being burgled and himself being assaulted and robbed. He took all possible precautions to ensure his home was safe, even if it meant not being able to get help in a crisis.

A post mortem examination showed he had suffered no external injuries and the cause of death was a fatal cardiac arrhythmia on 12 December 2006.

Michael O'Boyle, a neighbour, saw Joseph on 7 December and was the last person to see him alive. Michael recalled: 'We chatted for about ten minutes at 4pm. He told me that he would be travelling to Dublin to spend Christmas with his nephew. He was a good friend and was friends with everyone. He was a very fit, active man and looked younger than his years.'

Cock and Bull Story from Former Russian Policeman

When former Russian policeman Martin Seman came before Ennis District Court he not only learnt a little about Irish law but also something about the Irish way of describing tall tales.

Martin, 26, who lives in the town, pleaded guilty to stealing a bottle of vodka from Dunnes Stores. But he had an unusual rider to his story – he said he 'forgot' to pay for the Smirnoff. He had bought groceries, for which he paid, but left the store without paying for the drink. He claimed he went back to the shop to pay for it but met a friend and forgot about the drink again.

However, Garda Trevor Sheehan, who investigated the case, contradicted that claim saying closed-circuit TV footage showed Martin did not leave the premises and come back in again.

> Inspector Tom Kennedy told the court: 'I don't think he's as innocent as he makes out.'
>
> *The Clare Champion*

Judge Joseph Mangan then asked the Russian interpreter assisting with the case if she could translate the phrase 'cock and bull story', to which she raised a quizzical eyebrow and replied, 'I don't know that.'

The judge then remarked: 'Well, that's a new one for you to learn.'

Judge Mangan fined Martin Seman €300 and imposed a one-month sentence, suspended on condition that he stayed away from Dunnes Stores for six months.

The court was told Mr Seman had been in the police in Russia for a year, had been living in Ireland for six months and that he was 'not of bad character at all'.

Hollywood Beckons for Down-To-Earth Schoolgirl with Star Quality

Being around actors almost since she bawled her first cry, Saoirse Ronan took to the silver screen like the proverbial duck to water. Things began to happen seriously for her when she landed a role in RTÉ's *The Clinic* in 2004. A year later, she played the daughter of actress Orla Brady in the RTÉ drama *Proof 2*.

Following that, the Carlow girl got parts in feature-length movies and the offers continue to roll in. By the end of 2007, she will have appeared in four multi-million dollar movies alongside household names such as Guy Pearce, Catherine Zeta-Jones, Keira Knightley and Michelle Pfeiffer.

She is also working on a fifth, *The City of Ember*, produced by Oscar-winning actor Tom Hanks and due to be screened in 2008.

> In the midst of all this, Saoirse remains incredibly grounded, enjoying hanging out with her friends from Ardattin national school, playing tag rugby and basketball . . . all the normal pursuits of a 13-year-old.
>
> 'She doesn't really talk about who she works with. She just brushes it off. She's very down-to-earth, God she's not a diva. We'd put a halt to that nonsense straight away if there was any sign of it,' explained her dad, Paul.
>
> *Carlow Nationalist*

Her parents, Paul and Monica, are both from Dublin but they lived in New York for 12 years where Paul first became an actor, mainly doing theatre work before going into the movie industry. Eight years ago the family returned to Ireland and eventually settled in Co Carlow.

As a baby, Saoirse was used to being on sets. 'It just happened when she was seven or eight that they needed a child for a short film I was working in and Saoirse did it. We quickly found out she was very good,' recalled Paul who has appeared in *Ballykissangel*, *The Devil's Own*, *Veronica Guerin* and *Ordinary Decent Criminal*.

Saoirse's films in 2007 include *The Christmas Miracle of Jonathan Toomey*, *I Could Never Be Your Woman*, *Death Defying Acts* and *Atonement*.

But she also has to keep up with her school work. When she's away filming, the curriculum is sent on to her from her school and she has a one-to-one tutor on set for several hours at a time.

Cheers, Tears and Relief as Babies are Delivered

It was another normal day in a quiet estate in Castleisland until baby Aoibhin Mairead Ferris decided the time had come to make her entry on Earth. A crowd anxiously waiting for news gathered outside a house which had become a hastily set-up maternity ward.

Noreen Ferris was visiting her mother in St Stephen's Park when she went into labour. Noreen's husband, Eamon, was also in the house and he, along with others, carried her upstairs to a bedroom. None of them had even the slightest midwifery experience, but they kept Noreen calm and the delivery was completed without a hitch in a matter of minutes.

'My waters broke at 6.05 pm and my sisters were downstairs crying with every roar they heard out of me. Aoibhin arrived at 6.20pm, a mercifully fast labour and the ambulance came about ten minutes later,' Noreen said afterwards.

News of the impending birth travelled fast around the neighbourhood and Noreen's childhood friends and their parents came out in droves to support the young mother.

'They were fantastic. There must have been up to sixty of them outside the house and they gave us a great cheer and round of applause when they knew it had been a successful delivery,' Noreen said.

The Kerryman

Meanwhile, a County Meath mother was grateful to three gardaí who helped deliver her premature baby on the roadside after she failed to make it to hospital on time.

The ordeal for Audrey McMahon from Laytown started around half past eleven on a Saturday morning when she found her contractions were coming very quickly. Her mother rang the local gardaí to ask for an escort before setting off to Our Lady of Lourdes Hospital in Drogheda.

Gardaí Mary Farrell, Catherine Rennick and Brian Dolan, all based at Laytown, provided an escort through traffic in a patrol car. But things took a dramatic turn as they reached the old Dublin Road when Audrey's waters broke and she knew there wasn't time to get to hospital.

> Her mother flashed her lights at the patrol car, pulled in near the Europa Hotel on the N1 and little Dylan arrived just three minutes later with assistance from all concerned.
>
> 'Dylan was born with the [umbilical] cord wrapped around his neck and the guards unwrapped it. My mother rubbed his back and he cried and raised his hand. I was in shock, we were all in tears, my mum, Patrick [her partner], even the guards. It was unbelievable,' she [Audrey] said.
>
> *The Meath Chronicle*

Baby Dylan was 15 weeks premature and weighed just 1lb and 6 ounces. 'When it was happening, we just had to get on with it, but it was quite emotional afterwards,' Garda Rennick said.

The tiny new arrival was wrapped up warmly in towels and clothes

Audrey was bringing to the hospital with her. An ambulance arrived about 15 minutes later and immediately provided oxygen to Dylan.

The Butcher with No Meat to Sell

Michael Griffin opens his butcher's shop in Waterford city centre every day but doesn't have any customers. He sits on a well-worn wooden bench just inside the door holding court with various people who drop in regularly for a chat.

The 73-year-old, who worked in the family meat business since he was a teenager, quit trading as a butcher in 1983. The reason was that he felt he couldn't source the same quality meat he had sold prior to Ireland joining the EU.

> 'I couldn't get the quality cattle that I wanted so I stopped selling. For a while I used to supply some of my old customers from other butchers but I don't even do that any more,' he explained.
>
> 'The good old days are gone and there's no going back now. People wonder why they have to put an Oxo [cube] and Bisto into their meat to make it taste of something. All the juices are gone from the meat into the paper and packaging and the quality of the meat is just not the same. People will look back and see how right I am.'
>
> *Waterford News and Star*

To enter Michael's shop is to step back in time for it has scarcely changed since 1912. The concrete floor and marble worktops have been there for almost a century. In fact, the only 'modern' bit of equipment that was introduced was a cool room installed by Michael's father to keep meat at the correct temperature.

Michael never married and, despite having several nephews and nieces, there are no butchers in the family to continue the family trade. He also hasn't driven a car since he stopped trading. He lives a simple life, doesn't drink but enjoys a smoke and a flutter on the nags.

His shop-cum-home is in a prime location at Blackfriars but he has no plans to close and sell up. It looks as if the premises will continue to be a meeting place for people that want to discuss hurling, horses and life in general. It's also a great port of call for people from distant shores trying to traces their 'Decies' roots. Meanwhile, Michael sits there and watches the world go by.

She'll Be Singing down the Mountain

A regular walk to the corner shop or church might be regarded as exercise by many octogenarians, but definitely not by Dr Ursula Dethinger. The 82-year-old German woman still climbs mountains and getting stranded at night on Ireland's highest peak didn't knock a shake out of her. In fact, she only burst into song.

Having reached the summit of Carrantuohill at well over 3,000 feet, she felt uncomfortable about descending via the dangerous Devil's Ladder, a steep gully with lots of loose stones. Ursula and a 16-year-old boy, a family friend, decided to go down a different route planned out by her son, Michael.

Darkness, however, came upon them so they opted wisely to stay put on the mountainside, waiting for either daylight to come or help to arrive. Michael raised the alarm and a party from the Kerry Mountain Rescue Team set off for the mountain. The party made contact with Ursula and the boy at 12.30am and the mission was accomplished by 2.30am.

The pair were in good spirits and were guided to the foot of the mountain with the aid of strong lighting. Neither required medical assistance. The Dethingers have been visiting Ireland for the past thirty years and it was Mrs Dethinger's third time climbing Carrantuohill.

The Kerryman

Ursula was in party mood. She thanked and shook hands with each of the 20 rescuers before giving them of a blast of 'It's a Long Way to Tipperary' . . . and planning her next foray into the hills.

Politics – At the Parish Pump

Queen Banished from County Laois

Joy in the rebel Midlands. After 500 years, Laois finally gained its independence from the British Crown with the repeal by Dáil Éireann of a law which gave the Queen of England rights to seize lands in the county.

Laois was once known as the Queen's County, but local Fianna Fáil TD Sean Fleming, whose uncles were active in the fight for freedom, was happy to reveal that old legislation was being erased from the statute books. 'The Queen of England is to be banished from County Laois . . . I am also pleased that we are getting rid of the title King's County as a reference to County Offaly.'

Legislation passed in 1556 allowed for the confiscation of lands owned by Gaelic families – land which would be given to English settlers and 'good' English men. Despite years of independence, Dáil Éireann never repealed this old Act.

However, Deputy Fleming stated: 'We are now abolishing 3,188 Acts that are still in force, which were passed by the English Crown from 1171 right up until the beginning of the

1920s. I have ensured that, as part of this exercise, the legislation dealing with the Queen's County and King's County are to be deleted.

'Strangely, there are still 1,348 old Acts that have not yet been repealed and are still being examined as some of this legislation may have some degree of modern relevance.'

The Land Registry website continues to this day to refer to the county as Queen's (Laois).

Laois Nationalist

Trim Says 'Yes' to Jimmy but 'No' to Big Ian

Few people outside his native Trim ever heard of Jimmy Finnegan. But his fellow townspeople obviously think a lot more of Jimmy, who died a decade ago, than they do of Dr Ian Paisley, or any other luminary for that matter.

The first new street in the Meath town in several centuries is to be named after the late Jimmy who was known as 'the weatherman' and somebody who would always make time to stop for a chat with both locals and tourists.

A leading local historian, Noel French, had suggested it would be a 'magnanimous gesture' to call the street Paisley Parade, given the DUP leader's contribution to the political settlement in the North. It was a suggestion that led to a rumpus worthy of the North's First Minister himself and strong opposition from Sinn Féin in particular.

Others felt it should be called after Brian Boru, Bobby Sands, or even be named Stella Street in honour of Jonathan Swift's girlfriend. However, Jimmy Finnegan was given the signal distinction after a long debate.

Born in 1923, Jimmy emigrated to England where he worked in foundries and on the land. He returned to Trim in the mid 1950s, getting work in the bogs cutting turf and with farmers. Jimmy lived with his nephew, also Jimmy Finnegan, who said the family, who have been in Trim for nine or ten generations, were 'absolutely over the moon' that a street should be named after their uncle.

> Jimmy was a great local historian and earned his nickname from strolling around and commenting on the weather. He was also a great accordion player and an avid reader, loving history books, biographies and autobiographies, according to another family member.
>
> *The Meath Chronicle*

He had an extensive knowledge of local history and those seeking to find out about their family history would often go to him first to avail of his considerable knowledge of the old families of the town.

During his lifetime Jimmy Finnegan would have laughed at the idea of giving his name to a street in his own place. But this much-loved 'character' and ordinary man will be remembered in Trim long after Ian Paisley and other statesmen are forgotten.

'Big Apple' Junket Leaves a Sour Taste

It was like a state secret in Waterford – the identity of the councillors who went gallivantin' to New York for Paddy's Day. Nobody was told who the lucky ones were before they left and details were also scant when they got back. They spent five nights in the Big Apple on a €17,000 trip funded by the taxpayer and were accused, on their return, of making a 'mockery' of the public.

Remarkably for councillors who are rarely stuck for words, none of them would confirm at their subsequent monthly meeting that they had been on the trip. The names had not been released prior to their journey for their 'privacy and security' but the Council said all would be revealed when they came home.

Mayor Mary Greene gave a detailed report of the visit but failed to specify, apart from herself, the names of those who had travelled. Sinn Féin's Brendan Mansfield demanded that all be disclosed, but was told by officials that they didn't have those details to hand and would forward them on to him the next day.

> At the time, five of the councillors who travelled were present in the Council chambers but none of them volunteered that they'd been on the trip.
>
> *Waterford News and Star*

'I just found it amazing that when I questioned the make-up of the delegation at Tuesday's meeting of Waterford County Council that the veil of secrecy still remained even though five of the councillors that travelled with the Mayor were in the chamber. None of them had the courage to say that they were part of the delegation. I think they are making a mockery of the public,' Councillor Mansfield later said.

Seven councillors accompanied Mayor Greene on the trip that cost in total €16,623.46. One of the councillors, Fianna Fáil's Pat Daly, paid his own travelling expenses. The others who went were: Fianna Fáil's Tom Cronin and Kevin Wilkinson; Fine Gael's John Carey, Declan Doocey and Pat Nugent; and Labour's Ger Barron.

Mayor Greene described the trip as 'tough' as they had met with a lot of different groups including IDA Ireland, Enterprise Ireland, Tourism Ireland and the Waterford New York Association. They also marched in the St Patrick's Day Parade and attended the Mayor's breakfast at Mayor Bloomberg's.

Historic Cashel 'Worse than Baghdad'

If Cashel of the Kings does well in the Tidy Towns competition, nobody will be more surprised than the townspeople themselves and their local councillors.

The famous Rock of Cashel and its monastic ruins are visited by thousands of tourists, but if tourists heard what the town fathers had to say they might give the Tipperary town a wide berth.

Letting off steam at a meeting, councillors painted a picture of an unkempt town with sites which were 'worse than Baghdad' according to Councillor Michael Browne, who also claimed the council had no interest in keeping the town tidy. Others talked about bags of rubbish thrown around the place, rat-infested Traveller sites and graffiti daubed on walls.

Councillor Sean McCarthy expressed his 'amazement' that Cashel had received so many marks in the National Tidy Towns competition because, if he was responsible, he would give the town '0 out of 20'.

The situation was becoming intolerable throughout the country as people had developed a tolerance for dirt, filth and rubbish, he maintained. On a recent visit to a few towns in the south of France, the single most striking thing he noticed was that 'you could throw your sandwiches on the footpath and eat them, they [the streets] were that clean'.

There was no dirt, filth, empty chip boxes or broken bottles because the people had a culture of cleanliness that had been inculcated in them and taken on board by the local council.

> Another councillor claimed the Cashel council was a worse offender than the Travellers in regard to tidiness and there was a call for the enforcement of a policy whereby each Traveller family was allowed keep just one horse.
>
> *Clonmel Nationalist*

Oil back in Oylegate as Pellets Rejected

It was a chilly winter for some people living in Oylegate, County Wexford. They claimed they were treated as guinea pigs for a disastrous pellet burning heating system by Wexford County Council.

The council lauded the system as being cost-efficient and good for the environment, but it did not work and the €90,000 spent on it went up in smoke, so to speak. The burners brought nothing but problems, proving difficult to light and emitting fumes and smoke. They went on fire in two houses.

Prior to Christmas, the council began to reveal it was going cold on the idea when it removed the timer switches from burners in 28 houses in the Cum an Tobair estate, requesting that the burners be turned on manually and only when people were at home.

A couple of weeks later, a letter was issued asking residents to stop using the burners altogether. In their place, the council delivered one electric fan heater per house and seven bags of coal.

As the central heating in the houses was operated solely via the pellet burners, the only room in the house which could be heated properly was the sitting room. This did not last long either as the coal ran out within three weeks with the council refusing to provide any more.

> Seven mothers gathered, wrapped in coats, in the home of Laura O'Leary at number ten to speak to *The Echo* of their concerns, most having been left without heating since before Christmas . . . Sinead Somers, from number four, also had problems with the wind, as well as smoke coming into her kitchen from the front of the burner and an awful stench from the material being burned . . . Initially Sinead was told by the council that any problems were in her head, that the burners were 'safe as houses'.
>
> *The Enniscorthy Echo*

In February, the Minister for Justice Michael McDowell visited the shivering estate to see how well the pellet burners worked. Some residents claimed they had been told by council employees to keep their mouths shut when the well buttoned-up Minister graced them with his presence.

Despite this apparent show of confidence in the heating system, a message from the council was delivered by hand to each household, on 7 March, saying the pellet burners would be replaced with back boilers or oil heating.

A letter from the council asked residents not to use the pellet stoves until further notice and added: 'Wexford County Council is obtaining prices for the replacement of the wood pellet stoves with either oil burners or back boilers . . . prices will be in next Wednesday, 14 March, and WCC will endeavour to have the alternative heating options installed as soon as possible thereafter.'

Couple Live in Misery because of Faulty Letterbox

In a house of non-stop rattles and shivers, going to bed early is one way of surviving. That's what pensioners Leslie and Bernadette Broadhurst were forced to do as biting draughts continued to sweep through their home – all for the want of a letterbox.

The elderly couple living in Cox's Demesne, Dundalk, were at their wits' end from trying to get their local town council to carry out what they felt were just minor repairs. A broken letterbox and ill-fitted windows were making their lives miserable.

As well as the constant noise from the flapping letterbox, the couple were spending a fortune on central heating costs – heat that was, literally, going out the window because of draughts.

> 'It is costing us a fortune to try and keep the house warm and we have even resorted to going to bed early to try and save some money . . . My husband is only recently out of hospital and the place is freezing because of the draughts coming though the windows in the sitting room,' said Bernadette.
>
> *The Argus*

The letterbox flap rattled all the time giving the impression there was someone at the door when there wasn't. In stormy weather there was absolutely no peace.

Bernadette herself also needed to go to hospital at the time. The couple contacted Sinn Féin TD Arthur Morgan who had already been working on the case. He was confident his efforts would eventually strike a compassionate chord in the town hall and action would be taken to help the aged couple.

'Anyone who had met the Broadhursts couldn't but feel buckets of sympathy for them as they were suffering from cold and ill-health as a result of official inaction,' he remarked.

War of the Buses in Mallow

All was quiet on the transport front in Mallow – until the private bus company, City Link, arrived. Tensions flared and there were allegations of one bus company trying to block the spaces of another.

City Link started using the Mallow route in January 2007 and tensions soon rose between it and its competitor Bus Éireann, resulting in appeals for assistance from the gardaí and Cork County Council.

Cathy Cullen, the managing director of City Link, claimed it was only in Mallow that they had experienced Bus Éireann physically blocking their spaces. Her buses had to pick people up from the side of the road as their access to the bus park had been blocked. Their drivers were getting tired of this carry on, she complained.

Bus Éireann's Cork area manager, Joe Fitzgerald, argued that issues of space were primarily driven by safety, saying they could have up to 50 movements of buses on a Friday alone.

> 'We have kept records – some pictures can be worth a thousand words,' Joe added. He also had photographs that drivers had taken of buses entering the bus spaces in recent times to portray what he claimed were unsafe conditions.
>
> *The Corkman*

Having thought long and hard about the problem, the powers-that-be decreed that the two companies should be kept as far apart as possible. For the sake of peace, Cork County Council agreed to provide an extra space for City Link, about 100 metres away from the Bus Éireann stop.

Death Warrant Signed for the Dangerous Dog of Ruan

A stray dog that terrified the populace in the Clare village of Ruan wouldn't be fooled by the softly, softly attempts of would-be captors to lure him off the street. Even cans of Pedigree Chum were not enough to make this wily canine take the bait.

The black collie with a rope around its neck was 'snapping and biting' at children who were afraid to go out and play because of its behaviour. Parents armed themselves with hurleys as they brought their children to school, in case of an attack.

A dog warden made every effort 'humanly possible' to catch the stray but failed, according to Councillor Joe Arkins of Clare County Council. 'The time for running up and down the street with a can of Pedigree Chum calling "Fido, Fido" has gone and it's not enough to do that. If the dog can't be caught, then surely a tranquiliser gun is the humane answer,' he said.

This prompted chants of 'who let the dogs out?' from other councillors, which only added to Councillor Arkins' frustration. Some said their own children had been bitten by dogs and warned that dogs that didn't look suspicious could also be dangerous.

> But Councillor Colm Wiley jumped to the defence of 'dangerous looking' dogs. 'I have to defend the madra. Who will tell me what a dangerous dog is? I have been bitten by dogs three times, but if I'd known which ones would bite me, it wouldn't have happened. It's not the ones who look like they'd bite you that would, but the quiet ones. Councillor Arkins needs to have a bag of Pal going around with him so he'll befriend dogs.'
>
> *The Clare Champion*

The matter came before Shannon District Court where Clare County Council asked that the Ruan stray be put down under the Control of Dogs Act. A dog warden told the court he had tried to catch the dog and to sedate him with the help of a vet. Also, he had tried and failed to locate the dog's owner.

Judge Joseph Mangan signed the execution order and people can again walk safely through Ruan.

Paisley Crosses the Border for Shirts

Ian Paisley's new-found goodwill to the Republic now extends to the shirt on his broad back.

Unlike the late Charlie Haughey who went to Paris for top-of-the-range Charvet shirts, the North's First Minister doesn't go too far – just across the border to Donegal, in fact.

Big Ian's love affair with republican cloth started when the Doherty brothers, who own the Moville Clothing Company, sent him a sample shirt at the suggestion of local Donegal minister, the Reverend Jim Rea, in December 2006. The Reverend Rea has had his shirts made by the company for a number of years.

So impressed was Dr Paisley with the 100 per cent two-fold cotton shirt that he ordered a further five shirts, collar size 16.5 with a 44 inch chest.

> 'It was one of the nicest shirts I have ever seen. The material is so soft and comfortable,' the Free Presbyterian minister said.
>
> *Donegal News*

The Dohertys, who run the last remaining shirt factory in Donegal, also sent shirts to the North's Deputy First Minister, Martin McGuinness, and Sinn Féin leader Gerry Adams. However, the particular style of shirt is more suited to clerical wear.

Harry Doherty said: 'We're very proud that Dr Paisley has chosen to . . . get his shirts made with us. Hopefully it's a sign of the good things to come between the North and the South.'

Mayo Council Group Travels to Germany in Strength

Call it a study trip, a plain junket or, in the best tradition of Knock Shrine, an excursion, but when you're going at all you might as well go in numbers.

When Westport Town Council decided to travel to Germany in search of inspiration, it was felt a large group of people would learn more than a few. Thirteen people went – six councillors and three officials with four members of the media thrown in to keep an eye on them.

Sinn Féin councillor Dave Keating, who was not in the touring party, did not think it was necessary. 'I would learn more about the traffic in Westport by watching it in Westport than going to Germany,' he declared.

To which the town manager, Peter Hynes, reacted: 'To be the best, you have to see the best.'

> The group visited Baden Baden where they met local town hall officials for discussions on transportation, parking and environmental policy. They also met the lord mayor of the town who outlined the workings of the council and how funds were raised for the development of the town.
>
> *Western People*

They also took in Heidelberg, a tourist town like Westport, where they saw how the old parts of the town were preserved and were acting as a major tourist attraction.

Peter Hynes maintained the trip was absolutely a worthwhile investment, stating that if the Westport Council limited its vision to what it could see from the top of Sheeaun it would be to the detriment of Westport.

The trip cost between €10,000 and €12,000 and officials were quick to point out that it did not cost the taxpayer anything as proceeds from conferences run by the council met the bill.

At a meeting of the council, which was chaired by Councillor Keating due to the absence of the mayor, Councillor Keating wished the members present who were making the trip, a safe journey. He said later he had no problem with conferences or study trips if they were of some use to the council but asked: 'Why send a big group when just two or three could have gone?'

Mayor Sparks Chain Reaction

Wearing a chain of office is an honour to which every councillor aspires, but can the silver emblem of power be abused? Important-looking people with chains of glistening silver on their breasts pompously turn up at a whole variety of functions, from the official first flushing of public loos, to pub and supermarket openings, to football matches, to the Paddy's Day parade in New York, to formal booze-ups for foreign dignitaries.

It has been claimed that Mayor Flan Garvey of Clare wore his chain at 'inappropriate' events including weddings, funerals and Fianna Fáil church gate collections.

Fellow Clare councillor Martin Lafferty said it had been brought to his attention that the mayor was 'overusing' the chain for party and political purposes. 'Any inappropriate use of the chain devalues the whole decorum attached to the office of mayor,' Martin maintained.

Other Clare councillors called for proper protocols to be drafted in relation to when, where and how the coveted chain should be used.

Clearly unwilling to provoke further chain reaction, Mayor Garvey, whose term of office finished at the end of June 2007, said he was proud to wear the chain and represent the council at home and abroad.

'I will give all these comments the charity of silence,' he said and declined to be drawn any further on his colleagues' statements or claims.

The Clare Champion

Outside his native village of Kilgarvan in Kerry, a life-size image of Independent TD Jackie Healy-Rae has stood for over a decade. He is smiling broadly and wearing the Kerry County Council chain. The sign has become something of a tourist attraction and people regularly pose beside it to have their photographs taken.

Nobody there seems unduly bothered by the Kilgarvan *pièce de resistance* which, like the man it portrays, is unmissable on the roadside.

No Tipp Invite for Queen Elizabeth

It's a long way to Tipperary for the Queen of England, and getting longer by the day. Queen Elizabeth's ancestors are reputed in some quarters to have come from Thurles, but that doesn't mean an official invitation to visit the cradle of the GAA will ever find its way to Buckingham Palace.

Former Thurles mayor Lucy McLoughlinn had the temerity to raise the issue of a royal invitation at a local town council meeting. She stressed that she had been merely requested to start a debate, which turned out to be farcical.

Councillor Mae Quinn thought the whole thing ridiculous. 'Are we losing the run of ourselves? The Queen has never even been to Ireland. She's hardly going to make Thurles her first port of call, or any port of call for that matter. Have we gone completely mad?' she asked.

Chiming in, another councillor remarked that it was hard enough to get Bertie Ahern to come to Thurles, never mind the Queen of England.

However, Councillor Noel O'Dwyer said he would love to see the Queen coming to Thurles and, while they were at it, they should also invite 'poor auld Philip cause he gets to go nowhere' and Charles, Camilla and the 'two young lads' as well.

> He added, tongue in cheek, that they should wait until Councillor David Doran, of Sinn Féin, was mayor to send the invites. And he suggested that if the Queen would not be coming, perhaps instead Oscar winning actress Helen Mirren might dress up as her for the St Patrick's Day parade.
>
> *The Nationalist and Tipperary Star*

Councillor Doran wouldn't hear of any such thing, stating: 'I cannot see the benefit of everyone waving Union Jacks in Liberty Square for a woman whose predecessors presided over a million Irish people losing their lives during the Famine.'

Having got all that off their chests, the Thurles elders were told by officials that councils had no authority to issue royal invitations as any invitation to a Head of State had to come from the government.

The Final Word on Charlie Haughey

Charlie Haughey's family just wanted a simple headstone to mark his grave. The only thing they really specified was that the image of a cross found on his Kerry holiday island, Inishvickillane, should be depicted in fine detail on the granite slab.

Clare sculptor Michael McTigue was thrilled when he got a phone call from the ex-Taoiseach's son, Conor, inviting him to do the job. He had already created a statue for Charlie in Kerry and guessed that the family might make him an offer because they were pleased with that work.

'It [the Kerry monument] was controversial. Half the people said it should be put up and the other half didn't. But sure with Charlie you always had that bit of controversy,' Michael, from Kilnamona, recalled.

Charlie himself never saw it (he was too ill to travel down from Kinsealy) but his family were at the unveiling and that put Michael McTigue in the frame for another commission. The centuries-old Inishvickillane cross is in Trinity College and he went there to see it. Michael, who is assisted by his son, Eamon, had to use Irish stone and also decided to use some Dublin granite.

> With historic moments comes a sense of pressure; the bigger the occasion, the more people who will see any mistake that's made.
>
> 'I did feel some pressure. Whether you liked him or not, he was Taoiseach of the country for a long time. I got my wife down to proofread the inscription six or seven times, backwards and forwards. The bloody *Irish Times* or someone is only waiting for something to be wrong with it!'
>
> *The Clare People*

A bit like Charlie himself, the speckled headstone has two sides to it. It's a rough-cut boulder with one smooth face and could be said to reflect both the turbulent and suave sides of the man whose mortal remains lie beneath it.

While he was erecting the stone in St Fintan's Cemetery in Sutton, a few down-to-earth Dubliners came over to Michael for a look. Some touched it, at the same time remarking on Charlie's virtues and what he did for the elderly. One asked, 'Are yiz doin' him up for de election?'

But Michael had the final word on Charlie, carving the following inscription in Gaelic lettering:

Charles J Haughey 1925–2006

'Be my epitaph writ on my country's mind;

He served his country and loved his kind.'

End is Nigh for Neighbourly Gravediggers

In North Tipperary and other areas around the country, there's a time-honoured tradition that when someone dies, family members and friends come together to dig their grave.

Like many old customs, however, it is dying out with a little help from officialdom and obstacles put in the way by bodies (pun intended) such as the Health and Safety Authority. The powers-that-be have an attitude that one funeral at a time is enough for any community and there's no point in creating a situation that could lead to another – like a man with a 'drop taken' falling into a grave.

Karl Cashen, the council executive with responsibility for graveyards in North Tipperary, said the practice of inexperienced people opening graves was 'potentially dangerous' and needed to be regulated. He cited health and safety reasons.

But Councillor John Hogan wasn't a bit happy with what he saw as an interference with local traditions. It was commonplace for ten or twelve men to open a grave and he had often given a hand himself in such neighbourly operations in his own parish, he pointed out.

Some councillors wanted to ensure people were fully sober before they caught a pick or shovel to prepare the last resting place of someone they held dear.

> Councillor Hogan said he had heard of people getting drunk over a grave but he had never heard of anybody being hurt as a consequence. The council should not be creating problems where none existed, he declared.
>
> *Munster Express*

When an official claimed the practice of amateur gravedigging was not as common as it once was, he was assured by a number of councillors that the custom was alive and well.

However, despite the sensitivity and tradition involved, the officials' view was that time was moving on and the council would have to abide by health and safety guidelines and sacrifice yet another lovely way of doings things on the altar of present day correctness.

There have, of course, been cases of people with drink taken falling into graves and living to tell the tale at many a funeral thereafter. But such incidents generally happen on the day of the burial and not while a grave is being dug when the hardworking pick and shovel men are generally dead sober.

Spare a Thought for all those Hard-Pressed Mayors

All you thankless people out there have no clue how onerous the job of a mayor can be. Think of all the bashes the chain-wearing dignitary has to attend, all the home and overseas junkets he or she must go on – and then only to get abuse from punters and the horrible 'meejia' when they come home.

Judging from some of the remarks passed when Labour's George Lawlor took over as Mayor of Wexford in June 2007, it's sympathy the poor man should be getting from the public for putting in all those long hours of work that no one sees.

George had to listen to the following consoling words from Councillor Anna Fenlon who was almost moved to tears: 'It is a heavy burden for you to carry, but your shoulders are quite broad and I am sure that you will be able to carry the burden easily.'

It seems that the unappreciative and demanding general public do not fully grasp how labour intensive and stressful the position of first citizen can be.

Family members and Labour Party colleagues, including Deputy Brendan Howlin, were delighted to finally see Labour emerge victorious from a vote, even if the result was decided in advance and the nomination process a mere formality.

> When the time came for the symbolic transfer of the ruby ceremonial robe and the heavy golden chains of office, cameras flashed and applause thundered.
>
> Any concerns about the strain of the forthcoming job seemed to dissipate as the new Mayor beamed and spoke about his grandfather, Eddie Hall, who served as town Mayor in 1955 ...
>
> County Manager Eddie Breen congratulated the new Mayor on his election. He spoke about the qualities that a Mayor should possess and said that Philomena Roche [the former Mayor] had all of these attributes in spades: 'First of all you need to be a lady, and Phil is nothing if not a lady. Secondly, you need to be a good Mayor and Phil carried out her functions with style and grace.'
>
> A puzzled look crossed the new Mayor's face at this point, but he has nothing to worry about. Even though Mayor Lawlor is definitely not a lady, councillors of all political hues confirmed that he is a gentleman.
>
> Additionally, now that Wexford's first-citizen will be wearing the striking mayoral gown and chain at official functions, he is sure to be the most stylish man in the room.
>
> As one of the youngest Mayors that the town has ever had, hopefully his energy levels will be such that he will be able to face the strain of his official duties.
>
> *Wexford Echo*

At celebrations in a local pub after his election, George rendered his favourite song, 'This Is the Moment'. It was the greatest moment of them all, he sang, with supporters and friends from the Wexford Light Opera Society joining in.

Bertie's Christmas Card and Phone Call to Bev

The Christmas after Bev had been kicked out of Fianna Fáil she had no contact from Bertie. Not a word. The following year she received a Christmas card but no phone call. At Christmas 2006, however, the prodigal daughter from Castlebar got both a card and a phone call from Bertie.

'And I must say I was delighted he rang,' she told her Mayo constituents just as the campaign for the 2007 general election was cranking up. And no wonder she was.

The political wooing of Beverley Flynn, whose partner is a multi-millionaire businessman, had started. She and the Taoiseach had a 'light-hearted Christmas chat' but there was much more to it than that – Bertie's renewed interest in her showed that if Fianna Fáil was returned to power and she herself was elected she would be back in the fold.

She was duly elected as an Independent TD. As soon as the election was over, Bertie made it clear that once she had settled a little matter of legal costs with RTÉ, she would be welcome to return to Fianna Fáil and might even become a minister in the fullness of time.

She owed RTÉ €2.84 million in costs from the failed libel case she brought against the station arising from a report which stated she helped people dodge tax while she worked for National Irish Bank. She made a final settlement for less than half the sum owed and RTÉ, in turn, withdrew a bankruptcy action against her.

Award her full marks for a brass neck, but in Bev's Mayo queendom there were mixed emotions in Fianna Fáil following Bertie's giving of absolution. The forgiving of the comeback kid, who was once memorably described as a 'class act' by her father Pee Flynn, would not heal Fianna Fáil wounds in Mayo.

Frank Chambers, a defeated Fianna Fáil candidate in the election, felt particularly let down, according to Mayo pundits. He had been assured by party headquarters during the campaign that he was the authentic Fianna Fáil standard bearer, the man on whom the party was pinning its hopes for a return to its old glory days in Mayo.

> Those assurances were less than convincing following Beverley's well-timed revelation about the phone call she received from Bertie at Christmas. Releasing the information as the canvassing gathered momentum was a brilliant piece of opportunism and Chambers' chances were dealt a mortal blow.
>
> In making that call when Fianna Fáil ratings in the opinion polls were low, Bertie had his eye on the outcome of the election, clearly anticipating Beverley's return to the Dáil and hoping for her support in the event of a hung result.
>
> *The Connacht Tribune*

Huge Vote for Lowry in North Tipperarary

Michael Lowry always maintained the plain people were on his side regardless of high-powered tribunals or other controversies in which he was involved.

Sure enough, the voters of north Tipperary again cocked the 'two fingers' at tribunal-land and Dublin 4 by putting the Independent TD at the head of the poll for the third successive election. Let no one have any doubts, Michael Lowry is the most popular man in north Tipp.

Some months earlier, the man who had been investigated by the McCracken Tribunal, the Moriarty Tribunal and the Revenue Commissioners announced that he had settled his tax irregularities with the Revenue for €1.5 million and there would be no prosecution taken against him.

However, even when he had not sorted his tax affairs, his own people were giving him impressive mandates to represent them – his reward for hard work on the ground and service to the public. While he had endured many long days and dark nights when he could not sleep with worry, he was touched by the 'non-judgmental attitude' of what he called ordinary people. 'I was only judged by hob-nobs,' he claimed.

Before the 2007 election, the former Fine Gael minister said he had drawn a line under his prolonged tax difficulties and was now tax-compliant. He had to sell off some assets and re-mortgage his house. He had accepted payments of close to €400,000 from Dunnes Store in the form of work done at his home in Holycross. The payments were due for work carried out for Dunnes by his company, but the benefit was undeclared to the Revenue at the time.

A rally to launch his election campaign was attended by more than 600 people in Thurles, including Tipperary hurling manager Michael (Babs) Keating and former Munster GAA Council chairman Sean Fogarty, reflecting his massive popularity in the constituency. After five elections, he said he had the distinction and privilege of being trusted by the people of north Tipperary to represent them.

'I have built my reputation and support on the basis of caring for individual needs in the community,' he said.

The Nationalist and Tipperary Star

A keen racing man, Michael Lowry held his seat in a proverbial canter with 12,919 votes, more than 5,500 votes ahead of second-placed Maire Hoctor of Fianna Fáil who was appointed a junior minister. Lowry is also one of the Independents supporting the government, which should send further 'goodies' to north Tipp.

In Thrall to a 'Tache

It's not easy to faze Willie O'Dea but he was surprised when told of an unusual request from his number one fan. Mary O'Connor, a student teacher in Limerick, simply wanted to stroke his trademark moustache and sit on his lap.

The vivacious 20-year-old was caught up in election fever and her big moment came courtesy of *The Ray D'Arcy Show* on Today FM which is in the business of making people's dreams come true. An election was on and it was a request to which the Defence Minister simply had no defence.

> 'I was amazed that anybody would want to meet me like that, especially a beautiful young girl like Mary O'Connor. But I was very flattered that she did want to meet me. She seems a highly intelligent young girl and I wish her all the best in the future,' said the minister.
>
> *Limerick Leader*

Afterwards, the Mary Immaculate College student, who named her Bebo site 'callmewillie' in the run-up to the election, was inundated with comments from friends and complete strangers congratulating her on the 'ultimate Willie-fest'.

One social networker on her Bebo site wrote after the programme: 'I'm another stranger who thought you were hilarious on Ray this morning. In what other country could a girl get on the radio, sit on the lap of the Minister of Defence and play with his moustache?'

Nearly 40 of Willie's posters adorned Mary's site showing him in a variety of poses. One election poster had a pink bra over Willie's eyes and another showed him drinking a can of Bud.

Willie wasn't aware if other women also had a burning desire to stroke his moustache. 'But there could be legions of them out there for all I know. They certainly haven't come forward yet,' he joked.

Whether they wished to get that close up and familiar didn't really matter. For thousands of women did the most important thing for Willie the supreme vote-catcher – they gave him the stroke on the ballot paper helping him yet again to a poll-topping 19,082 number ones in Limerick East – more than twice the required quota.

Would Want to Be Mad to Run for the Dáil

You'd want to be out of your mind to stand for the Dáil according to Listowel wit and writer Billy Keane, who decried the fact that people are always making demands on politicians.

The son of the late John B Keane related a bizarre story which he had heard from a female TD. It concerned a woman looking for a sex change on the medical card. Though not a surgeon himself, Billy speculated that there would be absolutely no bother in turning a man into a woman, but doing the opposite would be a different story altogether. Where, after all, would you find a man volunteering the necessary organ for transplant?

> The politician said she would check it out and suggested the woman suffering from penis envy should try attaching a prosthesis . . . The lady in search of her manhood attacked the politician for not setting up surgical intervention for the dose of penis envy forthwith.
>
> *The Kerryman*

Billy is a close friend of north Kerry Fine Gael TD Jimmy Deenihan and the Keane family's politics has always been a deep shade of blue. At one time, Billy himself had notions of going for election but his father put him off the idea by telling him about a man from their hometown who once secured only two votes in an urban council election.

The broken man took refuge in a local pub to drown his sorrows and also to drown all those that promised to vote for him but didn't.

'Well,' said the consoling publican, 'I voted for you anyway.'

'My wife must be a liar so,' retorted the defeated candidate.

Ring Wakes Up Sweating

So busy is Mayo Fine Gael TD Michael Ring that people believe he scarcely finds time to sleep. But he does manage to get some rest, even during elections.

During the election campaign he had a dream, or maybe the politician's ultimate nightmare would be a more accurate description. 'I had a dream the other night that I lost my seat and I woke up in a sweat,' he revealed breathlessly.

Ring's seat has come to be regarded as 'safe' though that's the last thing he wants to hear people saying. Having come up the hard way, insecurity is never far from his mind – just a case of being ready in case the worst ever comes to the worst. In the election he had Fine Gael colleague and potential Taoiseach Enda Kenny 'up against him' (no worry about Fianna Fáil though).

A man with an insatiable appetite for hard work, his preparations for the 2007 election started the minute he topped the poll in his constituency in 2002.

> 'I'm not one of those politicians who gets elected and then hibernates for three and a half years and then when the election comes around again the cuckoo comes out. This is one cuckoo that has been on the ground for 52 weeks of the year.'
>
> *The Connacht Tribune*

In the 2007 election Michael Ring received 11,412 number ones, 3,300 votes behind Enda Kenny who headed the poll. He cruised back to Leinster House in comfort and was one of the first people to irk the new Ceann Comhairle, John O'Donoghue.

Video Nasty Returns to Haunt Bertie

It was a case of 'roll it there, Joe' when Joe Maloney came out with his camera to capture Bertie's visit to O'Briensbridge many moons ago. Little did Joe, who happens to be the long-serving secretary of the local Fianna Fáil cumann, think he would end up holding the Taoiseach to ransom over what the great man had said on tape and video.

In May 1997, when Bertie was canvassing in Clare, he promised O'Briensbridge a sewerage scheme during the five-year term of the incoming government. But by the time Bertie returned in 2002 and again in 2007, the promise had not been fulfilled.

> Since then (1997) I have raised the issue with the Taoiseach on no less than four occasions, the last time being last December when I had a face-to-face meeting with him at the GAA club in Killaloe,' said Joe.
>
> *The Clare Champion*

Joe pointed out the growth of O'Briensbridge was being stymied because of the lack of a sewerage scheme. The place had depended on septic tanks for far too long, with some of the waste flowing into the Shannon.

Joe and his friends, meanwhile, are hoping that Bertie will deliver for the village during the lifetime of the current government. But if Bertie doesn't, he won't be around when they start throwing the manure in

O'Briensbridge when the next election comes. He has said he will have retired by then. And that's a promise he'll surely keep.

God Supporting the Healy-Raes

Life was so good for the Healy-Raes before and after the election that even God was on their side, says the gospel according to Danny.

For a family that has seen ups and downs since father Jackie first entered Kerry County Council in 1973, all seemed rosy for once. And it wasn't just that Jackie was elected to the Dáil as an Independent TD for the third time.

On a momentous day for the dynasty, cap-wearing son Michael (obviously the anointed one in the family succession stakes) became Mayor of Kerry. But it was his big brother, Danny, who won the prize for the most humorous contribution on a day when a lot of hot air was blown around the council chamber.

> Danny, who was elected Deputy Mayor, had his say when most of the other councillors were finished. 'God is on our side,' he proclaimed. 'He's on the side of the Healy-Rae organisation.' Profound words, indeed, and we all waited breathlessly to hear what his next revelation would be.
>
> *The Kingdom*

When the laughter abated he proceeded to give them chapter and verse. Danny, one of the biggest civil engineering contractors employed by the council, explained that his tractor and trailer, which had been missing for two weeks, had been found by the gardaí during drug raids near Fermoy, Co Cork; his father had been elected to the Dáil; his father's pet pony, Peg, which had been missing, had been found in rich pastures in County Limerick; and now kid brother Michael had the glistening chain of office around his neck.

Sitting in the public gallery was Jackie Healy-Rae who chuckled almost uncontrollably as he watched his dynasty tighten its grip on Kerry politics.

Costa del Provo in Donegal

Chilling out by the sea in Donegal is now a favourite form of relaxation for redundant Provos from the other side of the border. The famous song, 'The Homes of Donegal', has a new resonance for leading Sinn Féiners and some people once active in the IRA who are buying up property in the county and pricing locals out of the market.

A *Sunday Independent* article claimed the large number of holiday homes owned by republicans from the North was a major source of annoyance in Donegal as it has driven up prices for young, first-time buyers. Clusters of holiday homes owned by northern IRA people have sprung up in places like Gortahork, earning that stretch of coastline the soubriquet Costa del Provo, the article stated.

One of the 'handsome' properties above Gortahork is owned by Gerry Adams even though he claimed the bank owned it, according to the article by Jim Cusack under the headline, 'SF Show That Home Is Not Always Where Their Vote Is'.

Predictably, some well-known Donegal auctioneer reacted to this negativity and Manus McGroddy was fast out of the traps. He described as 'outlandish' and 'highly unfair' the description of Gortahork as the Costa del Provo. The article had done little for the image of Gortahork in his view.

'There is no correlation between Gerry Adams purchasing a holiday home in Gortahork and the need to give that parish the name Costa del Provo. I'm sure Sinn Féin supporters have bought property in different parts of the country like Kerry and elsewhere and they're not labelled in this way,' he said.

'The holiday home market is not competing with the first time buyer market. They're two different markets and the County Development Plan positively discriminates in favour of local people to build or buy in their own localities. To me, the imposition of the government's stamp duty has greater cost implications than Northern Ireland people who wish to buy holidays homes,' Mr McGroddy said

'In trying to get at Sinn Féin and Gerry Adams, the article claims that Provos have bought so many houses they are outbidding local people who would like to purchase sites. This is untrue because the County Development Plan means that now locals have greater rights to apply for planning permission than ever before,' he concluded.

Donegal News

The Pope, Ian Paisley (who already buys his shirts in Donegal) or anybody else who wanted to purchase a holiday home in Donegal had a right to do so, Manus insisted.

Fairy Revenge for Tara Motorway?

Storyteller Eddie Lenihan once convinced a county council to reroute a dual carriageway around a 'fairy tree' after warning that misfortune could later befall users of the road if the tree was destroyed.

Believing that the fairy tree of Latoon, near Newmarket-on-Fergus, County Clare, was a stopping place for the Connacht fairies on their way home from their great battles with the Munster fairies, he argued that to interfere with it would be dicing with the evil side of the supernatural. The human powers-that-be did not take any chances and duly paid heed to what the seanchaí with the deep, expanding eyes and outsized glasses had to say.

Whiskered Eddie, who has made several television programmes and written books on folklore, has now warned of serious consequences if the government goes ahead with its plans to build a section of the M3 motorway close to the Hill of Tara. His chilling prediction is that drivers using the motorway will pay the price if another route isn't found.

> 'There are forces in this world besides money and physical things. Otherwise, all people who believe in religion are idiots . . . There are certain places on the landscape, fairy forts and that sort of thing. We have all heard the stories of unfortunate things happening to the people who interfere with them because they don't know what they're messing with,' he said.
>
> *The Clare People*

The very motorists who are clamouring for the new Tara motorway will be the ones who pay the price, according to Eddie, who called on politicians and planners to show some 'common sense' on the issue.

'We now live in a pagan country. People forget that physical things wear out but spiritual things do not. Are we turning out idiots from our universities? Are the planners fools? I think they are, in fact, or most of them. They don't seem to be able to admit they are wrong and change around the decision,' he maintained.

Eddie, who lives in Crusheen, County Clare, suggested the power of the supernatural world should never be underestimated. 'A lot of good ideas have come out of the spiritual rather than the physical. With that in mind, if that road is built that way, you will see trouble,' he predicted ominously.

However, Mary Deevy, a senior National Roads Authority

archaeologist, was unmoved. She thought fears about the impact of the controversial motorway on the Hill of Tara were being overestimated. The proposed road would not affect the Tara landscape and was further from the ancient site than the existing roadway. But Eddie has grave forebodings about the contentious project. They have been warned!

Eye in the Sky Spying on Farmers

In the bad old days, it was the gardaí that people making poitín in Connemara had to fear. There was a song with lines such as, 'keep the smoke from rising, Barney' and 'run like the devil from the excise man' – all about the joys of illicit distilling and the need not to give clues away to the eyes and ears of the law.

But now farmers in the hills of Connemara have more to fear from people travelling by air than those on the ground. Department of Agriculture inspectors hover in helicopters at points west of Galway, counting sheep to ensure farmers receiving payments comply with EU laws, according to Senator Ulick Burke. Spending taxpayers' money in such a way is 'quite shocking' behaviour, he claimed.

'We now have a situation where Department of Agriculture inspectors are flying over Connemara counting sheep while others are sitting down watching farmers milking cows,' he claimed.

> 'What is happening in parts of Connemara now is that parts of it are becoming overgrown because of the grazing restrictions in place. This ongoing hounding of the farming community by the Department of Agriculture will only serve to finish farming as a family business in the west of Ireland – young people just won't stand for this kind of harassment,' said Senator Burke.
>
> *The Connacht Tribune*

Both Senator Burke and the Irish Farmers' Association took the case to Agriculture Minister Mary Coughlan who agreed to take it up at EU level. The farmers demanded 14 days prior notice of inspection, the same as applies in Germany. The state of vegetation and effects of grazing on commonages and the mountainsides are also inspected from the air.

Puck Fair Pints Flow Freely into the Small Hours

It's rare enough for a judge to have deep, personal experience of a matter which comes before him. Judge James O'Connor, who presides over district courts in Kerry, is a native of the Killorglin area and has first hand knowledge of the age-old Puck Fair for which Killorglin is famous.

In his own understated words, the judge attended Puck 'once or twice' for the three days of the fair and never saw any thuggery even at 2.30am. Pubs are allowed open until 3am each day of the August fair but the gardaí are not happy about that.

When Killorglin publicans sought their usual exemption to serve drink into the wee hours, Superintendent Michael O'Donovan objected. He asked Judge O'Connor to curtail the opening hours to 2am, arguing that the late hours were 'putting a strain' on the gardaí's resources to keep order on the streets.

The superintendent pointed out that organised street entertainment ended at 11pm each night and the only entertainment for the following four hours was drinking. But the judge refused to reduce the hours, saying that the gardaí had not given him any proof of public order offences during Puck. Neither did he agree with the superintendent on the entertainment issue.

He described the Superintendent's references to a lack of entertainment after 11 pm as totally wrong saying, 'You'll always find some fella on a melodeon in the corner bawling out "Barr na Sráide" [a popular Kerry ballad]. It's this organised mayhem that lends itself to the happy, merry atmosphere of Puck Fair,' the Judge said.

The Kerryman

Until 1967, Killorglin's 20 or so pubs opened continuously for 72 hours during Puck, perhaps closing for an hour or two in the dawn light to clean up and allow revellers sleep off the effects of indulgence. Hardly surprising then that the event earned a reputation for being one of the country's most notorious drinking festivals.

Bacchus, the god of drink, is still worshipped copiously at Puck and while the essentials of the fair remain much the same, the event has changed in other ways. Street fights, for instance, are rarely seen nowadays and Puck has become more of a tourist event than the purely local festival it used to be.

It has traditionally been a great gathering place for Travellers who would sort out their own disputes with honest fist fights among young men stripped to the waist and 'bating' each other up and down the streets. That was long before they upgraded to machetes and slash hooks. In recent times, Travellers have felt less welcome at Puck and have, for example, very few places in which to park their caravans in Killorglin.

Puck Fair, meanwhile, is in safe hands as long as Judge O'Connor is on the bench. 'This is one of the most important fairs in Ireland and it has to be protected,' he said, telling the gardaí he did not expect to see any objections from them to late night opening for the next few years.

Religion – Spirited Tales

St Brigid Still Working Miracles

Where medical science is failing, one of Ireland's most venerated saints continues to work miracles. At least that's what devotees of St Brigid firmly believe. A man that visited the shrine at her birthplace in Faughart, County Louth, claimed to be cured of blindness. He had been diagnosed with permanent blindness in one eye, but returned to his consultant with his eyesight regained after making a novena at the shrine. According to Fr Richard Naughton, the man was insistent that St Brigid cured him and, while the man wished to remain anonymous, he wanted people to know the details.

> He had been suffering severe head pains and was told by doctors that his condition could result in blindness. He didn't tell his family but when he covered one eye, he couldn't see anything with the other eye. A consultant then told him the blindness was permanent.
>
> *Dundalk Democrat*

Fr Naughton described the man as being of 'very sincere religious conviction'. He had been persuaded by his sister to go to the shrine.

There was a dramatic change by the time he next visited his consultant who told him his sight was back and that she had never known of a person with his diagnosis to get their sight restored.

News of St Brigid's miraculous powers reached Faughart in the run-up to the saint's feast day on 1 February with all the talk being about the 'cure'. Most people go to St Brigid's wells just to pray, but the hope of seeing an elusive eel still draws the faithful in their hundreds to the saint's well in Liscannor, County Clare, on 1 February. An old tradition of praying and 'doing the rounds' continues in this peaceful place.

Everyone keeps an eye out for the eel which, according to ancient legend, brings good luck and health to those who see it. Nora Kelly of Lisdoonvarna is one of the few people claiming to have seen the eel. She was heartbroken following the death of her husband, Vincent, in 1998 and thought her grief would never go away.

While on a drive with a friend one day, she decided to stop off at the well. She just wanted to be alone with her thoughts and stood staring into the water. Very soon, however, things started to happen.

> Nora recalled, 'I was lost in my world of thoughts but suddenly I saw the eel I had heard so much about as a child. I immediately screamed and jumped back. I was so frightened but so excited at the same time. When I went back out to the car I was shaking so much. It was so amazing. I had cried so much after my husband died, but I can honestly say I never cried after the day I saw the eel.'
>
> *The Clare Champion*

Noreen O'Shea of Lahinch also has good reason to have unshakeable faith in St Brigid. More than 40 years ago, she was told by four eminent surgeons in London that she was losing her sight. She bathed her eyes in the Liscannor water and began to feel an improvement.

When she went back to the surgeons they noticed the difference and said they had 'stabilised' her condition. But Nora is convinced to this day that it was water in St Brigid's well that cured her eyes – not the learned medicos.

Is the Pub the New Church?

Never talk about politics or religion in a pub – a commandment that Irish drinkers have long been advised to obey. But that all changed in Mountmellick where members of the local Presbyterian Church started a course in religion in The Druid licensed premises.

The ten-week Alpha Course, billed as *Two Pints of Lager and the Meaning of Life Please*, was described by the Reverend William Hayes as a relaxed, informal and easygoing way of discussing the big questions in life, such as 'who am I' and 'is there any purpose in life?'

> He explained: 'For many people church is where you go for the big formal occasions in life, baptisms, first communions, weddings, funerals and the pub is the place where you relax with your mates and talk about the things that really matter to you.
>
> 'We are holding this course in The Druid because it is such a relaxed and welcoming place so that people who would not normally feel comfortable in church can come along and join in without feeling they are being pressured into doing something religious.'
>
> *Laois Nationalist*

There were no objections from The Druid's regulars to religion being discussed in their local. In fact, a few of them would ear-wig on occasion according to the Reverand Hayes.

But some of his 14-strong congregation had initial reservations about giving their blessing to the idea of bringing religion to the pub. 'They had asked was it the right thing to do? But in the end they felt it was the right thing to do, to bring the message to where the people are,' he said.

The Presbyterian Church in Mountmellick dates back over 300 years and is practically falling down, forcing the Reverand Hayes's congregation to meet every Sunday morning in the local Methodist Church.

Meanwhile, up to 20 people attended the religion course in The Druid. And there was no free drink.

Feakle Stays Faithful to Gay Priest

If a priest is gay, so what? But if his sexual inclination is towards the opposite sex and he has an affair with a woman he has to get out of the area, if not the country, with all speed.

When the faithful in Feakle, County Clare, learned that their parish priest was gay they were shocked but stood by him. And unlike the experiences of previous errant clergy, including Bishop Eamonn Casey, they asked him to hold his ground and not to run away.

Fr Michael Hogan had been in Feakle for four years when he was 'outed' by *The Sun* newspaper and forced to stand aside. His activities on a gay website were exposed when a reporter posed as a prospective date and met him in a hotel. The paper printed photographs of the 54-year-old priest in his underwear, which he had sent to the incognito reporter on the website.

Fr Hogan reacted by apologising for any hurt caused to parishioners and by asking Bishop Willie Walsh to allow him time away from his ministry to reflect on his position.

There was a groundswell of support for the cleric and the bishop got the all-clear from churchgoers to allow him remain in the parochial house as a temporary measure. Typically enough, there was a flood of calls to Joe Duffy's *Liveline* radio show and statements of support from community leaders in east Clare.

The chairman of Flagmount Parish Council, Ger Hoey, stated the reaction locally was of huge sympathy for Fr Hogan and the predicament he found himself in.

> 'He was and is a tremendous worker and has a lot to offer as a priest. This is a personal issue for him. Most of the people I came in contact with felt sympathy for Fr Hogan. No one expressed anger to me. People were so gobsmacked that a reaction wasn't forthcoming and it could take a while for some parishioners to express their feelings,' Mr Hoey said.
>
> *The Clare Champion*

A woman who asked not to be named said most people wanted the priest to stay on. 'He's gay. So what? It's not the end of the world,' she declared.

RTÉ sports commentator and Clare native Marty Morrissey, who knew the priest for many years, also got into the tribute act. The commentator found space in his local sports column to sanctimoniously support the cleric, as follows:

> He did nothing wrong or anything illegal. He was silly to say the least and totally naïve, but show me a man or woman that hasn't made a mistake in this life. None of us can throw stones. None of us are saints . . . it struck me how lonely a life the priesthood is and how difficult, even impossible, is a life of celibacy.
>
> *The Clare People*

One of the debatable questions thrown up by the Fr Hogan issue is: are people more tolerant of gay priests than, say, priests who have affairs with women? The Feakle case smacks of a Christian-like, forgiving approach. But there are plenty of examples of how priests who fell for women and sometimes fathered children were just booted out of a parish, with the least possible said publicly about them.

Or could it be that people have become so accustomed to clerical sexual scandals that they're not really surprised at anything anymore? However, a priest who falls in love with a woman could still come out much worse than a gay priest – especially if he has a child with the woman.

Limerick Still Keeps the Faith

Know-alls in the media might claim that the Catholic Church is all but dead in Ireland, but if they visited Limerick in June during a religious event that continues to draw the crowds they wouldn't be long getting their come-uppance.

The annual, nine-day novena in Limerick's famous Redemptorist Church draws about 12,000 people each day – a notable feat considering the 'trials and tribulations' being endured by the Church, according to the Redemptorist rector, Fr Seamus Enright.

> 'There is almost an assumption among certain media commentators, particularly in the national media, that religion is dead in this country. The general impression portrayed by commentators is of a people angry, disillusioned and seriously alienated from the Church. There is undoubtedly a certain amount of this and we have to admit that there are historical reasons for it, but for more than 30 years it [the novena] has been an outstanding witness to the faith of the people in this city,' said Fr Enright.
>
> *Limerick Leader*

Gone are the days when lukewarm Catholics were pressganged into attending such events, only to be bellowed at by pulpit-thumping zealots frightening them about the evils of 'company keeping' and threatening them with the fires of Hell.

Now, people go along without force or persuasion, a point also referred to by Fr Enright. 'I think the attendances we get today are more remarkable considering that everyone who comes is there of their own free will and because they want to be there. It's a tradition,' he remarked.

Ten daily sessions started at 7am, with the final service beginning at 10.30pm. One hundred and fifty laypeople were involved in the organisation of what some dubbed a 'festival of faith'. Polish, Slovak, Portuguese and French-speaking priests were brought in to cater for the members of overseas faithful now living in Shannonside.

However, Bishop Christopher Jones of Elphin wasn't as upbeat about the state of the Church as the Limerick Redemptorists.

Preaching in Birmingham, he said he was saddened by the 'corrosive' effect of the new prosperity on faith and family. We had plenty of beautiful houses but they were so expensive that both partners had to go out to work to keep up the mortgage payments, he pointed out.

> He added: 'Today, one has to stop and wonder why prosperity seems to have always a negative impact on faith and family life in the community. Today, with both parents working all day and children in schools, playschools and crèches all day, families have so little time and energy morning or night for themselves or for their God in prayer. Indeed, mainly for economic reasons, couples are living together outside of marriage and give up on the Church and Mass because they think the Church has no place for them.
>
> 'Then, of course, there are people whose hearts and minds are so preoccupied with things material that they have no place or time for God in their hearts or lives. Consumerism becomes

God for so many and the supermarket becomes the cathedral, the place of worship on Sundays.'

He went on: 'We are told today that people prefer to escape into the world of work, sport and entertainment rather than confront themselves through prayer in the presence of God.

'The happiness of every human person is rooted not in things material but in the life of the heart and spirit. The loneliness and unhappiness of so many today is rooted in the neglect of their spiritual lives, the neglect of prayer, reflection and worship,' he said.

The Sligo Champion

The Statue That Never Moved

In 1947 Bernd Rosenberger was among hundreds of German children who came to Ireland to be cared for by host families while their homes were being rebuilt after the second world war.

The programme was known as Operation Shamrock and Bernd was sent to the home of John and Hannah O'Carroll in the small village of Ardfert, County Kerry. The minute the ten-year-old stepped over the threshold he was marched upstairs by Hannah and told to kneel down before a statue of the Blessed Virgin which stood on a little pedestal on the landing.

Being a good Catholic Irishwoman, Hannah instructed him to ask the Blessed Virgin to mind him during his stay in Ardfert and he duly obeyed his proxy mother whom he was to call 'Auntie'.

Bernd spent three happy years in the O'Carroll household and was treated as another member of the family. After resettling with his own family in Dusseldorf, he kept in touch with Hannah O'Carroll but lost contact with Ardfert following her death in 1953. The years rolled on but Bernd and the O'Carrolls never forgot each other.

Fast forward to May 2007 and a member of the O'Carroll family renews long lost links with Bernd who arranged to return to Ardfert the following July, 60 years after he first set foot in the village.

The old O'Carroll home is now occupied by Noreen O'Mahony, a daughter of John and Hannah, who had a warm welcome for Bernd. The minute he walked in the door he asked a question: 'Is the statue still there?'

Noreen immediately turned to a hallway switch and on came a light showing the Blessed Virgin in exactly the same spot at the top of the stairs. In keeping with tradition, Noreen then asked Bernd to go up and say a prayer to the Virgin for looking after him all those years and bringing him back to Ardfert. Which he duly did.

Tears of joy welled up in his eyes as he went on to recall attending school in Ardfert and playing hurling and football with local boys. He was also confirmed in the village and learnt to speak Irish and English with a rolling Kerry accent.

> 'There were seven children in our family and most of us were grown up when Bernd arrived. As our family ran the post office and shop, which were on the premises, you could say he had a wide variety of language teachers,' said Noreen O'Mahony.
>
> *The Kingdom*

Meanwhile, one of the few statues that didn't stir in the mass statue 'movement' of the mid Eighties is going to remain rock solid in its position in Ardfert.

Norris Turns the Other Cheek

The Brigidine Sisters were hardly thinking of publicity stunts when they set about organising celebrations to mark their two centuries in Tullow,

County Carlow. But by inviting gay rights campaigner Senator David Norris as a guest speaker, they provoked an unexpected reaction.

Stephen Abbott, a 71-year-old Catholic from Tullow, kicked up a racket and shot off a scud-like missive to the bicentenary celebrations committee. 'To honour a man who constantly lambasts the Catholic Church and its priests and who promotes sinful homosexuality is inexcusable and reprehensible,' he wrote.

Explaining himself further in the local press, he objected to bringing an 'anti-Catholic to a Catholic celebration', claiming Senator Norris would go out of his way to destroy the Catholic Church if he got a chance.

> 'I am not homophobic which I see as a fear or hate of an individual but I do think that homosexuality is abhorrent and sinful. I favour tolerance rather than promotion. To promote homosexuality as an alternative way of life is unacceptable to me and that's what Senator Norris does. He doesn't waste any opportunity to remind us of his gay lifestyle,' Mr Abbott said.
>
> *Carlow Nationalist*

Strong stuff surely, but the senator, a doughty survivor of many battles, took the tirade in his stride. 'My, my, this is a flashback to 20 years ago. This must be the first time this has happened in years. I have to say I had a very warm and lovely reception in Tullow. It was a marvellous day and occasion and I didn't mention homosexuality once. So clearly, I'm not as obsessed with it as this man seems to be,' he said.

Senator Norris clarified that he was a Catholic but not a Roman Catholic and rejected suggestions that he lambasted individual priests. He was not anti-Catholic, he emphasised, but he opposed the political dimension of the Roman Catholic Church which could lead to interference by the Vatican in political life, specifically elections.

He was delighted to receive an invitation from the celebrations committee to speak at their educational conference about his own family's connection to the order's founder, Bishop Daniel Delaney.

His final words for Stephen Abbott were that he would love to meet the man for a discussion. 'I think this man has a problem but I will turn the other cheek and pray for his soul. He may be Catholic but he's not very Christian,' Senator Norris concluded.

Bishop Warns of Home Drinking

Corks are popping and the wine is flowing in Deckland. No point in having a mansion unless you can show it off to your friends and what better way than by having a drinks party or barbeque on those expansive, rose-scented lawns. In the past ten years, the amount of drink consumed in Irish homes has increased by a staggering 40 per cent while sales of alcohol in pubs have dropped severely, though not by quite as much, over the same period.

In continental Europe, 70 per cent of drink is consumed in the home. Given our ingrained pub culture that figure is unlikely to be replicated here, but there is a definite shift in Irish drinking patterns. A huge change, in fact, in a short few years and enough to get some bishops – many of whom have gone strangely silent in recent years – exercised.

According to recent figures from our biggest drinks player, Diageo (Guinness), which relies heavily on the pub trade, there has been a seven per cent decline in pub sales and a seven per cent increase in off-licence sales.

But the most alarming figure for the pub trade – not to mention bishops, doctors and others dealing with growing addiction problems – is that 30 per cent of alcohol sales here are now from off-licences, and this figure is growing.

Rather than going to the pub, more people are buying their tipple in the local petrol station or supermarket and bringing it home with them. Sitting by their own fires, they can smoke away to their heart's content and have no worries about driving. And while the pub will survive as an Irish institution, rural and small town hostelries are feeling the squeeze as indicated by the large amount of such premises being offered for sale.

The Bishop of Killala, Dr John Fleming, chose a receptive audience when he spoke in Knock about cut-price drink in off-licences and supermarkets and about the big increase in the number of people drinking at home.

He told members of the Pioneer Total Abstinence Association that all this presented many people with the opportunity to drink heavily or secretly at home, alone or with friends. This meant that the social aspect associated with having a drink was often eliminated, or limited to a few, and support for moderation was sometimes undermined.

> He noted the 200-year history of the temperance movement, speaking of its cycles of progress and failure, stating that the culture of drinking has established itself firmly in our time.
>
> *Western People*

A sober statement, indeed, in a country drenched in alcohol. The man never said a truer word.

Mystic Who Gave Glimpses of Heaven

A funny thing about John Moriarty, the mystic, was that everyone loved listening to him, but hardly anyone understood what he was saying. He was also a writer and philosopher whose words flowed as gently and poetically as a stream after a summer shower.

He had triple cancer and the reality that death was imminent was well flagged by him on the Liveline Show on RTÉ radio and other media. After travelling overseas and working as a teacher and lecturer, he settled in a modest house on a hillside outside Killarney.

John chose that spot on the edge of Killarney National Park because there was a 'radiance from the landscape' and he found inspiration there very easily. With a fine mop of curling hair going grey, he would often be seen around Killarney chatting to the locals who savoured the eloquent words that tripped from his lips.

Some would say there was never another human being quite like him. Others knew him from television programmes he made featuring unique people such as himself, and if they didn't understand, what matter!

> I first met him about twelve years ago at the launch of one of his books in Killarney. I hardly understood a sentence he spoke, or he wrote, but I loved the flow of his words.
>
> John exuded peace and tranquillity [sic]. I never spoke to him. I listened to him on stage, on radio, launching some project or telling of facing up to his cancer. He spoke on everything that mattered – Kerry, its beauty, its people and so often he spoke about his friend, God.
>
> It surprised me that John found followers and promoters in the mainstream media. They allowed him the canvass on which to stretch out his visions. I was surprised also that there were never scoffers. Dream-breakers are always around.
>
> He did not look for followers but was a solace to many who were lucky enough to have John introduce the big picture of a God that he understood. He gave listeners, or readers, a rare glimpse of Heaven in this life.
>
> *Kerry's Eye*

Vocal Priest Quacked Quacked on Words

Fr Kevin McNamara is the first to confess that his verbal wanderings and sermons are a bit long-winded, but he's in the penny-halfpenny league when measured against bureaucrats in Brussels.

The charismatic, Clare-born padre regales his congregations with tales about his everyday experiences, meetings with unusual people, travels at home and abroad, hurling and whatever they're having themselves. Truly a man that's never stuck for words, he has something to say about everything – even duck eggs.

He writes a weekly column called 'Looking Up' in *The Clare Champion*. By his own admission, he fills the space with fishy tales, the wonder of simple things, things that don't matter and little pearls of common sense that could in time be up there with the best quotes of Oscar Wilde.

> As a priest who is always accused of talking too much and always using far too many words, I still think I am running far behind civil servants. Just look at the following: the Our Father contains only 56 words; the Ten Commandments, 297 words; the American Declaration of Independence, 300 words; and the EEC Directive on the export of duck eggs contains 26,911 words. And by all accounts, the Ten Commandments were a lot clearer!
>
> *The Clare Champion*

Some of Fr McNamara's ten-second sermons:

Love your enemies, for they tell you your faults; there's only one really nice thing about egotists, they don't talk about other people; some people never say anything bad about the dead or anything good about the living; an expert knows all the answers if you ask the right questions; some church members are like wheelbarrows – they go only when they are pushed.

A Bit on the Long Side for a Wake!

The Irish wake, which has been dead and buried since those chilling funeral parlours took over, is undergoing a bit of a resurrection. But it could now be described as a 'half-wake' and not the same at all as the old-style 'full Irish' way of saying farewell to loved and not-so-loved ones.

On the first night, the body reposes at home but the whole country is not meant to descend on the house: that night is intended only for family, relations, neighbours and close friends and is usually not mentioned in public death notices. Gawkers and nosy people who come for a peep around the house and talk afterwards about their observations are not encouraged; they are supposed to wait for the second day. Some rural families now insert a 'house private' line in death notices, something that would never have dawned on them in the past.

The body is given a professional touch of make-up, coffined and presented in a downstairs front room where the only light is from flickering candles. Women with pious, long faces – yes, they're still around from the old days – sit by the walls, fingering their rosary beads, whispering to each other and nodding silently at mourners that step into the room.

Using a downstairs room is a very sensible tradition that survives from a time when wakes were actually full of life and far from dead affairs. Having mourners traipsing up and down the steps of a stairs was always regarded as high risk, especially when they were all drunk.

Drink is not dispensed at house wakes in the same quantities any more, indeed there are wakes where there's no visible sign of alcohol. But there's always a man in a back room with a bottle who'll shove a glass containing a generous measure of Paddy into your hand. This man never takes no for an answer, in fact he would be offended by a refusal. However, you must feign reluctance before accepting the libation –

another important part of the ritual – and praying, 'The Lord have mercy on the dead.'

On the second day of a half-wake, the body is taken to the funeral home where the public can turn up and show their respects.

But those that really wish to attend a funeral 'properly' go on the third day for the mass and burial. A few years back things got out of hand with eulogies from family members and friends during masses. But most priests now tightly control what happens in the church so there's no chance of getting in a blast of 'The Wild Rover' or any other such song, even though the verses might be highly appropriate to the lifestyle of the deceased.

If the mourners feel so inclined, they can sing or play tunes at the graveside but the real tributes – musical and otherwise – come in the pub after the dead man or woman has been laid to rest with due dignity.

Irish people are not the only ones who go in for lengthy wakes. When Valerijs Gaurjuncenko, a Latvian man living in Gort, County Galway, didn't turn up in the local court for a case, his excuse was that his brother had died and he was involved in bringing the body back to Latvia.

> However, Judge Joseph Mangan noted that the defendant's brother died in March and he had failed to appear in court on May 28. 'It's a bit on the long side for a wake,' the Judge remarked.
> *The Clare Champion*

Was there ever an Irish wake that went on that long?

The Unforgettable Brother Columbanus

Seán Deegan, better known as Brother Columbanus, made a lasting impression on everyone he met – an unforgettable character in every sense. Always welcome wherever he found himself, he didn't need tickets to get into shows and was known to hitch free lifts on ships going to other countries.

Born in Dublin's Usher Island in April 1925, he was an adventurous lad. He joined the British Army when he was only 17, trained as a Royal Air Force navigator just before the D-Day landings and smelt death on the Normandy beaches as his comrades coming ashore were blown to pieces by German machine gun fire.

Those awful images haunted him and the stench of death occasionally returned to his nostrils during the rest of his life which he devoted to helping his fellow man and woman. After the war, he tried a few jobs before becoming a Franciscan friar and a pacifist. Around 1981, he moved to Waterford where for many years he was chaplain to thousands of industrial workers and helper of people with all sorts of problems.

But it was his work with Breadline (an organisation that provides a 24-hour service for people down on their luck) that brought him into close contact with Waterford's homeless community and had him on call 24 hours a day.

When he died in July 2007, the Suirside city felt a genuine sense of loss and mourned the passing of an exceptional man who, in the words of Fr Pat Cogan at his funeral mass, loved life and lived it to the full with total fearlessness.

> Occasionally, some of us [in the friary] might get exclusive tickets to some new show in the Theatre Royal or somewhere and we'd be thrilled. Then we'd go down and there we'd see Colum ahead of us there, with no ticket!
> If you were travelling to Holland too, you might think of going by plane or getting the boat from England. Colum, when he wanted to go, walked down to the quays and spoke to the captain of a container ship. He asked if there was a place for him and his bike on the boat – and three days later he arrived in Holland to meet his friends!
>
> *Waterford News and Star*

Many people wept openly at his funeral service. Others touched the coffin on its journey to Ballygunner cemetery, bidding a fond farewell to a man that gave so much to so many.

Saint Patrick Works Another 'Miracle' on Reeks Sunday

The 30,000 souls who climbed Croagh Patrick on the last Sunday in July couldn't have hoped for a better day. On a rain-sodden summer, Saint Patrick was credited with working yet another miracle – getting a reluctant sun to peep through the clouds.

Mountain rescue teams had warned about the dangers of the climb and appealed to people to wear suitable footwear and clothing, as well as carrying enough water and refreshments with them. But a huge amount of pilgrims ignored the advice and came along in flip flops, wellingtons and other unsuitable footwear such as football boots – clearly putting all their trust on the saint to get them safely up and down.

Traditionalists were out in bare feet and many could be seen picking their steps ever so carefully as they moved onwards and upwards.

West of Ireland travellers turned up in droves for the annual pilgrimage with many fingering rosary beads and paying homage to St Patrick. One traveller woman who made the climb had given birth just five days earlier. She was determined the momentous event wouldn't stop her from being there on a special day.

> There's no point lying to ourselves . . . Croagh Patrick can be a difficult climb at the best of times and most of us have a habit of forgetting just how trying the hike can be, just as soon as we arrive back on flat ground. This writer had last climbed Croagh Patrick on Wednesday January 24, as part of Johnny Oosten's

seven-day fundraising climb for Mayo Autism Action and, in six short months, it had completely slipped my mind that I couldn't just breeze up and down the mountain without as much as breaking a sweat!

As we progressed up the mountain and the air became thinner, the fresh gusts of wind provided great relief and, with a few water stops along the way, it wasn't long before we reached the section of relatively flat ground in the middle of the climb.

Even for the most seasoned climbers, the cone is always the most difficult part of the climb, with stones and rocks likely to loosen from all angles on the final ascent. The weather throughout July did nothing to help in this regard and, on the whole, the stones and rocks all over the mountain had loosened considerably since January. But, while the steep slope at the top may have been difficult to manoeuvre, the views from the peak of Croagh Patrick on such a gloriously clear day made up for the heartache on the way.

Western People

But then, isn't penance for sins an essential part of this annual endurance test! On the day nobody sustained serious injuries on the reek but there were the usual cuts, scrapes and bruises and a couple of minor sprains.

After the climb, the intrepid *Western People* reporter enjoyed a relaxing jacuzzi and hot shower in Westport Leisure Centre followed by a delicious dinner, making for a perfect end to a perfect day as she described it. Who said Croagh Patrick was all about fasting and hardship?

Odds and Ends

Lots of Love but no Songs from a 'Hurt' Dolly

It was all quiet on the country 'n' western front for 6,000 fans who had been looking forward to a Dolly Parton concert in Millstreet. The busty blonde and her crew had been on site at the Green Glens Arena since seven o'clock that morning getting ready for a sell-out performance.

From two o'clock in the afternoon, folks in coats of many colours started arriving in the north Cork frontier town. Some sported cowboy hats and wore glitter costumes. Laid-back Millstreet was set to become Dollywood for a day.

Fans were humming some of their idol's best-known songs, but their happy mood suddenly went downbeat after the shock news was broken to them that the show could not go on because of 'technical difficulties'.

Inadequate rigging for the lighting was blamed by the 61-year-old gal from the Smokey Mountains and the arena's management for the decision to cancel, just four hours before she was due to swagger onto the stage.

Thomas Duggan, the arena manager, categorically refuted all other 'suggestions and malicious rumours', saying the cancellation was not the fault of Green Glens as the rigging was not supplied by his company but by an outside agent.

As for Dolly, she said she was ready and excited to do the show but wasn't told until late in the day that mechanical and technical problems were 'too severe' to be solved in time to get the gig underway safely.

During her all-too-short time in Millstreet, she asked to be taken on a tour of the surrounding countryside and brought a lump of clay from the foot of Clara mountain home to America with her as a memento of the non-event.

The bewigged Dolly left without singing a note in the Green Glens, which was the venue for the Eurovision Song Contest in 1993, but she had a farewell message from the heart for her fans:

> No one could be more disappointed and hurt than I am. I promise to try to make it up to you somehow some day. Just know that I will always love you.
>
> *The Corkman*

Oh Heavens Above! What a Fuss!

Sirens screamed and there was an unholy panic in Wexford – as if things weren't mad enough at the height of the St Patrick's Night festivities. And, no, the drama wasn't caused by alcohol for a change, but by a few drops of mercury.

A mercury thermometer broke in a wine store and it was decided to call the emergency services. Two units of Wexford Fire Brigade, two ambulances and several gardaí were summoned to the scene after a decision was taken to treat the spillage as a 'chemical incident'.

A section of South Main Street was closed off for about two hours. Customers were cleared from The Sky And The Ground pub, the

Heavens Above restaurant and Café Paradis after a staff member made a 999 call looking for advice.

'We were packed. The restaurant was full. I was a bit stunned that this was happening. We had no option but to follow instructions. I would say the thermometer contained about a teaspoon of mercury,' said Johnny Barron of The Sky And The Ground.

He described the incident as a business disaster for both the pub and Heavens Above on what should have been one of their best nights of the year.

Johnny's wife Nuala was still trying to get her head around the drama when she woke up the next morning. 'Did this really happen?' she asked herself. The bill for the attendance of the fire service was estimated at around €1,500.

> Wexford Fire Service has defended its action in sealing off South Main Street and evacuating the three premises. A Fire Service spokesperson said the decision to evacuate the entire building was taken as a precautionary measure in the interest of public safety.
>
> *Wexford People*

No Books Burned as O'Brien Comes Back to Clare

There were no smoke trails, heaps of burning books or raving zealots to be seen when the distinguished writer Edna O'Brien came back in glory to her native Clare. Once angrily rejected by Church and State, she returned like a queen. All was forgiven.

Almost five decades after her first novel, *The Country Girls*, was banned by Irish censors and set alight outside churches, she was welcomed as a 'renowned daughter of Clare' at a civic reception held in her honour in Ennis. Long ago, she took flight from a hostile, repressive environment in Ireland and has lived for much of her life in England. But Clare has now officially made amends.

The task of bestowing the 'greatest honour' they could give fell to the deputy mayor of Clare, Brian Meaney, who hoped it would 'make up for much of the unfair criticism you have received from within and outside your beloved Clare'.

He went on: 'As a writer you never really left your homeland. You may have been writing in London, but I feel you carried Clare in your heart ... I came across an interview you gave to *The Clare Champion* in 1965, a period in which your books were banned here. In the interview you said that if you were born in another country you would have been a "more tepid writer" and we are the beneficiaries of that circumstance ... we finally are pleased to honour you and it is not before time.'

Edna, now 77 but looking much younger, was gracious and said it was a great privilege and reassurance to be welcomed back to Clare. But, clearly, she hadn't forgotten the past, commenting: 'I know there will be no more books banned or burned. Let's hope there will be more books read.'

> Then the emotional side of her emerged, as she recalled her upbringing and parents in Tuamgraney: 'When I am in America giving talks, I say I am so thankful for where I came from. When I was young I had a great longing for getting away, as many young people do. But I didn't realise that you don't ever get away and the richest experiences you have are where you begin your life. I am so thankful for the landscape around where I grew up. It had a magic that I cannot begin to explain.'
> She also acknowledged her parents, describing her father as a 'gifted storyteller' and her mother as being 'masterful in the letters she wrote to me'.
>
> *The Clare Champion*

The adulation continued when she later gave a public reading to a packed house as guest of Ennis Book Club.

Roar of Landslide almost Rouses Peig

The peace of a quiet Sunday evening in the Dingle peninsula was broken by an 'unmerciful bang' as a large section of a cliff collapsed and tumbled into the sea. The thunder-like rumble was almost enough to wake Blasket Island writer Peig Sayers from her long slumber in the nearby graveyard at Dún Chaoin, according to shocked locals.

A Blasket ferryman, Mick Sheeran, was just finishing for the day when the landslide on the spectacular Slea Head road occurred at around 6.30pm. He first heard the roaring sound and then saw hundreds of tonnes of earth and stones falling into the Atlantic, with great clouds of dust billowing upwards.

'It reminded me of the Twin Towers in New York. I could see some figures on top of the cliff and I wondered if, maybe, some people had been swept down in the landslide, because from where I was I couldn't tell if the main road had gone as well,' he said afterwards. Mick then alerted the coastguard, gardaí and other emergency services.

> Mr Sheeran's quick action may well have saved lives because a number of serious cracks appeared in the main road within yards of the collapse. If buses and cars had continued to use the route, it could have precipitated a further collapse. Faced with this possibility, the authorities decided to close the road immediately.
>
> *The Kerryman*

The stretch of coastline at the scene is notoriously unstable because of the underlying soil and rock formation and the road has had to be rerouted there in the past.

The Slea Head route is an essential part of tourism in the area and Kerry County Council surprised itself by responding so fast that a temporary stretch of road was opened in less than three days. This meant that tourist buses and other traffic could again travel as usual.

The only snag for the council is that it has now set itself a precedent for acting with the kind of speed local authorities are generally not noted for.

Pat's 13,000 Train Journeys and a Million Breakfasts

Everyone on the train knew Pat English and he knew more about what people had for breakfast than anybody else. During his 30 years looking after first class customers on the early morning train from Limerick to Dublin, he learned a lot about people and their tastes.

He was into little secrets like how leading politicians and business people liked their eggs done and whether they liked black pudding. He could remember a whole carriage full of people's breakfasts from memory.

The diplomatic Pat also encountered many celebrities. A man that stood out on the train one day was the hard-drinking and hell-raising actor, Oliver Reed, who lived in north Cork at the time. Did Pat find Oliver in his usual form? 'All I'll say is that he was in good spirits,' replied a smiling Pat, ever the soul of discretion.

Pat's day started when he stepped onto the 7.50am train at Limerick station. He reckons he had completed around 13,000 journeys between the cities by the time he retired in early 2007.

More often than not, he would know a person's order the minute he saw their face. A lot of people took the train regularly, so they would not even have to ask him what they wanted.

Pat, a friendly man, served prominent politicians such as Jim Kemmy, Michael Lowry and Michael Noonan and was just as well known to the train's passengers as they were.

During the two and a half hour journey from Monday to Friday, Pat's role was to ensure that every need of the customer was catered for, no matter what.

> 'Sometimes we might have someone who was sick on the train, or got a nosebleed. Another time, a woman had brought her friend onto the train to get her seated, but the train pulled off before the friend had a chance to leave the train. We had to wait for the next stop and get someone to drive the woman back to Limerick,' he recalled.
>
> *Limerick Leader*

Post Office Closes after a Hundred Years

The last few stragglers had left the post office cum shop in a County Cork village after Saturday evening mass. Then, with a heavy heart, Pat McAuliffe turned the key in the door for the last time.

After over a century of business had been carried on there, she decided to close down in Carriganima because of lack of support and the growing trend to bypass local businesses for bigger towns – even for basics such as bread, milk, old age pensions and children's allowance.

Pat's grandparents had run the business. They did teas for the local dance hall and when food and other essentials were rationed in wartime, they were able to procure some provisions for customers. Pat remembers a busy trade when she was young. 'There were two masses on Sunday morning and it took four of us to do the shop,' she recalled.

For 60 years Pat's mum and dad, Cathleen and Matt McAuliffe, ran the business. Cathleen gave her life to the community: filling forms, giving references and dispensing advice were part and parcel of what she did.

> 'She even sent envelopes and stamps to people, so they could write to tell of the birth of a child . . . A lot of the older people were amazing. They were just fantastic to support the shop and post office. Mum always said that for each pensioner that died she lost a great customer and often a great friend,' said Pat.
>
> *The Southern Star*

Willie Riordan had been getting milk and the newspaper in the shop for 70 years. Now, like the rest of his Carriganima neighbours, he has to travel to Clondrohid or Macroom.

New Low in Rural Crime

Local hero Denis P (Battie) O'Sullivan had just collected his newspapers in a nearby shop on a Sunday morning. He then collapsed and died only yards from his home in the Kerry village of Kilgarvan.

Within hours of his passing, burglars kicked in a side door to enter the post office-cum-shop in which the 86-year-old bachelor lived alone. As he reposed in the village funeral home, they ransacked the house scattering GAA cuttings and records he had kept lovingly for 60 years.

That a crime so low could happen in Kilgarvan, where crime of any kind is rare, sickened people to the core. The man whose home was targeted had spent his life serving the community, chiefly as postmaster and GAA activist.

After the burglary was discovered on Monday morning, news spread quickly. People's grief at the passing of a much-respected personality soon turned to anger. Local GAA officials described the culprits as 'low-life scum'.

Along with his brother John, Denis P ran Kilgarvan post office for more than 40 years. It was also a traditional grocery and an open house for everyone, even when business was over for the day.

> Denis P was a man of old-world courtesy, a man who placed a deep value on human connections and family roots, a man who welcomed the stranger and who loved his native place.
>
> *Kerry's Eye*

He won three Kerry county hurling championships with Kilgarvan in the 1950s (Independent TD Jackie Healy-Rae was also on the team) and ran the local GAA club for decades. A man with influence in high places, he had the knack of getting gardaí who were good hurlers transferred to Kilgarvan to boost the local team.

He never owned a car, nor did he believe in hiring buses to take Kilgarvan juvenile teams to away matches. Instead, he would stand on the roadside with his young charges and flag down or, more accurately, commandeer approaching cars. His order to the drivers was direct: 'Take as many as you can as far as you can.'

The post office was the centre of intelligence in Kilgarvan and Denis P was the village's link with the wider world. He also wrote the local notes for *The Kerryman* for countless years. His last column was written just prior to his death and was published the day after he was buried. Typically, it featured news of Kilgarvan exiles.

His home was said to be better known to some people than Dáil Éireann, especially those tracing their roots. Denis P, a teetotaller and Irish speaker, had an encyclopaedic knowledge of local families. When baptism and other church registers failed to lead Americans and others to their old homesteads, he invariably put them on the right track.

In a graveside oration, Kilgarvan native Mairín Quill, former Progressive Democrat TD in Cork, recalled: 'His establishment in Church Street was a cross between the National Library and the American Embassy. It was a place to which second and third generation Americans came to find out where they could locate the family home.'

Meanwhile, some Kerry undertakers advised bereaved families not to give exact details of addresses in newspaper death notices, for security reasons.

Film Stuntman Training Helps Save a Life

Rapid action was called for when a car driven by David Cousins aquaplaned on a road near Castlebridge, County Wexford, and ended up submerged in a dyke full of water. David was trapped inside his Honda but, luckily for him, Gavin Fitzgerald was travelling behind him.

Gavin, from Dublin, saw David's car hit water on the road and then starting to spin. 'The water splashed up in front of me and I went completely blind. When the windscreen cleared, I couldn't see his car. It had disappeared.'

Looking to his left, Gavin, a technician who had completed a course in film stunts at the Australian Stunt Academy two years previously, spotted the rear of the car sticking up in a field.

> The car had flipped over on its roof and was covered in about five feet of water. David, who stands at five ft six inches, waded in with his head just above the water. He tried to smash the window but was unable to do so. Dialling 999, he jumped back out and flagged down a woman motorist, handing her his mobile phone so she could complete the emergency call.
>
> *Wexford People*

He went back into the water to resume the rescue. 'I don't know what came over me. I think the stunt training took over,' he said. He dived in and levered the car up onto the ditch with his shoulder.

David, a 35-year-old Wexford man, was stuck in the seat trying to get out, but Gavin managed to release the seatbelt and pulled him to safety. Both men were taken to Wexford General Hospital by ambulance and Gavin was commended by the gardaí and the fire service for his quick action and bravery.

Pop Goes the Hip Hopping Sean Bán Breathnach

When the irrepressible Seán Bán Breathnach wanted to present his own pop show on Raidió na Gaeltachta, fadó fadó, he was told 'never'. It was 1972 when he first broached the rather touchy matter during his interview for a job in the station. The interview board just laughed.

But it's Seán that's now laughing after eventually getting the all-clear to host his new pop programme. Being a balding fifty-something, he easily fits the description of an ageing rocker. And, after 35 years as a versatile broadcaster, that's just one of the roles he's now playing on Raidió na Gaeltachta.

The Connemara man, born and bred, admits he is one of the few 'old timers' working at the Irish language station who sees the potential and demand for entertainment other than sean-nós and 'diddly-ay' on Raidió na Gaeltachta.

> 'I've always believed that teenagers in the Gaeltacht reared with the Irish language are the same as [teenagers] anywhere else. They want pop, hip hop, whatever teenagers listen to.'
>
> *The Connacht Tribune*

At one time, there was a ban on English in Raidió na Gaeltachta but the station's bosses changed their attitude in recent years as they came to realise there's a market for music with English lyrics. Younger broadcasters are now presenting music which is not Gaelic or traditional.

In his youthful days, Seán listened to Radio Luxembourg and Radio Caroline and worked as a DJ in London. Material for his new programme is drawn from his own extensive personal record collection. The first programme was dedicated to *The Beatles*, whom he loves, with *The Rolling Stones* and many others coming after that.

Vasco the Fire Hero Helps Save 13 Lives

It was 5.45 on a Monday morning when Waterford city fire service received a 999 call about a fire in a building with people trapped inside.

The four-storey house in O'Connell Street was divided into eight flats providing accommodation for 13 people. The fire was on the ground floor, but a number of people were stranded on upper floors and on a rear fire escape. Three fire tenders rushed to the scene and the first was there within four minutes.

Luckily, one of the residents, a Portuguese man, Vasco Cordeiro, had just arrived back to his flat and was on his way to bed when the fire alarm went off.

When he opened his door, he was faced by a pall of black smoke. He climbed out the window and started banging on the windows of other flats to wake people, including Clarissa McCormack, a young Clonmel woman, and her 14-week-old baby, Hayden.

Clarissa, 22, was terrified and thought 'it was all over' for herself and Hayden. She didn't know what to do or where to turn. But when she heard the sound of banging on her window she saw Vasco outside.

'He was screaming the place was on fire and told me to get out, but I couldn't get out the door because the smoke was coming into my flat. I passed the baby out to him through a small window and then managed to squeeze through myself. I was never so scared in my life. I thought we were going to die. It was Vasco who saved us all – he was amazing. The fire fighters were just brilliant as well, they were just so helpful to us.'

Waterford News and Star

Another occupant of the house, Jim McNally, told how he was hanging out the window of his room on the second floor waiting for the fire fighters to come. 'They brought me down to the ground but I collapsed on the ground and the fire fighters gave me oxygen. It takes a lot to frighten me but this scared me. It was horrific,' he said.

When he awoke at about six o'clock, he couldn't see his hand in front of his face. Unable to get out the door, he then hung out the window. 'Just looking at the damage done now, I realise how lucky I was. I thought I was going to die. I'm okay now but I'm a bit weak and shook up. It's an awful shock,' Jim, a Dubliner, recounted.

The fire started in the hallway, 15 metres from the door of the building, and the stairwell acted as a chimney to funnel the billowing smoke upstairs. All 13 residents were rescued. Some were taken by ladder from the upper windows at the front of the building and others from the fire escape. Three adults and baby Hayden were taken to hospital.

All owed their lives to the quick thinking of heroic Vasco Cordeiro, a barman working in the city, and the prompt response of the Waterford fire service.

Lotto Millionaire Dolores Makes it to Top 100 Rich List

Dolores McNamara, the Limerick woman who scooped Europe's biggest lottery prize of €115 million, keeps a low profile and doesn't like flashing her wealth about.

She turned up at a local auction when 65 acres came under the hammer on the shores of Lough Derg, where she has a luxury home. But shortly after bidding started at €4.9 million, Dolores withdrew on learning a local person was interested. Afterwards, she was described locally as being 'very discreet' and someone that does not want to use her money to cut across others.

Her biggest splash-out since her Euromillions win in July 2005 was €1.7 million for the palatial pad overlooking Lough Derg – about €200,000 under the asking price. The house once caught the eye of actor Robert de Niro, but he wasn't among the bidders against her.

The unexpected lotto windfall changed her life forever and launched her into the media spotlight. After the initial publicity frenzy, Dolores appealed for privacy and moved out of her home in St Patrick's Road, Garryowen, in Limerick. She 'parked' her bundle in a Limerick bank account, earning interest of around €8,000 per day.

The new home of the mother-of-six, Lough Derg Hall, continues to attract sightseers and people who like to gawk from a distance, but it does offer privacy. Sitting serenely in Ogonnelloe, County Clare, the 930 square metre property has six en-suite bedrooms, each with four-poster beds. It also includes seven bathrooms, a large kitchen and the obligatory swimming pool.

Early in 2007, Dolores, aged 47, was placed at 85th in the Top 100 rich list by the *Sunday Independent* and was estimated to be worth €120 million – something that did not go unnoticed among her new neighbours in Clare.

She appears to have made a shrewd move purchasing a two-storey house situated on 38 acres with magnificent views over Lough Derg.

The Clare Champion

Though unable to completely avoid publicity, Dolores is trying to live as normally as possible. She has also been thinking about life on the 'other side'. One of her property purchases was a family plot at the new cemetery in Castlemungret, Limerick, for €2,000. Her mother has since been buried there.

Dolores has also got into the Sport of Kings, purchasing her first racehorse – a six-year-old bay mare named Carraig na gCapall for an undisclosed sum out of her massive winnings. It has a pedigree that could see Dolores in a winner's enclosure yet again; Carraig na gCapall's sire, Carroll House, won one of the world's most prestigious flat races, the Prix de l'Arc de Triomphe.

The horse runs in the colours of her husband, Adrian, and is trained by Ciaran O'Brien who has a string of 25 horses at his yard at Clonlara, County Clare. The McNamaras bought the mare after she won a point-to-point in Templemore.

As Carraig na gCapall is a jumping horse, Dolores won't be hob-nobbing with the Queen at Royal Ascot, which is for flat horses in the premier league. But she could be leading in winners in Galway, Cheltenham or Aintree.

Scratch Card Winnings Lead to Ticket Rush

Word spread around Tralee faster than you'd say 'lotto'; a shop in the town was reputedly selling winner-only scratch cards.

Customers queued outside Harry Hynes's shop in Shanakill from well before the eight o'clock opening time on the morning of 23 March 2007. Everyone wanted to buy the winning tickets before they were sold out.

The shop normally sells about 500 *Pot of Gold* scratch cards per week, with instant prizes ranging from €2 to €200. But thousands more were sold during the ticket rush, with sales rocketing to €15,000 in just a few days in the third week of March. At least €10,000 worth of these were winning tickets.

The more people won, the more people bought as the feeling that it really 'could be you' swept through the town. Many of the cards had winning cash amounts. Two local lads claimed to have won €700 and €500, according to Harry. 'It really has been a phenomenon,' he said.

> The craze began last week when a number of Eastern European customers found they had been winning on the scratch-offs, Harry explained. 'Once word got around, we sold four thousand tickets in three hours on Friday morning. Four thousand more tickets are due to be delivered to the shop today,' he said.
>
> *Kerry's Eye*

However, according to a spokesperson for Conquer and Care Lotteries, which operates the *Pot of Gold* lotto, any high level of winnings in a single shop is simply coincidence. 'In this particular case, there must have been many tickets sold. This would have led to them finding the winning tickets.'

Harry's scratch card customers struck it rich for a short time, with a much higher number of winning tickets than usual. But life soon returned to normal.

Sandra Uses Boat to Beat Traffic Chaos

Sandra O'Rourke-Glynn found a way of avoiding roads choked by traffic – she took to the water.

Tired of trying to negotiate her way through chronic congestion in the main streets of Athy, County Kildare, she collected her son, Ryan, and his friends from the local secondary school by boat. She felt she had no other option but to use the town's waterways for the purpose.

Sandra, who had been threatening for a long time to use the waterways as a means of collecting students from school, said: 'The traffic on the Carlow Road was so bad on Thursday last that I decided to pick the kids up from the slip at Batchelors and take them home via the river.'

While parents were seeking alternative routes to bring their children home from school, members of Athy Town Council were presented with a plan to help rid the town of traffic congestion.

A report drafted by the Athy Joint Policing Committee has recommended that some minor streets become one-way streets. And that traffic from the Dublin and Kilkenny sides be diverted in different directions.

> These short-term measures are being put in place until the proposed Southern Road is complete, which according to the county council's director of services, Joe Boland, is progressing well. He said a final report on the Northern Road would be published in June.
>
> *Kildare Nationalist*

Meanwhile, bring on the gondolas in Athy.

'Chuggers' Swoop on Unsuspecting Generous Folk

They've become known in some quarters as 'chuggers' and are now a common sight on the busy main streets of cities and towns. They hunt in packs and unsuspecting pedestrians unlucky enough to make eye contact with them are often snared.

The description, chugger, is an amalgamation of charity and mugger – a name for the new, aggressive breed of street fundraisers. Much more in your face than the usual church gate collector – who is often a shy, half-embarrassed individual wishing he or she wasn't there at all – chuggers have no inhibitions when it comes to stalking their quarry.

Once a potential victim is trapped into having a conversation, they can be persuaded into giving details of bank accounts so that standing orders can be set up to transfer money from an account to a charity.

Limerick is a popular and seemingly profitable city for chuggers who prowl around congested areas so as to blend in easily with the crowd. They wait to pounce on unsuspecting shoppers who in a moment of weakness will stop for a chat.

Nor are female chuggers beyond using their charms to lure males into parting with their money. A broad smile from a pretty young woman can often draw sizeable amounts of cash from an ageing male not accustomed to such flattering attention from the so-called fairer sex.

> There are several warning signs that you may be the target of a chugger. If a complete stranger approaches you on the street, shaking your hand and pretending to be interested in your affairs, be extremely cautious.
>
> Up until recently, faking interest in strangers has been the sole preserve of the politician. However, now that the election is over, it is far more likely being approached in such a manner means you are the target for a 'chugging'.

> If you are a middle-aged man of modest appearance and an attractive clipboard-carrying young lady asks can she speak to you for 'just a second' chances are it's a chugger. Super-friendly guy wants to tell you a joke? Chugger. Stranger wants to share a statistic with you? Chugger. Someone compliments you on how happy/pretty/generous you are looking today? Chugger.
>
> *Limerick Leader*

A poll by the above newspaper found that Limerick people had had enough of chuggers who sometimes followed them down streets when they rejected chuggers' initial approaches.

As for a solution to the problem, the answer could come from Britain where councils have set up exclusion zones where it is illegal for chuggers to operate. On the other hand, maybe inclusion zones could be set up where people could go and meet chuggers, if they so wished, and donate to the charity of their choice without harassment.

Gillian the Heroine of Fire Rescue

Gillian Downey was asleep in her apartment in Mallow when she awoke to desperate cries for help. Two people trapped in a fire in a neighbouring apartment were screaming her name. She jumped out of bed and woke her brother, Edward.

By now, smoke was wafting around the corridors and the fire alarm went off in the building. Edward grabbed Gillian's baby, Carly, from a cot and Gillian rushed to her neighbours' blazing apartment and kicked in the door. Sarah Byrne and Terry Fitzgerald, who had been calling her name, were inside.

She fought her way through thick, black smoke. 'I could hear my heart in my ears . . . The smoke was gushing, one inhale and you feel like you are dying,' she said afterwards.

Grabbing Sarah, she pulled her out of the apartment and threw a jacket over her. Terry was still screaming and calling Gillian's name, but she could not see him through the wall of smoke. Gillian then raced out of the apartment block where she found a local man, Peter Ruby.

The pair of them immediately ran back into the building to try and save Terry. But they were beaten back by the 'blackest smoke' they had ever seen. They did as much as they could, but their best attempts failed.

Fire brigades from Mallow and Kanturk arrived at the scene in Fair Green shortly before midnight. Every effort was made to revive Terry, who was aged 34 and from Carrigaline, County Cork, but sadly he died. The fire may have been caused by a dropped cigarette according to the gardaí.

Gillian Downey could not find words to describe the trauma of the fire. The saddest part of all, she felt, was that Terry was so near and they still could not reach him.

> 'I'll always be saying what if? The sound of the alarm is still with me. I'm very proud of what I did. I thought I'd run and would never look back. But I've never experienced screams like theirs. They were trapped and the one person they were calling was me,' she said.
>
> *The Corkman*

The deeply-shocked Sarah Byrne was fortunate to be taken out of the blazing apartment so quickly. She was treated at Mallow General Hospital for smoke inhalation and was discharged the following day.

Baffled by Man's Image on Wall

American artist Jeanne Cullen was spooked when she suddenly noticed what looked like the image of an old man's face on the wall of a thatched cottage in a remote corner of Kerry. It was several months after she moved from Atlanta to a house she and her husband, Michael, had purchased near the laid back village of Lixnaw. The disused cottage is in the grounds of their house.

At first Jeanne was taken aback when she spotted the image and pointed to the apparent eyes, a nose and a mouth. But she eventually came to accept it. She and Michael regularly visited the thatched house and if the image had been there all along, they felt they would have seen it.

> 'As an artist, I would have been aware of the image long before now, but it just seems to have appeared for no apparent reason. I have shown it to many people who are all amazed. It's really weird,' she said.
>
> *Kerry's Eye*

Jeanne speculated about what might have caused the phenomenon. Her thoughts focused on a nameless Black and Tan reputed to have been buried in an unmarked grave in a Lixnaw bog. Locals around Lixnaw believe he was shot by the IRA in Tralee during the War of Independence.

'The image on the wall could be a sign from the spirit of this man asking that his body be brought home to England. Then he can finally rest in peace,' Jeanne maintained.

No Joke as Cash Runs Out during Comedy Festival

'If ever you go to Kilkenny,
Look out for the Hole in the Wall,
It'll always work when not needed,
But on bank holidays,
It won't work at all.'

It was a case of 'no mun, no fun' for some of the estimated 30,000 people that packed into Kilkenny for a good laugh during the June bank holiday.

Crowded pubs certainly had ample supplies of drink in stock for the Cat Laughs Festival. Many comedy fans were not amused, however, when they were unable to find extra euros to spend on booze, chips and whatever they were having themselves. A new comic twist to the festival, some of the cash-strapped revellers mused.

From early on Sunday, the ATMs run by the major banks began to empty around the city. By late on Sunday night, only a few were still working and by the bank holiday Monday, any stragglers left in the city were hard pressed to find money.

The 'holes in the wall' simply dried up because, according to the bigger banks, it was such a busy weekend and as people queued for money, there were no bankers working to replenish cash stocks. 'Unfortunately, there is no way around it. The machines are loaded to capacity on the Friday but they are emptied over the weekend,' a Bank of Ireland spokesperson said.

A number of Allied Irish Banks ATMs were also emptied by lunchtime on Sunday. However, for the cute punter willing to have a search around, some of the city's smaller banks had functioning ATMs for the duration of the festival.

Kilkenny People

In his column in the same paper, a satirical Gerry Moran quoted the doggerel in the introduction. Beneath it, he set the following question in a 'Kilkenny' Leaving Certificate (higher level, of course) exam paper:

> In your own words explain why the banks cannot put enough cash in their ATMs at the weekends – especially the Cat Laughs Comedy weekend when there are purportedly 30,000 extra people in the city. Are they a) too stupid? b) too lazy? or c) too indifferent to their customers? that is yourself and myself. You may use bad language. Lots of it.

Nude Bathers Hang Out on Top Beaches

The bishop and his mistress were strolling along the glorious beach at Inch on the Dingle Peninsula when they encountered a German tourist in the nude. Bishop Eamonn Casey and Annie Murphy were taken aback and Eamonn told the tourist to put on some clothes. But the bishop didn't get a good response and bathers are still walking around Inch in their birthday suits.

That incident, as related by Annie in her book, *Forbidden Fruit*, happened several years ago and bum-baring bathers seem to be getting cheekier all the time. Over the June bank holiday weekend, hundreds of free and easy people disrobed at beaches in Wicklow, Sligo and Kerry in a bid to seek legal recognition for naturism and to celebrate World Naturist Day.

Public nudity is still illegal in Ireland and the campaign to decriminalise naturism is hotting up. Rarely, if ever, have people been prosecuted here for nude sunbathing, but they can be done for indecent exposure.

Ireland is the only country in the EU that does not provide

outdoor facilities for naturists, complained Irish Naturist Association president Pat Gallagher who confirmed that nude bathers took to the beach at Inch (Co Kerry) which is a real favourite location for naturists.

The Kingdom

Inch, Brittas Bay in Wicklow and Trawalua in Sligo are among the unofficial naturist beaches and councils are being lobbied to officially designate beaches. Naturists don't appear to be too worried about voyeurs and peeping Toms, but they do want signs put up saying, 'Nude bathers may be seen beyond this point', to warn people who may be offended by the spectacle of naked men and women. A case of out of sight, out of mind.

Pat Gallagher wants newcomers to take part in the campaign. He said that, despite what some people might think, naturism is very much non-sexual. 'It's all about freedom of expression and growing out of inhibition,' he explained.

But, according to Irish law, nudity in public places is an arrestable offence if there is an intention to offend. According to Pat Gallagher, no Irish naturist has ever been arrested and they always go to secluded areas. At least 5,000 people now enjoy naturism in Ireland. With EU directives now controlling much of our lives in Ireland, it seems only a matter of time before some bureaucrat in Brussels decides it's time we too have bare-all beaches.

An American guide has listed Brittas Bay and Inch (where some of the scenes for the epic film *Ryan's Daughter* were filmed) among the top 1,000 places in the world in which to go naked.

It described Brittas Bay as 'this special place' which more bare bathers enjoy than anywhere else in the Republic. The guide praised Inch for 'seclusion and open space for baring all – naturist nirvana'. Nakedly ambitious operators in the tourist industry, meanwhile, are looking at a potentially lucrative business.

Wheels of Fortune Man Advised to Buy a Lotto Ticket

A man who fell asleep on a railway track woke up to find he was covered by more than a duvet. The homeless man in his twenties did not realise what he was doing when he wandered onto the track and put his head down to rest.

It was around eleven o'clock at night when the incident happened on the track at Grangemellon Bridge between Athy and Carlow. According to local people, the man had a miraculous escape after a freight train drove over him as he slept in the middle of the tracks.

He told the gardaí afterwards that he hadn't even been aware of his unusual sleeping arrangements.

> It is believed the man, who was not from the area, was intoxicated and did not realise what had happened until the gardaí informed him of the seriousness of the events that had unfolded just minutes earlier. Although emergency services attended the scene, the lucky chap miraculously appears to have emerged unscathed and refused to go to hospital for a check up.
>
> *Kildare Nationalist*

Iarnród Éireann confirmed that an incident occurred on the line but disputed the claim by the gardaí that the train drove over the man. Iarnród Éireann also said the man had received some injuries prior to what was described as an 'incredible' incident.

A spokeswoman for the rail service said the train driver had been informed that a man was lying on the track and had reduced his speed. She also said the train made no impact with the man and had in fact stopped before it reached where he was lying on the track.

One of the gardaí who attended the scene remarked, 'It was extraordinary that the man was not injured – we told him to go away and do the Lotto!'

Landlady Discovers House Being Used as Brothel

Her house had been advertised for renting and a Sligo landlady was happy to get a phone call from a man who said he was urgently looking for a place in the town. His story was that he was relocating from Dublin and planned to live there with his girlfrend.

Later, the landlady met the 'girlfriend' in Sligo and showed her the house. She was Irish, was driving a Sligo-registered car, agreed to take the house and paid over a deposit of €700. She came across very well and the landlady, who was renting the house for the first time, had no suspicions.

The year-long lease had all the usual stipulations about not operating a business or keeping pets and having only friends around. But the landlady became a little suspicious when the woman was unable to give a telephone number for her boyfriend, the excuse being that he was waiting on a new company phone.

The next day when the landlady arrived at the three-bedroomed house to drop in a bin bag, she found two young foreign women there and neither appeared to be able to speak English. Nor did they seem to have any idea of who the other woman or man were and had no contact details for them.

Immediately the landlady went about evicting them and when she called back to the house again she met a man. He was leaving the property and handed her a business card with the name of an escort agency on it.

And he went further by 'highly recommending' the service. Within 48 hours of moving in, the two women in their twenties were operating a brothel through an on-line escort agency.

When the number on the business card was dialled, directions were given to the house. The landlady was totally stunned, but the prostitution could not have been going on there for long as none of the neighbours had noticed any unusual comings and goings. She again rang the woman, returned the deposit and the two girls had left the house by taxi inside an hour.

> 'I was duped and it was easily done. Many landlords don't ask for references and my advice to them is to keep an eye on their property. Only for the fact I had called on a regular basis to the house I would never have found out what had been going on,' she said.
>
> *The Sligo Champion*

'These two women had no English and they could have been brought to this country on the basis of being provided with jobs but instead they ended up working for an escort agency in Sligo,' she added.

The Celtic Tiger and the internet have spawned huge growth in prostitution countrywide, according to regional newspapers. Surveys have found that the number of men paying women for sex has doubled in ten years. In June, for instance, *The Kerryman* reported four fully operational brothels in Tralee, with hotels in tourist haven Killarney being used as temporary brothels by exotic, touring prostitutes, some reportedly from as far away as Indonesia.

Country Weather Experts Bamboozled by Global Warming

Time was when Tom Holmes had only to take a good look at the sky and he would then be able to give a pretty accurate weather forecast. But with the increasing unpredictability of the elements and varying seasonal temperatures, his task is becoming ever more difficult.

Local weatherlore and the signs on which the farming community once depended are all, literally, up in the air as Tom from Murroe, County Limerick, pointed out.

'I'm 83 years old and the only thing I can say for certain is that this is the worst month of June I've ever known. The wind is blowing from the north most of time and if it were any other month, I'd be predicting snow. It's impossible to predict the weather now. Even the scientists aren't getting it right,' he remarked on a bad day in mid-summer.

> Tom is usually a very accurate weather forecaster, taking his cues from the position of the new moon in the sky, the behaviour of animals and birds, cloud formations and the flowering of the hedgerows. He was the only one in Murroe to predict the last white Christmas we got.
>
> *Limerick Leader*

In the spring there was a strange sign that he had not seen too often – a profusion of whitethorn and crab tree blossoms in the hedgerows. But they turned pink very quickly and didn't last long. Not a great sign, according to Tom.

In the Dingle Peninsula, another amateur weatherman, TP Ó Conchúir, was also finding it very hard to give a forecast for 2007. He has a reputation for on-the-ball summer forecasts but his best early summer offering was 'a mixed year ahead, impossible to fully predict'.

There were no firm portents from the sea or air and none of the traditional weather watchers he consults around the country was prepared to put their heads on the prediction block. In June, there was a considerable amount of seaweed on the beaches and this was always taken by the old people as a sign of a poor year. Bees were also out in March and April and the old people used to say to beware of bees in March.

On a positive note, TP observed, hundreds of basking sharks were seen off the Kerry and Cork coasts and that was always interpreted as an indication of heat. In summary, his honest assessment was that the year would be *trí na chéile*.

What can the poor weathermen do with such highly unseasonable weather patterns? This has been one of the wettest months of June since records began, with temperatures in the south-west on Midsummer's Day falling to 9°C when they would normally be expected to be at least double that!

Christy Moore's Lament for Hometown Provokes Backlash

The town he loved so well has changed beyond recognition and balladeer Christy Moore is getting himself into a sweat about it. He decided to have a go at modern-day Newbridge which, he claimed, 'like every other town in Ireland, is victim to greed, bad planning, gombeenism, little or no thought to facilities for the young, the old and needy'.

Laneways and old 'coorting corners' were now full of townhouses and apartments forcing memories to be confused and obliterated by 'concrete and mock facades'. Newbridge's most famous son described the Whitewater Shopping Centre as a developer's wet dream and a 'right f**king kip'.

Strong stuff even from a man who doesn't usually pull his punches. As might be expected, the town elders were quick to hit back at his broadside which was made in an article by Pádraig Kenny entitled 'Death of an Irish Town' in *Magill* magazine. Christy said that when he was young, his home town was his 'city of dreams' but all had changed utterly and for the worse.

The outgoing Mayor of Newbridge, Murty Aspell, felt Christy had gone a bit too far. 'It's a totally different place than it was when he was growing up. I'm very disappointed in him for saying what he said. I don't give a damn who he is or what kind of celebrity he is, he doesn't even live here. Nobody can say this isn't a great town.'

Christy spoke of the families of Moorefield Terrace (Brannigans, Murrays, Moores and Molloys) but noted that the houses are now all offices.

The article went on to say that what were once state of the art apartments are now grubby and grimy, falling into seediness and in the first stages of becoming small ghettos. It added: 'The traffic is incessant. Thanks to the Whitewater Centre, the town has a new, specially-widened bridge to accommodate the increased traffic, and perhaps it's because of this that there is a feeling that Newbridge is just a place to get into and out of as quickly as possible.'

Eyre Street is dubbed a 'grim, rutted stretch of road, with its sad-looking, paint peeling pubs, and the grim functionality of the odd internet café'. Elsewhere in the article, Newbridge is described variously as a developer's playground, a dumping ground for economic refugees from both inside and outside Ireland and a soulless shell.

Some councillors thought Christy was being unfair to Newbridge. While conceding that people might be entitled to romantic memories about the hometowns of their childhood, life moved on and many things changed.

> Councillor Fiona O'Loughlin said she was quite shocked by the article. 'Everybody is entitled to their opinion and I don't take that away from this son of Newbridge. The town is going through a growing period and there are growing pains in terms of matching the social infrastructure with the number of houses being built over the last number of years.
>
> 'There's no doubt there are areas [in which] we have been

lagging behind and there is a sense of playing catch up. I can't think there is any other town in Ireland of equal size that has such a strong and vibrant community awareness and activism and if people want to see everyday examples of active citizenship all they need to do is come to Newbridge and witness it on a daily level.'

Leinster Leader

Choppers – the New Status Symbol

During the first week in August a trip to Galway for the races offered a few defining images of the new Ireland. And it's not just the millions of euro floating around the betting ring or all the Mercs and BMWs or the style of the fashionable and feathered ladies.

More than anything else, it's the scores of private helicopters heading west and touching down around Ballybrit that reflect the champagne lifestyle of the new rich. The number of helicopters officially registered here in the last six years has trebled to more than 140. There may also be 50 or 60 others which are used and mostly based in Ireland but registered overseas.

Flying by 'chopper' to the Galway Races, the K Club or the Old Head Golf Club in Kinsale may be the trendy thing to do, but we've also reached a stage in corporate Ireland where such aircraft are seen as almost a necessity, even commonplace, in certain circles. Easy to understand given the clogged up Irish roads – a case of just flying over all the traffic.

The sky around Martinstown, County Limerick, was 'black' with helicopters on the Saturday in July when Cian Foley married Sue Ann McManus, daughter of billionaire tycoon JP McManus. Several of the 1,500 guests came by helicopter, while limousine was the first choice alternative transport on *terra firma*. An air traffic control system was even in place, giving pilots individual landing slots.

Property developers are among the prime users of this form of transport, but frazzled executives for whom time is definitely money also use them to get to business meetings.

Helicopters start at €180,000 for a two-seater but prices go steeply skywards to as high as €10 million.

Millionaire business tycoon Bill Cullen has long been a high flyer, but he got into a spot of bother with Kerry County Council which refused him planning permission to retain a helipad at his Killarney home. The former Renault chairman and best-selling author had used the landing area for over a decade as he hopped from his base in Dublin to his five-star Muckross Park Hotel, near his residence in sylvan Killarney.

According to a statement issued for him to *The Kerryman* on 28 February:

> Bill, personally, has always taken great care to ensure these activities have been conducted so as to minimise any disruption to the area.

However, he later withdrew his appeal to An Bórd Pleanála against the council's decision.

Meanwhile, a woman who's certainly not a high flyer was on cloud nine for her 97th birthday. As a treat, great grandmother Maudie Monaghan, from Headford, County Galway, enjoyed a surprise flight in a helicopter in the hands of granddaughter Yvonne, herself a pilot with EasyJet.

> 'It was lovely to see all the places I know from above – especially my own and those of my friends and neighbours. I'd do it again tomorrow,' she said.
>
> *The Connacht Tribune*

Widowed and left with six children before she was 40, Maudie spent her long life working on the family farm. She always had a philosophy that 'sitting on your backside won't boil the kettle', still enjoys an active lifestyle and is a steadfast follower of Galway football.

New Money's Now in K4

Kildare is definitely becoming to place to live and not just for the horsey set. Some people are now claiming that the thoroughbred county has eclipsed Dublin 4 as the property hotspot for the rich and aspirational.

K4, as it is better known in elevated circles, is the new D4 according to property pundits who consider that everyone who is anyone now has a place there. The posh address aside, the plains and gallops offer the joys of country living, proximity to Dublin, a high-profile location and high-flying neighbours.

> The attraction lies in the status associated with living alongside the likes of soccer star Niall Quinn, Renault millionaire Bill Cullen and, of course, the potential to join the local pony club or hunt safe in the knowledge that you now have room for a pony. Shopping hotspots such as the Whitewater Centre, Kildare Village and the traditional boutique haven that is Naas are also being dangled as carrots for the fashion conscious.
>
> *Leinster Leader*

Ordinary people had moved in well before the elite, exploding the population of Kildare towns, living in 'semi-ds' in sprawling estates and commuting each day to workplaces in the capital. But it took the wealthier set that followed them to the country to earn the appendage K4.

Mayor of Kildare Mary Glennon is not exactly over-enthusiastic about having K4 in her realm: she's not convinced K4 attention bodes too well for the county. 'I have heard this phrase [K4] before, especially in regard to Ballymore Eustace where some enormous haciendas have been built around Mullaboden in what is now known as the D4 of Ballymore,' she said.

'I don't mind who comes to live in Kildare but I often wonder about some of these enormous monuments to cash and bad taste that seem to get planning permission when people who just want to build a modest family home are put through enormous hoops by the planning system.'

As professed urbanites and affluent Dubs threaten to colonise the Lilywhite county, Mayor Glennon also warned of a mentality that threatened to 'obliterate all country life'. Less than half of the people currently living in Kildare were born here and there are almost as many Dubs in the county as Lilywhites.

According to Central Statistics Office figures, Dubs now make up just over a quarter of the entire population of Kildare. Kildare has the second lowest percentage of native-born residents still living in the county. Only County Meath has a higher percentage of 'non-natives' living in the county.

Kildare currently has a population of 186,000 people, only 76,000 of whom were born in Kildare. In the last census, 50,000 people in the county listed their place of birth as Dublin.

Willie Week's Special Magic

The letters have Japanese, American, Norwegian and Australian postmarks and they arrive in Miltown Malbay in late summer from musicians and their followers who have just enjoyed a real taste of traditional Irish music.

People in trad circles know the event simply as Willie Week – the Willie Clancy Summer School – a magnet that has been drawing thousands of musicians to the small west Clare town for a week each July for 35 years.

It's not a fleadh cheoil or even a music festival. It has no flashy PR campaign behind it and doesn't have a website, an email address or any other new-fangled communications to promote itself. And it doesn't need gimmicks. Most of the aficionados who go there first hear of it through word of mouth. Having experienced it, they then go on to tell others and so the occasion continues.

The organisers don't care a whit about image. They just want people to learn and play Irish music in a truly genuine setting and to the highest standard. The Oscar-winning actor Jeremy Irons was among the students at the fiddle workshops this year.

Miltown Malbay is a down-to-earth, old-fashioned place with plenty of small, cosy pubs, some of which have been spared the plastic 'modernisation' that has destroyed good watering holes in every town and village in Ireland. It's a place where cars and tractors are still abandoned rather than parked and where everyone seems to have time to chat and pass the day at leisure. People visiting for Willie Week bring their sleeping bags and lay down their heads where they like for the night.

While the business end of Willie Week (dedicated to the memory of a famous piper, Willie Clancy) is in the 135 workshops, it's the impromptu sessions in the pubs the followers come for.

> The Willie Week campers who dot the campsite that overlooks Spanish Point beach awake to a sight and sound that money will never buy. The sight of the beach and the combined sound of the sea and wafting music lull all who stop there into the essence of the festival.
>
> *The Clare Champion*

People cast aside their watches, switch off their mobile phones and just float along with it, all enjoying the unique aura and atmosphere of Willie Week.

Christmas Comes in June for Kate

On 18 November 2006, Kate Flannery was chatting with friends outside a pub in Edinburgh when she suffered horrific injuries in a bizarre incident. The young Galway woman was hit by a traffic cone which had been launched 40 feet off the George IV Bridge in the Scottish city.

It resulted in a smashed skull and three fractured vertebrae in her spine. At first, doctors feared her injuries would leave her paralysed. In December, she underwent surgery to repair damage on her spine using bones from her hip and she gradually regained strength in her arms and legs. By March, the 24-year-old occupational therapy student was back in Galway, much to the surprise of her physicians.

During her long stay in hospital, Kate missed out on Christmas at home. Something she had always looked forward to was a traditional Christmas Eve drink with her parents in Ward's Hotel and Bar in Salthill. It was her father John, anxious to keep a cherished custom alive, who came up with a plan for a belated Christmas drink with Kate.

John and Anthony Finnerty, the host in Ward's and a former Mayo footballer (respectively), arranged to have the Christmas Eve tipple in June as they believed Kate would be well enough to celebrate by then.

She certainly was and the pub was cheerfully adorned with fake snow and Christmas decorations for the unique occasion, while festive music played and finger food was served. According to Anthony Finnerty, the local community was 'quite cut up' about Kate's incident as the Flannerys are well known in the area for being 'good neighbours and great people'. Thus, it was with great pleasure that Ward's hosted the belated celebration.

Western People

Kate, meanwhile, is walking with the aid of a cane, swims regularly and hopes to resume her studies in Edinburgh.

In a subsequent court case, Australian Andrew Smith admitted hurling the cone from the bridge after a drunken night out in the Scottish city centre. He pleaded guilty to culpable and reckless conduct on the occasion.

In a letter to the court, Kate and her family asked for him to be shown leniency and said they did not want to see him jailed.

Fury After 'Jewel' Fails to Make Tourist Guide

Mayor of Killarney and man about town Niall O'Callaghan barely had the chain of office around his ample shoulders when he got into a fight with Fáilte Ireland and Cork/Kerry Tourism. He couldn't believe how his hometown, which likes to dub itself as the capital of tourism in Ireland and the jewel in the crown, could be ignored in an official guide.

There was no mention of Killarney among the main attractions on the Ring of Kerry, even though the Ring begins and ends in Killarney.

Fáilte Ireland quickly acknowledged that a simple howler had been made and promised to correct it in future editions of the *South West Holiday Guide*, 120,000 copies of which are given to visitors to the area. But the promotion bodies refused a request by Mayor O'Callaghan to withdraw the guide and reprint a corrected version.

'It is unbelievable that such a mistake has been made. It is totally unacceptable that this guide is being handed out to visitors at tourist offices, in hotels and elsewhere . . . here we have the two premier tourism promotion bodies who are doing the job full-time and they can't get it right,' he went on.

The Kingdom

Fáilte Ireland replied: 'We thank the mayor for bringing this simple printing error to our attention and we will correct it in future editions. But we wouldn't see it as a useful way of spending taxpayers' money to reprint this booklet.'

Something that really got up the noses of some snootier tourism elements in Killarney was that the unpretentious village of Kilgarvan, which was never on the Ring of Kerry, was included in the guide.

Independent TD Jackie Healy-Rae and the pub with his name in bold letters over the door might be tourist attractions in their own right but they are miles off the Ring. Then again, maybe Jackie insisted on Kilgarvan being put on the Ring as part of his deal with Bertie to support the Fianna Fáil/Green Party government! That will never be known, however, because the deal is secret.

As far as the Ring goes, Killarney is the big winner as most visitors doing the day trip stay there. A Caherciveen hotelier, who couldn't conceal his envy, once remarked that his town 'only gets the steam out of the buses passing through'.

In July, another row flared in Killarney with claims, yet again, that some pony men in the spectacular Gap of Dunloe were trying to stop motorists from driving through the Gap. Though the road through the mountain gap is public, visitors are not encouraged to drive cars or other vehicles on it; instead they are expected to take a pony ride or go by pony and trap.

Kerry Fine Gael Councillor Pat McCarthy took the whip out and lashed some people in the pony business for 'bullying and intimidating' tourists. He knew of a couple from Mayo who had twice been turned back as they tried to drive into the Gap and they would certainly not be returning to Killarney, he pointed out.

Elderly Postmaster Frightens Off 'Armed' Teenager

High noon came to a tranquil Cork village as elderly people arrived in dribs and drabs to collect their old age pensions. It was the same as any other Friday in any rural post office – until a raider appeared from nowhere and announced his arrival by stating, 'This is a f****ng robbery.'

Just before midday, a youth wearing a balaclava burst into Kiskeam post office brandishing what turned out to be an imitation gun. A woman standing at the counter thought it was all a joke and coolly told the agitated intruder, 'Go 'way you bledy eejit.'

He was dead serious, however, and ordered postmaster John Murphy to hand over what money was in the safe, but John immediately pressed the security buzzer to alert the gardaí. The raider also ordered the contents of a drawer to be emptied but made a critical mistake by placing the 'firearm' on the counter as he piled €500 from the drawer into a bag.

An alert John Murphy grabbed the gun and pointed it back at the intruder who then fled with the bag of money. John chased him out the door and within minutes everyone in the village knew what had happened. Villagers were soon on the trail of the raider who had taken to the fields.

Locals who heard the commotion gave chase and the normally

quiet village became alive to the sound of sirens. Five units from Kanturk garda station were quickly at the scene and a helicopter was also dispatched.

The Corkman

Local people helped gardaí to arrest the man less than two hours after the robbery. The money was also found and returned to the post office.

The 72-year-old postmaster who braved the teenage raider personified the spirit of Kiskeam, an area famous for the freedom fighters it produced during the War of Independence, notably Sean Moylan. To celebrate their feats, a book called *Kiskeam Versus The Empire* was once published. When asked who won that particular war, a wise local man replied, 'Kiskeam is still there . . . the British Empire has long since disappeared from the face of the earth.'

Are Ye the Band?

A Memoir of the Showband Era

JIMMY HIGGINS

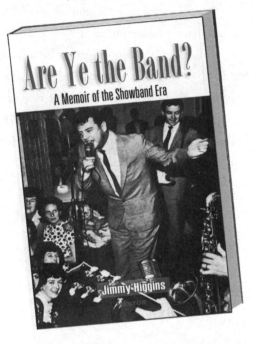

Jimmy Higgins, a veteran of the showband era, recalls the heady days of life in showband Ireland. As an innocent 14-year-old from Tuam, Co Galway, Jimmy started out as a trumpet player in the Paramount Showband. In this book, he recounts the many untold tales from this golden era in Ireland's social history. The characters, the clothes, the managers, the groupies, the near-hits and the close calls are all recounted in this nostalgic trip down a musical memory lane. Packed with photos showing the movers and shakers of the time – a must for anyone who ever danced on a Saturday night in an overheated ballroom to the music played by the 'pop idols' of the day.

Up the Poll

Great Irish Election Stories

SHANE COLEMAN

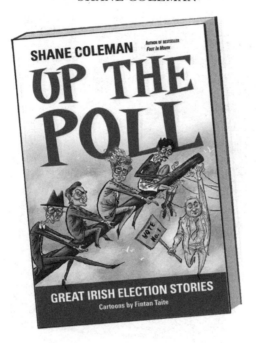

Up The Poll gathers together all the comical, tragic and farcical moments from Irish election campaigns from 1917 to 2007.

- Michael McDowell's shimmy up a poll in 2002, which kick-started the PDs' campaign and landed them in government. Surely the most profitable poll-dance in Irish history?
- The senior Fianna Fáil politician seen assembling a machine gun in a phone booth in Dáil Éireann after the 1932 election.
- The clash of the titans – Charlie v Garret in three RTÉ television debates. Would Garret's hair get any wilder? Would Charlie postpone dinner at Mirabeau's?
- Bertie's run-in with Vincent Browne about spending *his* money how *he* wants. So there.

. . . and many more.

Great GAA Moments 2007

FINBARR McCARTHY

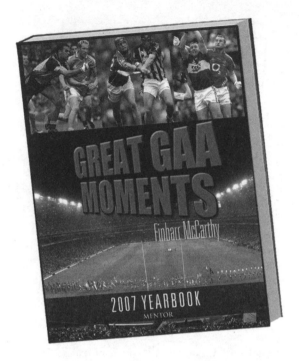

Sports journalist Finbarr McCarthy serves up another action-packed book chronicling the ups and downs of the 2007 GAA season. Kicking off with the first floodlit game in Croke Park in February, the season's most spectacular moments are captured in eye-catching colour photos. The Allianz Football and Hurling Leagues, the club finals on St Patrick's Day, the sublime and the best-forgotten moments of the Championship season are all covered in this book, along with many other GAA-related events. A perfect gift for any GAA fan.

The Great Irish Bank Robbery

The Story of Ireland's White Collar Villainy
LIAM COLLINS

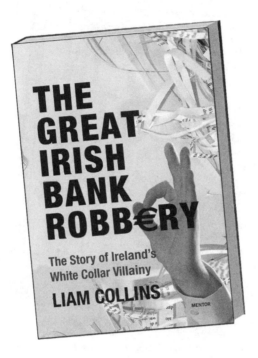

In this mesmerising book, Liam Collins weaves a fascinating tale of the biggest financial scandal ever witnessed in Ireland. Ten years after uncovering the shocking conduct of AIB Bank, Collins explains in clear, concise language the web of deceit involving some of Ireland's most prominent business figures, the banks they ran, the greed of their customers and the negligence of the tax authorities. A fast-paced saga of financial avarice that tainted almost every village and town in Ireland.

Foot In Mouth

Famous Irish Political Gaffes

SHANE COLEMAN

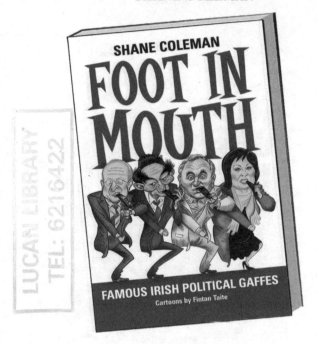

Foot In Mouth – Famous Irish Political Gaffes recounts the gaffes that rocked governments, shocked public opinion and mocked accepted uses of the English language.

Containing over 70 cringe-inducing gaffes, including:

- Pee Flynn's musings on the *Late Late Show* on life on a measly income (how will he pay for that third housekeeper?)
- Jack Lynch's memory loss concerning two British agents
- *That* Fine Gael Ard Fheis
- The PDs' excessive housekeeping (let's dump these sensitive financial records in this skip!)
- De Valera's notorious response to the death of Hitler

. . . and many more.